INCOME AND STATUS DIFFERENCES BETWEEN WHITE AND MINORITY AMERICANS

A Persistent Inequality

INCOME AND STATUS DIFFERENCES BETWEEN WHITE AND MINORITY AMERICANS

A Persistent Inequality

Edited by

Sucheng Chan

With the Assistance of
Jenni Currie

Mellen Studies in Sociology
Volume 3

The Edwin Mellen Press
Lewiston/Queenston/Lampeter

Library of Congress Cataloging-in-Publication Data

Income and status differences between white and minority Americans : a persistent inequality / edited by Sucheng Chan, with the assistance of Jenni Currie.
p. cm. -- (Mellen studies in sociology ; v. 3)
Papers from the 1st and 2nd All-UC Conference on the Comparative Study of Race, Ethnicity, Gender, and Class, held at the University of California, Santa Cruz in May 1986, and at the University of California, Davis in Dec. 1987.
Includes bibliographical references.
ISBN 0-88946-635-1
1. Income distribution--United States--Congresses. 2. Social status--United States--Congresses. 3. Discrimination--United States--Congresses. 4. Minorities--United States--Economic conditions--Congresses. 5. Minorities--United States--Social conditions--Congresses. I. Chan, Sucheng. II. Currie, Jenni. III. ALL-UC Conference on the Comparative Study of Race, Ethnicity, Gender, and Class (1st : 1986 : University of California, Santa Cruz) IV. ALL-UC Conference on the Comparative Study of Race, Ethnicity, Gender, and Class (2nd : 1987 : University of California, Davis) V. Series.
HC110.I5I47 1989
339.2'2'0973--dc20 89-12659
CIP

This is volume 3 in the continuing series
Mellen Studies in Sociology
Volume 3 ISBN 0-88946-635-1
MSS Series ISBN 0-88946-630-0

A CIP catalog record for this book is available from the British Library.

The Edwin Mellen Press
Box 450
Lewiston, New York
USA 14092

The Edwin Mellen Press
Box 67
Queenston, Ontario
CANADA, L0S 1L0

The Edwin Mellen Press, Ltd.
Lampeter, Dyfed, Wales
UNITED KINGDOM SA48 7DY

Printed in the United States of America

INCOME AND STATUS DIFFERENCES BETWEEN WHITE AND MINORITY AMERICANS

A Persistant Inequality

Contents

Acknowledgments

The essays in this volume are based on papers presented at the First All-UC Conference on the Comparative Study of Race, Ethnicity, Gender, and Class held at the University of California, Santa Cruz in May, 1986 and at the Second All-UC Conference on the Comparative Study of Race, Ethnicity, Gender, and Class held at the University of California, Davis in December, 1987. I thank Frank C. Child, then Dean of Social Sciences on the Santa Cruz campus, for funding the first conference and Calvin C. Moore, Associate Vice President for Academic Affairs, Office of the President, University of California, and Frank J. Samaniego, Assistant Vice Chancellor for Academic Affairs on the Davis campus, for supporting the second. The Davis conference could not have been organized without the enthusiastic cooperation of my colleague, Vicki L. Ruiz of the History Department, to whom I express my warmest appreciation.

Jenni Currie helped to edit the papers and did the tedious work of checking and standardizing everyone's footnotes, which came originally in many different formats and with all kinds of missing information. As my secretary during 1986, she also made the local arrangements for the first conference, while Peggy Hurley of Oakes College at Santa Cruz kept track of the finances. Charlotte Honeywell and Deborah Shields of the History Department at Davis took care of the local arrangements and the bookkeeping for the second conference. Thoreau Lovell provided technical support for the production of this volume. I am most grateful to all of them.

Introduction: American Dream, American Reality

Sucheng Chan

From the time English colonists founded Jamestown in 1607 to the present, more than fifty million people have come to the territory that became the United States. Immigration statistics for the colonial period are unreliable, but it has been estimated that almost four-fifths of the newcomers were English, Scottish, and Irish. With the exception of enslaved Africans, the rest also came mostly from countries of northwestern Europe. The influx after 1820 has been better documented: between that year and the mid-1870s, about two-thirds came from the British Isles, with the proportion from Ireland rising steadily vis-à-vis those from England and Scotland after 1840. Then, in the late 1860s, German and Scandinavian immigrants began increasing in numbers until they surpassed those from Great Britain by the 1880s. In the next two decades, people from central, eastern, and southern Europe became predominant in the immigrant stream. However, the 1924 Immigration Act sharply reduced that flow, so that northwestern Europeans were favored once more. Entrants from Canada, Mexico, and other countries of the western hemisphere were also important from the 1920s to the

1960s. During the entire three and half centuries before 1965, Asian immigrants formed a minuscule part of the total influx, but after the "national origins" basis of United States immigration laws was abolished in 1965, more and more Asians began coming. They now represent about half of all immigrants into the United States.

Most Americans believe that an overwhelming proportion of these millions of people have come in pursuit of the American dream, at the heart of which lies a democratic system of government and a capitalist economy. Both systems are attractive, because in theory they allow people to be rewarded according to their individual merit and hard work. But for many, the reality of life in America has been almost diametrically opposite to what the dream has promised. The essays in this volume examine a central paradox in American society: unlike the case for white immigrants, a majority of nonwhite Americans continues to suffer from persistent inequality, living under conditions that fall far short of the image that lured them here; yet people from Asia and Latin America keep coming. Why? Several of the essays suggest that one possible answer is that small cracks in the structural barriers confronting nonwhites--what might be called "windows of opportunity" or "entering wedges"--allow some members of nonwhite groups in this country to partake of the rewards of capitalism and democracy, thus keeping the dream alive for everyone.

The studies collected here rely on several kinds of data to evaluate the relative status of minority Americans: quantitative measures of economic and social standing, subjective perceptions of life satisfaction, and assessments of how nonwhites are represented in the mass media and in scholarly journals. The first six essays, by Paul Ong, Amado Cabezas and Gary Kawaguchi, Adalberto Aguirre, Jr., Refugio Rochin, Adela de la Torre, and Amado Cabezas et al. present objective measures of the economic status of blacks, Hispanics, and Asian Americans. Next, Edwin Almirol, relying on survey data, reports how Filipino Americans evaluate their own situation. Then Larry Shinagawa and Gin Yong Pang unravel the complexities of Asian American marriage patterns in order to challenge the underlying assumptions of assimilation theory. Silvia Santos et al. also use questionnaire data to tap at the perceptions of Mexican American and white students regarding their respective statuses. Finally, Federico Subervi-Velez and Chalsa Loo et al. examine the representation of nonwhite minorities on television and in community psychology journals, respectively. Although none of the authors addresses directly the paradox I have identified, each of their studies illuminates some of the contradictions that face people of color in the United States today. In this introduction, I offer my interpretation of what these studies reveal about the complicated nature of multiethnic America.

Paul Ong analyzes the earnings of American-born black and Hispanic males, compared to white males, based on data culled from the public use samples of four U.S. censuses of population in "Uncertain Economic Progress: Racial Inequality Among California Males, 1940-1980." Unlike many existing studies of income inequality, which look at data from only a single census year, Ong's longitudinal analysis reveals patterns that cannot be discerned in single-year studies. He shows how there has indeed been "progress"--as measured by a closing of the gap in earnings between white males and the two groups of nonwhites--over the entire period, but the rate of progress has been uneven. Most importantly, his data indicate that most of the progress came in a single decade, the 1940s.

In the 1940s all blacks, as well as more educated, urbanized, and older Hispanics (but not less educated, rural, and younger ones) managed to close part of the income gap between themselves and white males. In the subsequent three decades, only certain subgroups within the black and Hispanic populations made economic progress. Blacks, regardless of their socioeconomic characteristics, suffered a setback in the 1950s from the gains they had made in the preceding decade. As a matter of fact, the incomes of the more educated and less educated blacks converged. The only group that gained a little during the 1950s was "average Hispanics." The rest of the Hispanic population neither gained nor lost much ground. In the 1960s and 1970s, middle-class blacks gained the most economically, vis-à-vis white males, while other blacks and Hispanics overall experienced virtually no upward mobility. In 1979, the "cost of being non-Anglo," i.e., the size of the income disparity, was about the same as it had been in 1949.

Ong then tests the human capital theory of income inequality by looking at the "investments" in, and "returns" to, education for each of the three groups. He found that while the educational attainment of blacks improved over the four decades, the "returns" to education that they enjoyed were inconsistent: about the same as whites in 1940, higher in 1950 and 1980, and lower in 1960 and 1970. As for Hispanics, even though they experienced higher "returns" to education than white males did in all years except 1970, their consistently lower educational attainment level (i.e., "investment") meant that the gap between their income and that of whites remained unbridged.

Ong concludes that the gains of the 1940s were made possible not by ordinary market forces but by "massive structural changes" in the United States economy resulting from the vast expansion of defense industries during World War II--a boom that finally ended the Great Depression. He also suggests that the struggles of blacks during the Civil Rights era may have helped them to recover some of the losses they suffered during the 1950s, while raising the "possibility that the economic decline [of the 1950s] was an impetus for the Civil Rights movement." That is to say, political struggles may have both resulted from, and subsequently helped to counteract, the secular downward economic trend.

By calling into question the ability of competitive market forces to improve the socioeconomic status of certain racial/ethnic minority groups in the United States, Ong suggests that theories of assimilation do not seem to be borne out by reality. Rather, his data lend credence to "conflict" theories that claim that the upward mobility of nonwhite minorities is ordinarily blocked by structural barriers in the American economy as it is presently organized. During "normal" periods, most people of color are relegated to that part of the labor market that offers fewer rewards in terms of pay and working conditions, though the "upper echelons" of the minority groups--that is, the better educated young people who reside in urban areas, the cream of whom are professionals--are able to make some gains. It is only during periods of exceptional economic expansion that a sufficiently large number of "windows" open up to enable other nonwhites, women of all ethnic backgrounds, and certain "white ethnics" to make significant inroads into the better paid and more secure primary labor market.

The 1970s was a period of economic contraction, rather than expansion, so it is interesting to examine how nonwhite groups were faring when the 1980 census was taken. In "Industrial Sectorization in California in 1980: The Continuing Significance of Race/Ethnicity, Gender, and Nativity," Amado Cabezas and Gary Kawaguchi use the five-percent Public Use Microdata Sample of the 1980 Census of Population to study the placement of various groups in sixteen different sectors of California's economy. They argue that treating the state as a whole does not reveal the full extent of inequality in terms of employment; only by dividing its economy into "industrial sectors," according to a scheme first proposed by Robert Kaufman, Randy Hodgson, and Neil Fligstein, can we see clearly how race and ethnicity, nativity, and gender still operate to differentiate various groups in terms of the economic rewards they receive.

Choosing California for close study is useful because it has been a frontier in more than a geographic sense. Home of numerous social experiments, the state has led the nation in changing agricultural production from farming to agribusiness, in developing a high-technology and service economy, and in dealing with the challenges posed by the presence of an ethnically-mixed population. Thus, the findings of Cabezas and Kawaguchi are important because they not only document the current situation in California but also presage what the future might look like in some other parts of the country.

The "service" nature of the California economy is revealed by the fact that in 1980 only four of its sixteen sectors were of the "core" type, characterized by large size, ownership concentration, and capital intensity, and these four provided only one-fifth of the jobs in the state. But even this "core" manufacturing is more light than heavy, devoted mainly to the making of electrical machinery, apparel and accessories, and printing and publishing. About three-quarters of the state's employment is found in the periphery manufacturing and services, wholesale trade, small shops, local monopolies, and educational services sectors, where large proportions of the jobs are either clerical or blue-collar.

Glossing over some of the fine points in Cabezas and Kawaguchi's study, it can be said that in general the best paid and most prestigious jobs in management and the professions are primarily held by white men and secondarily by Asian American men. Clerical ranks are filled mostly by U.S.-born white, black, and Asian American women, while blue-collar jobs are mainly relegated to black and Mexican American men, regardless of their nativity, and to foreign-born Asian and Mexican women. The most significant numbers that Cabezas and Kawaguchi present are found in the bottom rows of their Tables 4 through 10. These show the "occupational distribution" within specific industries. In all sectors--with the exception of the educational services sectors, where professionals fill more than three-fifths of the available jobs in higher education and almost nine-tenths of those in elementary and secondary education--managerial and professional ranks represent relatively small fractions of the employment available and are greatly outnumbered by clerical and blue-collar jobs. That means the number of nonwhites and women who can achieve upward socioeconomic mobility via the managerial/professional route will remain relatively small. Moreover, white resistance to Asian American and female encroachment in these ranks is likely to increase, as competition for the limited number of positions at the top of the occupational hierarchy intensifies.

The findings of Cabezas and Kawaguchi remind us that though most *legal* barriers to inequality have been removed, there still exist many economic and social blocks embedded in the structure of the economy itself that prevent nonwhites, females, and the foreign-born from enjoying the same benefits that whites, males, and the U.S.-born receive. To be sure, there are *some* nonwhites who have managed to acquire good jobs and high social status, but they tend to be male and American-born. Their "success" camouflages the plight of the far larger numbers who do not possess the necessary ascriptive characteristics to advance in American society.

If the studies of Ong and Cabezas and Kawaguchi offer some glimmer of hope, the data in Adalberto Aguirre's paper, "Poverty in the United States: Race, Ethnic, and Gender Differentials," are completely grim. He shows that the percentage of individuals, as well as of families, living below the poverty line has increased in all three groups he studied--whites, blacks, and Hispanics. An increasing number of families are living in poverty despite the fact that median family income rose between 1970 and 1980. The contradictory trends indicate that the rise in cost of living outpaced the increase in median family income. More importantly, as shown in Aguirre's Table 3, the increase has been sharpest after 1980 for both individuals and families. With median family income falling between 1980 and 1983, more and more people are plunging headlong into poverty. This means that the general trend discovered by Ong--that during the 1960s and 1970s Hispanics and blacks, for the most part, recovered what they had lost during the 1950s--is rapidly being reversed in the 1980s.

In addition, Aguirre's data on female householder families reveal a development that should be taken very seriously by public policy-makers. Not only are women of all ethnic backgrounds earning much less than men--many studies show they have always done so--but the number of poor female-headed households is sharply growing. In the days when women's earnings mainly supplemented their husbands' incomes, their low wages had less dire consequences than at present, when female earnings constitute the sole source of income in an increasing number of households. As

Aguirre points out, nowadays when poor women start households of their own, given their low earnings (if they work) or their total dependence on welfare, they are simply duplicating the households they have left. In short, the reproduction of poverty is occurring at an accelerating pace in the United States. And this, in turn, "eclipses any likelihood of intergenerational improvement in particular households." In the lives of poor minority women who are the sole support of their families, race, ethnic, gender and class inequalities tragically converge.

Since the well-being of various nonwhite groups is not all alike, it is important to examine specific ones in detail. In "The Socioeconomic Status of the Hispanic Population in the United States," Refugio Rochin synthesizes what is known about different subgroups of Hispanics to illustrate the importance of not lumping them all together. Hispanics are internally differentiated by race, national origins, culture, immigration history, and region of settlement. By looking at demographic statistics, indices of income and poverty, educational attainment and other aspects of schooling, employment patterns, and entrepreneurial activities, Rochin paints a nuanced picture of the resident Spanish-speaking population in the United States.

In many ways, the Spanish-speaking population forms the pivotal minority group in the nation, if for no other reason than the fact that, due to a number of factors, in the last seven years it has increased five times faster than the U.S. population as a whole. Hispanics are younger, with a larger proportion of women in their prime childbearing years; they tend to marry at a younger age; the women have a higher fertility rate; and the group as a whole experiences a large net in-migration, both legal and undocumented. If these trends continue, the Hispanic population may well double in thirty years and possibly triple in sixty years.

Such increases are cause for concern, given the fact that in 1986 more than five million Hispanic families (25 percent of the total) live below poverty and the percentage of Hispanic children living below poverty in female-headed households exceeds that of black children (72 versus 69 percent, respectively). Although the dollar value of the median family income for Hispanics has increased since 1970, when inflation is taken into account real family income for the group has actually fallen by more than $2,000. Hispanic income is depressed not only because so many members of the group receive low wages, but also because the rate of unemployment among them is 1.6 times higher than among non-Hispanics. Having large numbers of wage-earners confined to jobs with inherently high turnover rates, thousands of recent immigrants who lack the skills needed to land desirable jobs in a high-technology and service economy, and a sizable group of young people who leave school to enter the labor market during their teenage years when they are least employable, the Hispanic population faces a very dire situation indeed.

Because there is such a clear correlation between economic deprivation and low educational attainment, Rochin concludes that unless Hispanic youngsters do better in school, the prospects for their communities as a whole are pessimistic. Researchers and public policy-makers differ on what they consider to be the causes of the poor academic performance of Hispanic children. Controversies rage over how best to change the situation. Scholars, politicians, and community advocates argue over the relative importance of improving such students' English-only schooling versus bilingual education, integration versus providing better resources for ghetto schools, and promoting assimilation versus maintaining the cultural heritage of the children in order to enhance their self-esteem. Rochin rightly points out that the burden of assimilating does not rest solely on the shoulders of Hispanics; rather, how receptive the dominant society is to their efforts also matters. Unfortunately, the lack of receptivity is a factor that many observers ignore or downplay. But they cannot afford to do so, since, in the words of Rochin, the situation facing Hispanics is a virtual "time bomb."

The brightest spot in an otherwise bleak picture is provided by Cuban immigrants, who have shown an extraordinary proclivity to enter small business. Scholars have tried to explain why that group has differed from the rest. The main reason seems to be that, unlike immigrants from Mexico or Puerto Rico, a large majority of the Cubans came from well-off or at least middle-class families trying to escape the strictures of Communism. After their arrival, they have used the wealth and "human capital"--education and work experience--they brought with them to create a firm economic foundation for themselves in the Miami metropolitan area where they are heavily concentrated. Although their success is largely a class phenomenon, Rochin argues that it will be possible for other Hispanic groups to follow in their footsteps, mainly because the Hispanic consumer market is increasing in size, despite the relative poverty of the group, and Spanish-speaking entrepreneurs are best able to understand, and consequently to capture, this growing market. Better schooling and entrepreneurship, therefore, are the two rays of hope Rochin sees for the Hispanic population.

Another aspect of Hispanic well-being, health, is examined by Adela de la Torre in "Latino Health in the 1980s: Critical Health Policy Issues." She shows that the status of Hispanic health care is poor. The adult mortality rate is higher among Hispanics than among non-Hispanics, with homicide as the leading killer. Although infant mortality thus far has not been alarming among Spanish-speakers, as the percentage of teenage pregnancies increases, without a concomitant improvement in prenatal and postnatal care, and as AIDS spreads to the Hispanic population, the statistics may soon worsen. De la Torre points out that the status of Hispanic health cannot be understood solely within a medical model, because poor health will incur long-term economic and social costs not only for the Hispanic population but also for American society as a whole.

In light of such pessimistic data, those who want to show that the American dream still works have turned to Asian Americans to prove their point. In the last two decades, journalists, television reporters, and scholars alike have touted Asian Americans as the "model minority" because they possess high educational attainment levels, enjoy high median family income, and show a low rate of "deviance."

In "Income Differentials Between Asian Americans and White Americans in California, 1980," Amado Cabezas, Larry Shinagawa, and Gary Kawaguchi investigate the truth of the assertion that the experience of Asian Americans is an exception to the general experience of nonwhites. First, they present figures from the 1980 published census to expose the flimsy empirical foundation on which the "successful" minority image of Asian Americans has been built. Next, they analyze data contained in the five-percent Public Use Microdata Samples of the 1970 and 1980 Censuses of Population for the San Francisco and Los Angeles metropolitan areas to measure the amount of "progress" various groups have made and to assess how well human capital theory accounts for each group's income gap.

By comparing various indicators for Asian immigrants--who now make up the majority of the population in all Asian American groups except among Japanese Americans--with U.S.-born whites, Cabezas and his coauthors show that, indeed, Asian immigrants, with the exception of the Chinese who show a bimodal distribution, have more years of schooling than whites, but their high educational attainment level is something that they brought with them; consequently, it reflects the selectivity of U.S. immigration policy (which favors highly educated professionals) rather than the "openness" of the American educational system. Most groups also have a median family income that is only slightly below that of whites, with the exception of Filipinos who have a higher median family income than whites. But this is due to the fact that there are more workers per family who pool their earnings. The labor force participation of all Asian American groups is high; that for Filipinos is nine points higher than the percentage for whites. The median *per capita* income of Asian Americans, in contrast to their median *family* income, is considerably lower than that of whites: in California in 1980, while white men earned $23,400 per capita, Chinese immigrant men earned only $15,900, Filipino immigrant men $14,500, and Korean immigrant men $19,200, or 68, 62, and 82 percent, respectively, of white male income. The income of women of all ethnic backgrounds was only approximately half that of white males: $13,300 (57 percent) for white women, $10,600 (45 percent) for Chinese immigrant women, $12,100 (52 percent) for Filipina immigrant women, and 11,500 (49 percent) for Korean immigrant women. There are also more Asian immigrant families as well as individuals living below the poverty level and a considerably larger percentage of them are in blue-collar or low-paid white-collar jobs.

The second set of statistics presented by Cabezas et al. contains two significant findings. First, only Japanese American men in Los Angeles now earn more than white men, by virtue of the fact that they receive higher "returns" for their human capital "investment." Every other group has lower "returns," while U.S.-born Chinese and Filipino men and women have both lower "returns" and lower "investments." Second, while every Asian American group has managed to narrow the income gap between itself and the comparison white male group between 1970 and 1980--in some cases, by significant percentage points--there is still income disparity across the board (with the exception of a small number of Japanese American men). In the 1970-1980 decade, U.S.-born Chinese American men and women made the largest gains in income, whittling away the gap between themselves and white males by 31 and 26 percentage points, respectively. They did this in spite of the fact that they have lower "investments" due to their relative youthfulness. Although Cabezas and his associates do not attempt to predict what 1990 census data will show, I think it is safe to say that in all likelihood, the Asian American group that will experience the most spectacular gains by 1990 will be these same U.S.-born Chinese Americans whose "investments" will have increased with age. The parallel rise in percentage points for U.S.-born Chinese men and women, however, camouflages the continued existence of gender inequality: the women earned only 53 percent of what white men earned in 1980, compared to the men, who earned 86 percent of white men's income.

The one Asian American group that deviates from the general pattern is Filipino Americans. Between 1970 and 1980, Filipinos, foreign-born and U.S.-born, male and female alike, made the smallest gains. That Filipinos have not shared in the economic advances made by Asian Americans in general can be seen very clearly by comparing them with blacks and Hispanics. As shown in Table 1 in Cabezas' essay, both foreign-born and U.S.-born Filipino men earned only 64 percent of the income of white men, while U.S.-born black men earned 70 percent and U.S.-born Mexican American men earned 72 percent. In contrast, the earnings of all other Asian American men, foreign- as well as native-born, exceeded those of black and Hispanic men.

Cabezas et al. do not explain why Filipino Americans' earnings lag behind, and neither does Edwin Almirol in "The Economic Adaptation of Filipino Americans in California, 1980." Almirol, however, does explore why, despite their low earnings in the United States, Filipino immigrants keep coming. He uses survey data to link the current socioeconomic status of his respondents to their motivations for emigration and to their own perception of their conditions before and after emigration. In the process, Almirol shows that people care about many things besides money.

Almirol's data underscore a fact that many observers already know from impressionistic evidence: Asian immigrants, particularly Filipino immigrants, are distributed bimodally in terms of occupation. If we aggregate Almirol's data, we find that among the fathers of his 1,500-plus respondents, 31 percent are professionals and 54 percent are working-class, while among the respondents themselves, 54 percent are professionals and 26 percent are working-class.

Professionals and working-class people apparently have different aspirations: among Almirol's respondents, the former seek "life fulfillment," while the latter are more interested in money *per se*. It can be inferred, therefore, that the two groups have different motives for emigration. The professionals want not only higher wages but also better "working conditions"--however these may be defined in the various professions--while the working-class people are lured primarily by the larger income they think they can earn in the U.S., but the picture is muddied by the fact that not only do many Filipino American families have multiple wage-earners but a good number of individuals often have more than one job. For example, it is not uncommon for professionals simultaneously to own small businesses. Such a dual-occupation pattern suggests that the immigrants are hedging their bets: they try to acquire social status by making sure that at least a few members of their families become professionals, while the rest work to reap whatever rewards that entrepreneurship or even menial labor may bring.

Whether their families are in the Philippines or here in the United States, Almirol's respondents care about being with their relatives more than anything else. Twenty-eight percent of them listed the desire to join family members already here as their primary motive for emigration. If we add the 15 percent (all women) who came because their husbands decided to, then 43 percent of them came for "kinship" reasons. Another indication of how kinship ties lead to chain migration is that 60 percent of the respondents have relatives who had preceded them to the United States, while 57 percent settled in California because they already had family members here. Almirol concludes that despite their relatively low earnings, Filipinos keep coming to the United States because, by pooling their earnings, they find their collective income is sufficient to "meet their needs," and so they are relatively satisfied with their lot in the United States. Also, joining family members already here gives them emotional satisfaction that helps to compensate for the economic discrimination they face.

By telling us something about the Filipinos' post-migration situation, Almirol has recounted only one part of their story. If we wish to get the whole picture, we must look at a host of reasons related to the political, social, and economic conditions in the Philippines that account for the large exodus of recent years. For example, if we are to argue that professionals come to the United States because they desire better working conditions, then we must ask what makes working conditions undesirable for them in the Philippines. To take another example, Almirol's data show that Filipino professionals are underemployed in California. Are they just as or even more underemployed in the Philippines, and if so, is that why they decided to emigrate? Or, if we hypothesize that investing in small business is one way that immigrants consolidate the middle-class standing of their families, then we must ask why those with savings don't invest them in their homeland.

Besides the opportunities that open up during a period of exceptional economic expansion, the entry of U.S.-born Asian American males into managerial and professional ranks, the achievements of Cuban immigrant entrepreneurs, and the pooling of income by Filipino immigrants, there is an additional phenomenon that makes a degree of upward mobility possible: marriage across ethnic and class boundaries. In "Marriage Patterns of Asian Americans in California, 1980," Larry Shinagawa and Gin Yong Pang offer a sophisticated analysis of the reportedly high rate of interracial marriage among Asian Americans. They show that although the raw statistics indicate that Asian Americans indeed outmarry more than other ethnic groups (30 versus 8 percent interracially), after the rates have been adjusted for sample size, the rate for Asian Americans no longer greatly exceeds that for the California population as a whole. Moreover, once the large number of "war brides"--foreign-born Asian women married to American military personnel--has been taken into account, then interracial marriage mainly characterizes well-educated Asian Americans with high incomes, rather than the Asian-ancestry population overall. (Among women of Japanese ancestry, only 14 percent of the U.S.-born are married to white males, compared to 42 percent of the foreign-born who are.) In short, like Cuban entrepreneurship, the tendency of Asian Americans to marry whites is a class-related phenomenon.

Shinagawa and Pang use their findings to challenge the conclusions of other scholars who have argued that the high rate of Asian American interracial marriage is "proof" that assimilation is indeed possible. Although many of these theorists base their analysis on Milton Gordon's conceptual scheme, in which he delineates seven different forms of assimilation, they ignore a central point Gordon makes: different kinds of assimilation occur *sequentially*. In particular, Gordon argues that structural assimilation (i.e., acceptance of members of minority groups into the economic, social, and political organizations of the dominant society) must occur before marital assimilation can take place. What scholars of intermarriages have done, however, is to trace the causal relationship backwards: they argue that since the rate of Asian American intermarriage is high, *ipso facto* it must mean that structural assimilation has occurred.

Shinagawa and Pang do not accept the prevailing wisdom. Instead, they interpret their data according to hypergamy theory, which posits that in a class, caste, or racially stratified society, women of higher caste or racial origins but lower class standing will tend to marry men of lower caste or racial status but higher class positions. The partners both gain by "exchanging" something each desires from the other. Shinagawa and Pang then examine the rates of interracial marriage according to class standing, using "labor force status," labor market position, and family income as "approximators" of class.

"Labor force status" is a term that Shinagawa and Pang have coined to refer to the employment status of individuals. It is not the same as "labor force participation," a *ratio* based on the number of individuals employed divided by the number who are working plus those who are actively seeking employment in a given period. They find that for U.S.-born Asian American men and women alike, a larger fraction of those who are interracially married are employed. As for occupational position in the labor market--which refers to the relative prestige and remunerative rewards of various categories of jobs--the authors find that in general, proportionately more interracially married Asian Americans occupy higher (i.e., managerial/professional) positions. An exception is found, however, among foreign-born women. In that group, a larger proportion of intramarried ones have professional jobs for two reasons: first, many of them had advanced training and considerable job experience *before* they immigrated and have managed to retain their employment status after arrival, and second, their comparison group is foreign-born Asian wives of military personnel with relatively little education.

The picture with regard to income is complex. When *individual* median income is examined, interracially married Asian American men as well as women have higher incomes than their intramarried counterparts. However, if *family* income is used as the yardstick, then intramarried households tend to have higher median incomes, due to the cohabitance of relatives outside of the immediate nuclear family who contribute to the familys' financial pool.

These refined data clearly support hypergamy theory. If assimilation theory is correct, interracially married individuals should be evenly distributed among the different classes of a minority population. Such is not the case for Asian Americans. The incidence of interracial marriage differs among the different socioeconomic strata and is most prevalent among U.S.-born, well-educated, and high-income individuals, with the exception of foreign-born women married to military personnel. Thus, it appears that, as in the labor market, the opportunity for upward socioeconomic mobility through marriage is also selective and limited.

What are the political implications of the uneven progress experienced by different segments of America's minority populations? None of the contributors to this volume directly addresses this issue. However, Silvia Santos, Raymond Garza, and Lisa Bohon-Hock offer a hint in "Perceptions of Intergroup Relations: A Comparison of Anglo American and Mexican American University Students." The three authors rely on Henri Tajfel's social identity theory to guide their research design. Tajfel argues that people usually try to maximize their self-esteem, and since individuals tend to define themselves mainly through their membership in social groups, in order to increase their self-esteem they will seek to belong to groups with positive social identities. In the United States, because white Americans have imposed a negative social identity on Mexican Americans, Mexican Americans today who wish to improve their situation must either leave their own group for a higher-status one or they must struggle to change the society that has relegated them to the bottom rung of its status hierarchy. Social identity theory hypothesizes, however, that before members of a group are prepared to take drastic action, they must perceive their situation to be illegitimate.

Santos et al. find that their Mexican American respondents in general *do* think their low status is unjustified and therefore they tend to favor a "social change" approach to improving their lot more than do whites. In other words, they believe that individuals can better their lives only when the standing of the *entire group* is upgraded through structural realignments, i.e., changes in the power relationships in American society. White students, on the other hand, think that individual mobility does exist, so they favor it. The results reported in the study by Santos et al. show that the respondents have an accurate perception of American society: for a good many whites, individual advancement *is* possible. Whether Mexican Americans can translate their desire for an enhanced social identity into action, and what form such action will take, are questions that require further exploration.

Though inequality between minority and white Americans is most glaringly apparent in economic terms, it is also manifested in other ways, including how people of color are represented in various media. In "Interactions Between Latinos and Anglos on Prime-Time Television: A Case Study of 'Condo'," Federico Subervi-Velez applies some widely used social science concepts to the analysis of television portrayals of minority groups.

The story line of "Condo" hinges on the interactions between a Latino family and its Anglo neighbors. Examining the length of time that members of the two families appear together, the contents of the statements they make, and the nature of the scenes portrayed, Subervi-Velez reaches several conclusions. First, the show is unusual in that interactions between the Latino and Anglo characters occur 61 percent of the time. Moreover, the Latinos are central, and not just background, characters. They are not stereotyped negatively and are shown to be more inclined towards pluralism than assimilation. Of twenty scenes that Subervi-Velez analyzes, only three reflect assimilationist values, ten lean towards pluralism, while seven show mutual accommodation.

Obviously, "Condo" is a great improvement over past

representations of minorities in film and on television. According to Subervi-Velez, the message imparted by the show is that "Latinos can be upwardly mobile, relate to Anglo neighbors, and still retain aspects of their own culture." Unfortunately, the show lasted only one season. Subervi-Velez is not certain why it was not continued. The show clearly suffered because it was aired in the same time slot as the highly popular "Magnum, P. I." and "Fame," but perhaps just as important was the fact that the writers and producers did not seem to have had much interest in promoting the series, possibly because the very fact that it conveyed such a positive view of Latinos made it suspect.

The short life of "Condo" is a pity, for, as Subervi-Velez points out, television can play a significant role in socializing viewers to positive ways of interacting with people of different ethnic backgrounds. Given the fact that many people have little first-hand knowledge of minority Americans, and the fact that many of them seem to rely on television as their main source of information, how minorities are represented on television can affect how people treat them in real life.

Whereas television is aimed at a popular audience, scholarly journals are published by and for academic specialists, who, being better educated than "Mr. and Mrs. Middle America," are conceivably more enlightened in their attitude toward minority groups. Such, however, is not necessarily the case.

In "Studies of Minority Groups in Community Psychology Journals," Chalsa Loo, Kenneth Fong, and Gayle Iwamasa examine more than 1800 articles in three journals in community psychology to assess the extent to which these works have promoted pluralism and cultural diversity in the last fifteen years. They chose community psychology for analysis because the field supposedly is more sensitive than are other social science disciplines to the concerns and needs of underrepresented and underserved groups.

Loo et al. find that over the period they studied, only 13 percent of the articles in the three journals promoted cultural diversity while the rest did not. Although the percentage of articles on minorities has risen over time, still, the overall proportion is considerably smaller than the approximately 20 percent that nonwhite groups comprise in the U.S. population in 1980. The authors believe they are justified in choosing a benchmark based on demography because the field of community psychology was founded to promote a better understanding and to serve the needs of hitherto neglected groups. They suggest that it will be useful to carry out similar studies of journals in other disciplines to see whether they have done any better in terms of promoting cultural pluralism. It is likely that we will find they have not.

The studies in this volume show that the general conditions faced by nonwhite minorities in the United States today are not sanguine. There still exist wide discrepancies in the income and social standing of nonwhites and women vis-à-vis white male Americans. Nevertheless, there are a few channels of upward mobility open to selected individuals within the minority groups--primarily young, well-educated, U.S.-born professionals and small-scale entrepreneurs. The fact that such groups are able to "make it" allows defenders of the American dream to ignore the harsh realities that saddle the lives of millions of impoverished people, many of whom are immigrants from Third World countries. But the question, "If things are so bad, why do they keep coming?" cannot be answered without an analysis of why some nations are poor and who is responsible for creating and perpetuating such destitution on a worldwide scale. Leftist scholars have argued that the foreign policies of the United States and the economic behavior of American corporations are in large measure responsible. If one accepts such a thesis, then one is led to the conclusion that the heavy immigration of recent years represents a global safety valve: by letting a "lucky few" obtain visas to enter the United States, and after their arrival making it possible for an even more choice group to climb the ladder of success, the revolutionary potential for the overthrow of capitalism is diminished. In this manner, the small number able to enjoy the fruits of American life are coopted and become its staunchest champions.

Uncertain Economic Progress: Racial Inequality Among Californian Males, 1940-1980

Paul M. Ong

Introduction

Despite California's image as a land of opportunity, from the days of the gold rush to the recent high-tech boom, not all racial groups have shared equally in its fortunes. American-born Asians apparently have reached income parity with whites, but the same is not true for the other two major minority groups, Hispanics and blacks.[1] The Treaty of Guadalupe Hidalgo, which ceded the Southwest to the United States, guaranteed equal protection to the Mexicans who chose to remain in the territory, but they soon became a subordinated minority.[2] Blacks have migrated to California since the second half of the nineteenth century and have experienced discrimination since that time.[3] Years of change have not eliminated a considerable income gap between white males, on the one hand, and black and Hispanic males on the other hand. At the same time, there have been periods when minorities did improve their relative economic status.[4] Thus, the issue is not whether there has been economic progress, but what has been its nature.

California shares some similarities with the nation in terms of long-run trends in racial inequality, but it is likely that the state also has some unique patterns due to two important factors.[5] The first is that racial progress in regions outside the South has been minimal at best, as hypothesized by Reich.[6] Much of the observed closing of the earnings gap at the national level has resulted from black migration away from a very oppressive South to relatively less oppressive regions and from a decline in racial inequality within the South itself, which nonetheless still exhibits the greatest racial disparity among the various regions of the United States. In the other areas, secular progress has occurred at a snail's pace or has been entirely absent. Consequently, national trends obscure a persistence of racial inequality in some regions. Reich's hypothesis suggests that, at the very least, racial inequality in California may not have waned to the same extent as observed for the nation as a whole.

The second factor that may cause California to deviate from the national trend is the state's more complex racial situation. Racial stratification is not merely along a black-white line, for there is a sizeable Hispanic population. In fact, Hispanics constitute the state's largest minority group. Whereas they represented only 6 percent of the state's population in 1940, by 1980, they comprised 16 percent.[7] By contrast, blacks comprised 2 percent of the population in 1940 and 8 percent in 1980. Theoretically, there is no *a priori* reason to assume that long-run changes in racial inequality in this setting with several ethnically diverse groups evolved in the same manner as in a setting with only two groups. There is also a methodological issue: the presence of a large Hispanic population can distort any analysis of the difference between blacks and whites because the census categorizes Hispanics as whites. For California, an analysis of racial inequality must include both Hispanics and blacks as minority groups, and must use Anglos (non-Hispanic whites) as the reference group.

This study examines the trends in racial inequality in California from 1939 to 1979 based on data from public use samples released by the Bureau of the Census.[8] The analysis includes Anglo, black, and Hispanic males who were born in the United States, are active in the labor market, and are between the ages of 24 and 64.[9] Foreign-born persons are excluded, so observed group differences are not confounded by the adjustment problems of immigrants.

There were three major findings:

1. From 1939 to 1979, racial inequality in annual earnings waned substantially, more for Hispanics than for blacks. However, the process was not linear. Much of the improvement occurred during the first decade. Blacks suffered a setback between 1949 and 1959, and after 1960, economic progress was either very slow or absent.

2. The cost of being non-Anglo followed a similar pattern: substantial progress between 1939 to 1979, with most of the improvements concentrated in the first decade, and with mixed results thereafter.

3. Differences in educational attainment played a role in

generating inequality between Hispanics and Anglos. Blacks experienced large fluctuations in their absolute and relative rates of returns to schooling, a pattern that suggests fluctuations in discrimination rather than in the quality of black education.

The remainder of this paper examines these points in detail: part one traces the trends in earnings; part two estimates the cost of being non-Anglo; and part three analyzes the effects of education on earnings. The last part discusses the implications of the findings on a broader debate over the relative effects of government intervention vis-à-vis market forces in promoting racial equality. The experience in California suggests that normal market forces played only a small role in the economic progress of minorities.

Technical details are placed in the appendix and footnotes.

Trends in Relative Earnings

An examination only of the end points between 1939 and 1979 leaves an impression of a long-term secular waning of racial inequality. (See Table 1.) In California, at the beginning of the forty years, Hispanics earned 55 percent of what Anglos earned, and blacks earned 53 percent.[10] By the end of the period, Hispanics earned 76 percent of what Anglos earned, and blacks earned 71 percent. The Californian pattern is consistent with two recent optimistic reports on the long-run improvement in the relative economic status of black males at the national level.[11] Smith and Welch report "a very

Table 1

Sample Characteristics

	Anglos	Hispanics	Compared to Anglos	Blacks	Compared to Anglos
Average annual income					
1940	$1,550	$847	55%	$819	53%
1950	$3,630	$2,540	70%	$2,500	69%
1960	$6,330	$4,880	77%	$4,010	63%
1970	$10,400	$7,830	75%	$6,860	66%
1980	$20,200	$15,400	76%	$14,300	71%
Average years of education					
1940	10.5	7.9	-2.6	8.4	-2.1
1950	11.1	8.6	-2.5	8.2	-2.9
1960	11.9	9.3	-2.6	9.9	-2.0
1970	12.8	10.4	-2.4	11.4	-1.4
1980	14.0	11.7	-2.3	13.0	-1.0
Average age					
1940	36.5	33.1	-3.4	35.8	-0.7
1950	36.7	33.6	-3.1	37.4	0.7
1960	38.3	35.4	-2.9	37.5	-0.8
1970	38.3	37.1	-1.2	37.4	-0.9
1980	36.4	35.6	-0.8	36.0	-0.4
Average Weeks Worked					
1940	44.1	39.2	89%	41.1	93%
1950	46.7	40.7	87%	44.4	95%
1960	47.5	46.1	97%	44.1	92%
1970	47.6	46.9	99%	45.4	95%
1980	47.4	46.1	97%	45.1	95%

Source: Pulic Use Microdata Sample, 1 percent sample from California

impressive rise in the relative economic status of black men over this forty year span," when blacks in the country as a whole improved their earnings from 43 percent of what whites earned in 1939, to 73 percent in 1979.[12] While their figures and those reported here are not directly comparable, both document a dramatic improvement in the economic status of minorities.

However, the story for California (and to a lesser degree, for the United States) is not simply one of linear progress. The bulk of the increase came in just one decade between 1939 and 1949. Unfortunately, thereafter improvements were not as spectacular nor always apparent.

Blacks lost ground between 1949 and 1959, when the black-to-Anglo earnings ratio fell from 69 percent to 63 percent. This sizeable drop is contrary to the notion of a continual waning of racial inequality. There are three potential explanations for this observed decline: one, the seeming decline could be due to random statistical error, since the figures are based only on samples; two, the decline was cyclical rather than secular; and three, it was a rare phenomenon restricted to California. Although these explanations are possible, the evidence indicates that they are not plausible.

Published census data for the country as a whole provide evidence that this setback is not a statistical fluke. In 1949, the median income of black males over the age of 14 was 71.5 percent of that of their white counterparts, but a decade later the equivalent figure fell to 69.5 percent.[13] Although the decline of 6 percentage points in my sample is larger than the 2 percentage points given in the published data, the discrepancy may be due to my use of Anglos rather than whites as the comparison group and the use of an older age group. In any case, the published statistics provide corroborating evidence that there was, in all likelihood, a real increase in racial inequality.

Neither did this increase appear to have been cyclical. Studies based on time-series analyses show that the black-white income ratio is positively correlated with the business cycle.[14] Since 1949 was a year of high unemployment, the 69 percent figure underestimates the underlying gap between black and Anglo earnings. Consequently, it is likely the observed drop understates the underlying secular downward trend.

Finally, the trend is not limited to California. Smith and Welch note a similar "anomaly" between 1949 and 1959 in the national data, which show that "relative black wages fell among younger workers and remained basically constant for the older male workforce."[15] Consequently, there was a widespread decline in the economic well-being of blacks by the eve of the Civil Rights movement.[16]

During the Civil Rights era, blacks in California recaptured what they had lost. By 1979, they earned on the average 71 percent of what Anglos earned. This is 8 percentage points higher than the rate for 1959, but only 2 percentage points higher than the rate for 1949. While there was progress, the rate of change was slow. A simple extrapolation shows that blacks will not achieve parity until several years after the second decade of the next century, and this is assuming that racial inequality will continue to wane.

Hispanics fared better than blacks in the post-World War II

period, but they encountered other problems. The two minority groups shared approximately the same economic status in 1939 and 1949, but Hispanics did not suffer the setback that blacks did during the 1950s. For the next three decades, Hispanics had higher earnings, which created a racial hierarchy with three distinct strata: Anglos on top, Hispanics in the middle, and blacks at the bottom. Race, however, remained paramount, since Hispanic income levels were closer to the income levels of blacks than of Anglos.

Despite the Hispanic people's relatively better position, they gained very little ground during the Civil Rights era. Their earnings relative to Anglos remained essentially unchanged through the 1960s and 1970s. Other studies have documented a decline in relative economic status for all Hispanic males, immigrant and American-born alike.[17] This decline was caused by a rapid increase in the alien population, which constituted only 19 percent of the state's Hispanic population in 1960, but 37 percent by 1980.[18] As the foreign-born population increased, average earnings dropped because immigrants earned far less than American-born Hispanics. While the demographic shift explains the decline, the figures in this study show clearly that while American-born Hispanics did not lose ground, neither did they make any progress.[19] The pessimistic recent trend in the economic status of Hispanics is not due simply to the changing composition of the population.[20]

Figure 1. Hispanic and Black Income Gaps and the Cost of Being Nonwhite

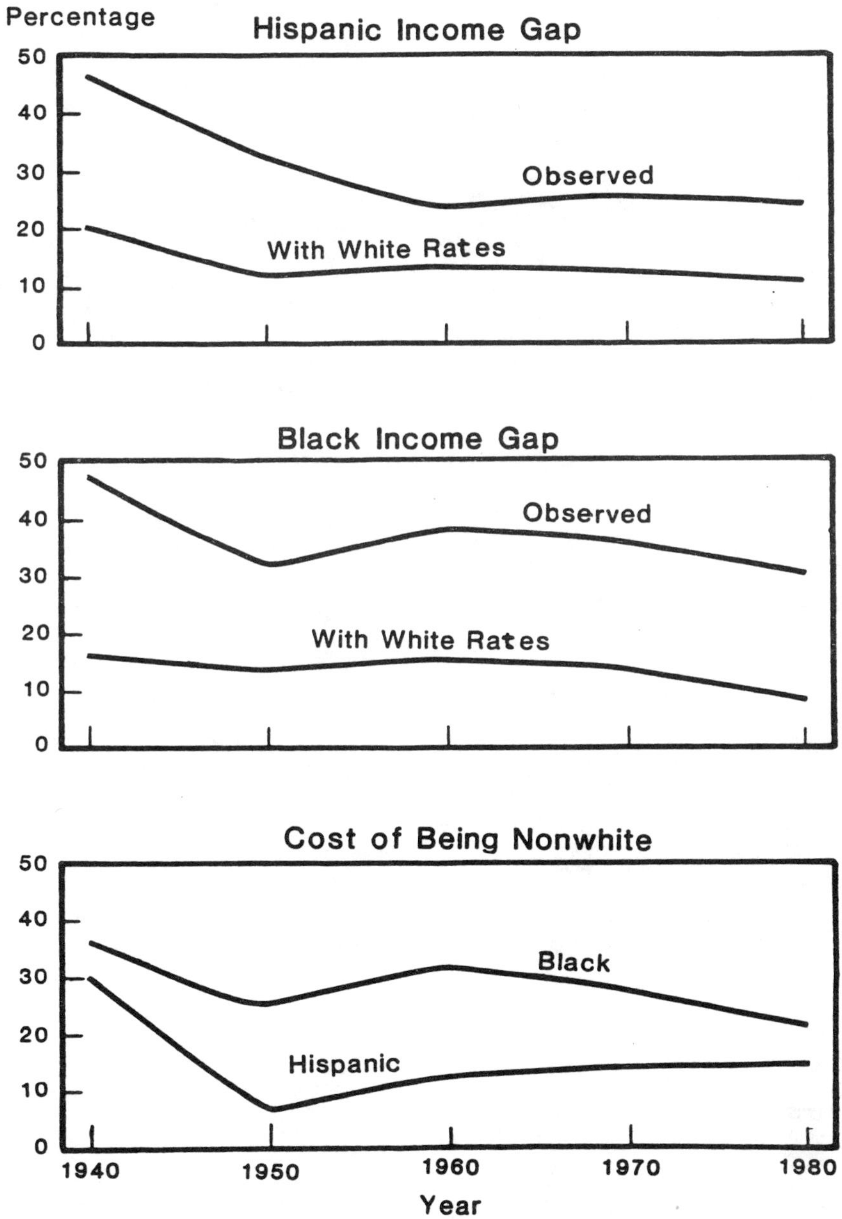

Table 2
Earnings Regressions

Dependent Variable: Log of Annual Earnings

1940	White	Hispanic	Black
intcp	1.3167 ***	0.599	1.7675 ***
school	0.08653 ***	0.1671 ***	0.06236
exp	0.06394 ***	0.1111 ***	0.06224
expsq	-0.0007728 ***	-0.001351 ***	-0.0009744 *
expsch	-0.002105 ***	-0.005695 ***	-0.001982
married	0.1642 ***	0.05074	0.1044
kids	0.02706 **	0.1526 *	0.01264
met	0.09882 ***	0.129	0.1674
lgwks	1.1008 ***	1.01016 ***	0.9813 ***
cencity	0.02222 *	0.03003	-0.03987
	R-sq = 0.4842	R-sq = 0.6289	R-sq = 0.5746
	n = 9248	n = 243	n = 243

1950	White	Hispanic	Black
intcp	2.3822 ***	3.5198 ***	3.4643
school	0.08573 ***	0.0589	0.1084 ***
exp	0.06142 ***	0.007234	0.04146
expsq	-0.0006771 ***	0.0001145	-0.0004074
expsch	-0.002264 ***	-0.000263	-0.002794
expcol	0.0009493	0.02209	0.002399
married	0.07124 ***	0.03525	0.03816
kids	0.06927 ***	0.1943 **	0.04192
vvet	-0.04491 ***	0.1363 **	-0.09348 *
met	0.04135 **	0.05266	-0.2055 *
lgwks	1.08925 ***	0.8707 ***	0.8786 ***
college	-0.04663 **	-0.313 *	-0.2345 **
cencity	-0.003411	0.1556 **	0.02382
	R-sq = 0.47	R-sq = 0.6	R-sq = 0.51
	n = 3951	n = 177	n = 265

1960	White	Hispanic	Black
intcp	2.8202 ***	2.9611 ***	2.9224 ***
school	0.07333 ***	0.06988 ***	0.05453 ***
exp	0.05482 ***	0.03732 ***	0.0626 ***
expsq	-0.0007326 ***	-0.0004739 ***	-0.0008932 ***
expsch	-0.001325 ***	-0.0007562	-0.001081
expcol	0.001905 ***	0.003383 **	-0.001081
married	0.1572 ***	0.1528 ***	0.1151 ***

	White	Hispanic	Black
kids	0.08536 ***	0.1067 ***	0.09165 ***
vvet	0.01715 **	-0.06175 **	0.009425
met	0.1206 ***	0.1894 ***	0.3957 ***
lgwks	1.09078 ***	1.05325 ***	0.9714 ***
college	-0.02792 ***	-0.05545 **	0.0284
cencity	-0.01276 *	-0.02068	-0.1032 ***
	R-sq = 0.48	R-sq = 0.54	R-sq = 0.51
	n = 19675	n = 1734	n = 1408
1970			
intcp	2.6901 ***	3.0752 ***	3.4796 ***
school	0.09574 ***	0.08732 ***	0.07939 ***
exp	0.06914 ***	0.06201 ***	0.06583 ***
expsq	-0.0008673 ***	-0.0007836 ***	-0.000856 ***
expsch	-0.001759 ***	-0.001268 *	-0.002131 ***
expcol	0.002104 ***	-0.0009351	0.00218
married	0.1363 ***	0.114 ***	0.1183 ***
kids	0.1019 ***	0.1187 ***	0.09878 ***
vvet	0.03184 ***	-0.07183 ***	0.0002805
met	0.1672 ***	0.1692 ***	0.2943 ***
lgwks	1.1199 ***	1.0211 ***	0.9081 ***
college	-0.2997 ***	0.01818 *	-0.01723
cencity	-0.02457 ***	-0.04088 *	-0.05252 *
	R-sq = 0.47	R-sq = 0.47	R-sq = 0.41
	n = 22391	n = 2126	n = 1895
1980			
intcp	3.000707 ***	3.7703 ***	2.4156 ***
school	0.11087 ***	0.0824 ***	0.1573 ***
exp	0.09002 ***	0.05544 ***	0.1116 ***
expsq	-0.00104 ***	-0.0006918 ***	-0.001185 ***
expsch	-0.002597 ***	-0.00113 *	-0.00423 ***
expcol	0.001855 ***	0.001667	0.003652 ***
married	0.1077 ***	0.05824 *	0.1027 ***
kids	0.07825 ***	0.1562 ***	0.06892 **
vvet	0.02052 **	-0.08813 ***	-0.01336
met	0.1156 ***	0.1004 **	0.1744
lgwks	1.147 ***	1.07141 ***	1.093 ***
college	-0.04352 ***	-0.0367 *	-0.07685 **
cencity	-0.0624 ***	-0.09255 ***	-0.06027 **
	R-sq = 0.46	R-sq = 0.51	R-sq = 0.52
	n = 24509	n = 2995	n = 2502

* p<.10 **p<.05 *** p<.01

The Cost of Being Non-Anglo

The raw income gaps discussed above resulted from both discrimination and variations in group characteristics. One method of measuring the extent of discrimination is to compare individuals of similar characteristics but of different racial origins. The regressions listed in the appendix are used to calculate two measures: one, the differences in earnings of the hypothetical average black (or Hispanic) with that of a hypothetical Anglo with similar characteristics; and two, the differences in earnings of the average white with that of a black (or Hispanic) with similar characteristics.[21] The results are reported in Table 2. These estimates of the cost of being non-Anglo include the effects of discrimination both within and outside the labor market, and no attempt is made here to disentangle the two.

The trends in discrimination parallel the racial gap in annual earnings. There was a sizeable decline between 1939 and 1979, about 10 percentage points or more, depending upon which measure is used. The progress was very concentrated in the first decade, with the decline in discrimination being the major factor accounting for the decrease in the size of the gap in annual earnings between Anglos and minorities. The individuals who benefited most from the decline in discrimination were those Hispanics with characteristics closest to the average Anglo--that is, the more educated, urbanized, and older Hispanics made greater progress than the less educated, rural, and younger Hispanics. At the same time, Hispanics made greater progress than blacks in general.

Some of the gains of the 1940s were lost in the following decade, as the indices of discrimination increased between 1949 and 1959 for average blacks, as well as for blacks and Hispanics with characteristics close to the average Anglo. Only average Hispanics experienced progress. These setbacks reinforce the notion that economic progress was not simply linear.

The results during the Civil Rights period were mixed. The measurable level of discrimination against Hispanics remained constant. While the average black experienced only a moderate decrease in discrimination, blacks closer to the average Anglo experienced a substantial decrease. This indicates that the more educated blacks were the major beneficiaries of the Civil Rights movement, which is consistent with what others have observed.[22] The diverse outcomes are consistent with Leonard's finding that the effects of affirmative action have been uneven.[23] In California, there were differences along both class and race lines.

The Role of Education

In most models of wage theory, particularly in human capital theory, formal education (along with on-the-job training) is considered a key causal factor of differential earnings.[24] Schooling is of particular interest to policy-makers because it has been widely supported by public funds in recent decades. There is no doubt that racial differences in levels of educational achievement generate economic inequality.[25] The crucial question is how important is education in this respect. Three aspects are examined here: years of education, the returns to education, and the contribution of differences in the educational level of particular minority groups to the income gap between themselves and Anglos.

All three groups generally experienced a secular increase in the average number of years of education. (See Table 3.) The exception is the decline for blacks from 8.4 years in 1940 to 8.2 years in 1950. This decline was probably due to an influx of less educated blacks from the South during World War II, a period when blacks were attracted to the state by the employment opportunities in the rapidly expanding defense industries.[26] Both Hispanics and blacks had lower levels of average educational achievement than Anglos, but blacks made gains in narrowing the gap while Hispanics did not. Blacks reduced the educational gap from a high of 2.8 years in 1950 to one year in 1980, but Hispanics continually lagged behind by about 2.5 years.

The marginal impact of education on annual earnings is estimated through the use of regressions listed in the appendix. The last three columns of Table 3 contain the net effects of an additional year of education on average annual earnings.[27] The fluctuations in the net rate of return to schooling for Anglos can be taken as short-run effects of the demand for workers with different educational levels.

For Hispanics, the rates of return were higher than those for Anglos with the exception of 1970, when the Hispanic rate was about one percentage point lower. Despite the relatively good returns to schooling--around 5 percent throughout the post-World War II period--Hispanics consistently lagged behind in educational achievement, as noted earlier. If the Hispanics had closed the gap in educational attainment, they could have eliminated over a third of the

Table 3
Weeks-worked Regressions

Dependent variable: log of weeks worked

	White	Hispanic	Black
1940			
intcp	3.1359 ***	2.442 ***	0.83
school	0.03028 ***	0.09425 ***	0.1565 ***
exp	0.01282 ***	0.04554	0.129 ***
expsq	-0.0001955 ***	-0.0005233	-0.001759 ***
expsch	-0.0002924	-0.002663	-0.003594 **
married	0.116 ***	0.07879	0.08594
kids	0.03757 ***	0.006579 **	0.008725
met	0.07753 ***	0.07194	0.1779
cencity	-0.0001825 ***	-0.02292	0.047
	R-sq = .055	R-sq = .049	R-sq = .131
	n = 9248	n = 243	n = 234
1950			
intcp	3.0627 ***	1.9147 ***	3.1444 ***
school	0.03972 ***	0.08081 *	0.06002 *
exp	0.02267 ***	0.1083 ***	0.02277
expsq	-0.0003067 ***	-0.001876 ***	-0.0003062
expsch	-0.0007626 **	-0.002004	-0.001306
expcol	0.002064 ***	0.02144	0.005131
married	0.1055 ***	-0.01594	-0.04166
kids	0.03726 ***	-0.0625	0.001439
vvet	0.02905 **	0.02291	-0.0207
met	0.0543 ***	0.1251	0.02371
college	-0.06385 ***	-0.2989	-0.1788
cencity	-0.02229 *	0.1025	0.02473
	R-sq = .042	R-sq = .137	R-sq = .014
	n = 3951	n = 177	n = 267
1960			
intcp	3.1418 ***	3.1613 ***	2.6205 ***
school	0.03823 ***	0.02914 **	0.05778 ***
exp	0.01692 ***	0.02288 **	0.04167 ***
expsq	-0.0001888 ***	-0.0003539 **	-0.0005614 ***
expsch	-0.0006018 ***	-0.0006116	-0.001655 **
expcol	0.0005417 **	0.001832	-0.002927 *
married	0.1075 ***	0.1027 ***	0.1485 ***

	White	Hispanic	Black
kids	0.0598 ***	0.1034 ***	0.03051
vvet	-0.002812	-0.03725 *	-0.005506
met	0.03097 ***	0.03071	0.149 **
college	-0.03811 ***	-0.04742 **	0.00734
cencity	-0.0139 ***	0.009293	0.01069
	R-sq = .060	R-sq = .069	R-sq = .046
	n = 19675	n = 1734	n = 1408
1970			
intcp	2.9523 ***	3.3379 ***	2.7853 ***
school	0.05089 ***	0.02358 **	0.03411 *
exp	0.02664 ***	0.01177	0.02542 **
expsq	-0.0002754 ***	-0.0001074	-0.0002744 *
expsch	-0.001086 ***	-0.0005914	-0.0009847
expcol	0.001295 ***	0.001054	0.001893 *
married	0.07947 ***	0.1284 ***	0.1126 ***
kids	0.05702 ***	0.02874	0.05177 **
vvet	-0.009287 ***	-0.04451 ***	-0.1838
met	0.05806 ***	0.0678 **	0.3003 ***
college	-0.05606 *	-0.03078 *	-0.0306
cencity	-0.01935	-0.03601 **	0.0334
	R-sq = .052	R-sq = .041	R-sq = .046
	n = 22392	n = 2126	n = 1895
1980			
intcp	2.3213 ***	2.6476 ***	1.9836 ***
school	0.1009 ***	0.06473 ***	0.1156 ***
exp	0.0445 ***	0.03385 ***	0.04687 ***
expsq	-0.0002496 ***	-0.0002874 **	-0.0001727
expsch	-0.002517 ***	-0.001392 ***	-0.002851 ***
expcol	0.002326 ***	-0.00005771	0.00186 *
married	0.06384 ***	0.07341 ***	0.05964 **
kids	0.04358 ***	0.05428 **	0.04827 *
vvet	-0.0006463	-0.02587	-0.03326
met	0.06952 ***	0.117 ***	0.1726
college	-0.0904 ***	-0.02988 *	-0.07954 ***
cencity	-0.02828 ***	-0.04547 ***	-0.04443 **
	R-sq = .043	R-sq = .045	R-sq = .036
	n = 24509	n = 2995	n = 2502

* p<.10 **p<.05 *** p<.01

gap in annual earnings. The low educational attainment suggests that Hispanics experienced significant institutional barriers to education.

Blacks showed a less consistent pattern. Their rates of return were higher than those for Anglos in 1950 and 1980, about the same in 1940, and lower in 1960 and 1970. The decline from 1950 to 1960 mirrored the increase in the cost of being non-Anglo and the drop in relative earnings for blacks from 1949 to 1959. The contraction in the rate implies that the more educated blacks suffered a greater setback than the less educated blacks, since the former's earnings drew closer to that of the latter. The situation was reversed by 1979, when the high rate of return favored the more educated blacks, leading to a greater proportional difference between their earnings and those of less educated blacks.

The movement in the rates of return for blacks are not consistent with the "vintage effect" hypothesis. Smith and Welch argue that the low rates observed in a number of studies are the result of black education being inferior to white education in the past, rather than just the result of current discrimination in the labor market.[28] Cross-sectional analysis that does not take into account the "vintage effect" would downwardly bias the estimated rate of return for educated blacks. If the rates in California were taken literally as indicators of the quality of education, then the conclusion would be that the quality of black education was on a par with Anglo education in 1939, superior to Anglo education in 1949, and inferior in 1959 and 1969. This fluctuation in the quality of education does not seem plausible, and it is more likely that changes in the intensity of discrimination against the more educated blacks was the driving force behind changes in the rates of return.[29]

Broader Implications

The empirical findings reported above provide insight into a major debate over the ability of the economic market vis-a-vis the government in promoting economic racial equality. Mainstream economists believe that competitive forces have been closing the income gap between whites and nonwhites.[30] An eclectic group of economists, on the other hand, argue that structural barriers hinder economic progress for minorities.[31] While the debate is mainly theoretical and ideological, it is also fought on empirical grounds, where the conclusions have policy implications, because the findings either support or undermine governmental intervention into the labor market on behalf of minorities.

The conservative position has received a boost from two recent reports which examine the long-run trends in racial inequality from 1939 to 1979. One written by the staff of the U.S. Civil Rights Commission states that black workers' earnings grew rapidly long before the 1964 Civil Rights Act.[32] Another by Welch and Smith asserts that "the general pattern of rising relative returns to black schooling emerged long before the Civil Rights activism."[33] Both reports favor the thesis that competitive forces have been instrumental in promoting this economic progress.

My findings for California suggest another interpretation. As documented above, much of the progress came in the first decade.

These gains were not the result of competitive forces; rather, they reflected the upturn following the end of the Great Depression, when employment opportunities expanded for minorities because of the extraordinary demand for workers in defense industries during World War II. In other words, the improvement in the relative economic status of minorities was the product of massive structural changes, rather than the normal workings of the economy.

The role of the Civil Rights movement should also be reinterpreted in light of the setbacks from 1949 to 1959. While Civil Rights legislation may not have produced the same progress that occurred in the 1940s, one could argue that the laws at least reversed the adverse trends of the 1950s and early 1960s. Things may have been worse without the Civil Rights laws. More intriguing is the possibility that the economic decline was an impetus for the Civil Rights movement.

The fact that we cannot assume that economic progress for minorities automatically results from competitive forces means that economic progress is uncertain. The reality is that if substantial declines in racial inequality are to occur, such improvements must also depend on structural changes and conscious political action.

Appendix

Definition of variables:

lgwage	Log of annual earnings
school	Number of years of education
exp	Years of potential labor market experience
expsq	Experience squared
expsch	Interaction term of school and experience
married	Dummy denoting whether married
kids	Dummy denoting presence of children
met	Dummy denoting whether in metropolitan area
lgwks	The log of weeks worked
cencity	Dummy denoting whether in a central city
college	Number of years of college
expcol	Interaction term of college and experience
vvet	Dummy denoting whether a military veteran

The recursive model:

Equation one:

lgwage = B*X + a*lgwks + e
where B is a vector of coefficients,
X is a vector of independent variables, and
e is a random term.

Equation two:

lgwks = D*X + u

where D is a vector of coefficients,
X is a vector of independent variables, and
u is a random term.

Corrections for sample-selection bias (James Heckman, "Sample Selection Bias as a Specification Error," *Econometrical* 47 [1979]:153-161) were examined but not used because the results were not consistently robust.

Notes

1. Victor Nee and Jimy Sanders, "The Road to Parity: Determinants of the Socioeconomic Achievements of Asian Americans," *Ethnic and Racial Studies* 8 (1985): 75-79.

2. Carey McWilliams, *North From Mexico: The Spanish-Speaking People of the United States* (New York: Greenwood Press, 1968); Joan W. Moore, *Mexican-Americans* (Englewood Cliffs, N.J.: Prentice-Hall, 1976).

3. Delilah Beasley, *The Negro Trail Blazers of California* (Los Angeles, 1919); California, Department of Industrial Relations, Division of Labor Statistics and Research, *Black Californians: Population, Education, Employment* (San Francisco: Fair Employment Practice Commission, 1963 and 1974).

4. This study is concerned with relative earnings rather than absolute earnings because the relative relationship can be taken as an indicator of racial discrimination. Annual earnings are analyzed rather than weekly or hourly wages because annual earnings determine living standards. The regressions in the appendix control for the number of weeks worked. Hourly data are not available for the early decades.

5. Reynolds Farley, "Three Steps Forward and Two Back? Recent Changes in the Social and Economic Status of Blacks," *Ethnic and Racial Studies* 8 (January, 1985): 4-28; James Smith and Finis Welch, "Closing the Gap-40 Years of Black Economic Progress," unpublished ms. University of California, Los Angeles, August, 1985; Civil Rights Commission cited in Joann Lubin, "Civil Rights Panel's Staff Drafts Report on Blacks' Status," *Wall Street Journal*, 4 Sept. 1986.

6. Michael Reich, *Racial Inequality: A Political-Economic Analysis* (Princeton: Princeton University Press, 1981).

7. Paul Ong, et al., "Socio-Economic Trends in California: 1940 to 1980," Employment Development Department, State of California, 1986.

8. The data set (CAL-PUMS) used for this study was prepared by this author and the California Employment Development Department. Categories and definitions that have changed from decade to decade have been standardized. While CAL-PUMS contains a 1 percent sample of the population, economic information is available for only a sub-sample of the 1950 observations. Consequently, the usable sample for that year is less than one percent. Weights are used for the 1950 sample in all statistical analyses to account for the sampling method. For most decades, the sample size for each racial group is large. They number at least 1,400 for 1960, 1970, and 1980. The smallest sample is for Spanish-surname in 1950, with 177 observations.

9. The analysis would be better if the Hispanic sample were restricted to those of Mexican ancestry, but unfortunately this is not possible since not all of the census years contain such an identifier. The only consistent identifier is Spanish-surname, which has three potential problems. One, the list of Spanish surnames itself has changed. Unfortunately, it is not known if this introduces any systemic biases. Two, an analysis of the 1970 sample, which contains both a Spanish-surname variable and a Spanish-origin variable, shows that the average socioeconomic characteristics for the Spanish-surname population is slightly higher than that for the Hispanic population. Consequently, the analysis in this study biases the Hispanic status upwards. Three, the Spanish-surname population contains some non-Latinos, with the Filipinos being the single largest group that falls into this category. This problem is minimized by excluding black and Asian individuals with Spanish surnames. Despite these problems, the data presented in this paper are probably the most valid and consistent available for California's Hispanic population. For convenience, the term Hispanic is used in place of Spanish-surname. American-born Asians were not included because of a low number of observations for each of the major groups in the early decades.

10. Two adjustments were made to the raw data on earnings. The highest income categories were open-ended and assigned values suggested by Smith and Welch ("Closing the Gap"). Extreme weekly earnings were excluded. Regression diagnostics show that the outliers are the product of the implausible weekly earnings which were the result of a combination of either a very high number of weeks but low earnings or a very low number of weeks but high earnings.

11. Smith and Welch, "Closing the Gap"; Civil Rights Commission, cited in *Wall Street Journal* (4 Sept. 1986).

12. Smith and Welch, "Closing the Gap," 6.

13. U.S. Bureau of the Census, *U.S. Census of Population: 1950, Part 5, California* (Washington, D.C.: Government Printing Office, 1952). U.S. Bureau of the Census, *U.S. Census of Population: 1960, California*. (Washington, D.C.: Government Printing Office, 1961).

14. Orley Ashenfelter, "Changes in Labor Market Discrimination Over Time," *Journal of Human Resources* (1970): 403-429; Richard Freeman, "Decline of Labor Market Discrimination and Economic Analysis," *American Economic Review* 63 (1973): 280-286; Richard Butler and James Heckman, "The Government's Impact on the Labor Market Status of Black Americans: A Critical Review," *Equal Rights and Industrial Relations,* ed. Leonard Hausman et al. (Madison: Industrial Relations Research Association, 1977).

15. Smith and Welch, "Closing the Gap," 64.

16. For the purpose of this paper, the Civil Rights era is defined as a period beginning in the early 1960s with the start of active federal intervention against unfair employment practices.

17. Vernon M. Briggs, Jr., Walter Fogel, and Fred H. Schmidt, *The Chicano Workers* (Austin: University of Texas Press, 1977).

18. Paul Ong, et al., "Socio-Economic Trends in California: 1940 to 1980," Employment Development Department, State of California, 1986.

19. The increase in the number of Hispanic immigrants may have an adverse impact on American-born Hispanics because of crowding in the sectors of the labor market where most Latinos work. Borjas provides some evidence of this effect (George Borjas, "Immigrants, Minorities, and Labor Market Competition," University of California, Santa Barbara, unpublished ms., 1986).

20. The decline could be due to an increase in the number of first-generation, American-born Hispanics. However, analysis of the 1970 data, which contain a generational identifier, indicates very little difference in earnings between the first and subsequent generations of American-born Hispanics.

21. This is a modification of the regression-simulation method presented by Oaxaca and Reimers. Ronald Oaxaca, "Male-Female Wage Differentials in Urban Labor Markets," *International Economic Review* 14 (1973): 693-709; Cordelia Reimers, "Labor Market Discrimination Against Hispanic and Black Men," *Review of Economics and Statistics* 65 (1983): 570-579. The first measure is the product of the average values of the independent variables for the minority sample times the difference between the estimated coefficients for the two samples. The model used in this paper differs from the usual wage models since it is a recursive one, where the log of annual earnings is a function of the log of weeks and other independent variables, and the log of weeks is a function of other independent variables. The term "average" refers to the vector of average values of the independent variables for the respective samples. The estimates of the amount of discrimination are not directly comparable to the observed gap in annual income because the former is based on the log of annual wages while the latter uses the untransformed annual wages.

22. Richard Freeman, *Black Elite: The New Market for Highly Qualified Black Americans* (Chicago: University of Chicago Press, 1977); William Wilson, *The Declining Significance of Race* (Chicago: University of Chicago Press, 1978).

23. Jonathan S. Leonard, "The Impact of Affirmative Action on Employment," *Journal of Labor Economics* 2 , 439-463.

24. Gary Becker, *The Economics of Discrimination* (Chicago: University of Chicago Press, 1957); Jacob Mincer, *Schooling, Experience and Earnings* (New York: National Bureau of Economic Research, 1974).

25. Of course schooling can have effects other than those posited by the human capitalists. See, for example, Samuel Bowles and Herbert Gintis, *Schooling in Capitalist America* (New York: Basic Books, 1976). However, this study uses education and schooling in human capitalist terms, and the empirical results can be taken as a test of the human capital position.

26. Keith E. Collins, *Black Los Angeles: The Maturing of the Ghetto, 1940-1950* (Saratoga, Calif.: Century Twenty One Publishing, 1980); France, *Some Aspects of the Migration of the Negro to the San Francisco Bay Area Since 1940* (San Francisco: R and E Research, 1974).

27. These net rates differ from those reported in most wage studies because the rates here include both the direct effect on earnings controlling for weeks worked and the indirect effect on weeks worked, and because the rates are adjusted for the trade-off from one less year of labor market experience.

28. James Smith and Finis Welch, "Black-White Male Wage Ratios: 1960-1970," *American Economic Review* 67 (1977).

29. A positive correlation between the intensity of discrimination and education would lower the rate of return to schooling, and a negative correlation between the intensity of discrimination and education would raise the rate of return to schooling.

30. The prevailing theory is based on Becker's work on the "taste for discrimination" in *The Economics of Discrimination.* His approach fits well within neoclassical economics, where outcomes are determined by atomistic action of individuals seeking to maximize utility and firms seeking to maximize profits. One important assertion is that unless there are major market imperfections, competetive market forces will, over the long run, eliminate any purely racial differences in pay. Since mainstream economics assumes that the economy is characterized as being competitive, then nonwhites should experience economic progress.

31. The writers in this category include those emphasizing market imperfections, e.g., Kenneth Arrow, "Some Mathematical Models of Race Discrimination in the Labor Market," in *Racial Discrimination in Economic Life,* ed. Anthony Pascel (Lexington, Mass.: DC Heath, 1972); Edwin Phelps, "The Statistical Theory of Racism and Sexism," *American Economic Review* 62 (1972); organized white labor, e.g., Anne Kruger, "The Economics of Discrimination," *Journal of Political Economy* 71 (1963): 481-486 and Ray Marshall, *The Negro Worker* (New York: Random House, 1967); internal labor markets, e.g., Peter Doeringer and Michael Piore, *Internal Labor Markets and Manpower Analysis* (Lexington, Mass.: Health Lexington, 1971); and class conflict, e.g. Gordon, Edwards, and Reich, *Segmented Work, Divided Workers.* Consequently, there are a number of explanations for the difficulties encountered by nonwhites. For example, one can argue that some unions create racial barriers through blatant discrimination in the past, and in more recent years through entry rules that lead to *de facto* discrimination. Other barriers may be based on more fundamental economic structures, with racial distinctions emerging as one way of operationalizing that structure. In models based on internal labor markets or class conflict, non-racial factors underlie labor segmentation but racial discrimination becomes a convenient mechanism for allocating workers among the various

sectors. While the literature is diverse, it shares a common assertion: structural factors impede mobility for nonwhites.

32. Lubin, "Civil Rights Panel Report."

33. Smith and Welch, "Closing the Gap," 36.

Industrial Sectorization in California in 1980: The Continuing Significance of Race/Ethnicity, Gender, and Nativity

Amado Cabezas and Gary Kawaguchi

Two factors can help explain income inequality among American wage and salary workers: differences in employment level in the economy, and differences in human capital investments and/or in rewards for such investments within given employment settings in the economy. Using 1980 census data, this study focuses on differences in employment level by race/ethnicity, nativity, and gender in the California economy. We divide the economy of the state into sixteen industrial sectors, using an empirically-based model developed by Kaufman, Hodson, and Fligstein in their study of sectorization in the national economy.[1] Within each industrial sector, we compare the employment level by occupational category of Californians by race/ethnicity, nativity, and gender relative to their proportion in the employed civilian labor force. To further clarify the employment patterns, we control for age and educational level and analyze seventeen key industries within the sixteen industrial sectors. The key industries selected either dominate or are representative of the employment in each sector. By presenting empirical evidence that the California labor market is divided along race/ethnicity, nativity, and gender lines that cut across industrial sectors and key industries in the state, the study shows the utility of considering race/ethnicity, nativity, and gender in developing structural approaches to understanding economic inequality.

Theoretical Considerations

Previous studies by Cabezas and Kawaguchi, Wong, Nee and Sanders, and Chiswick have explored both differential human capital investments and differential returns as causes of income inequality.[2] Table 1 shows the extent of income inequality in California, revealing significant differences by race/ethnicity, nativity, and gender. U.S.- and foreign-born white men and U.S.-born Japanese and Chinese American men have the highest incomes, while women of all races and nonwhite Americans in general have lower incomes. Human capital investments by themselves do not explain the income differences. Cabezas and Kawaguchi found that from one-half to two-thirds of the income gap between Asian Americans and white men can be explained by lower returns to investments rather than by deficiencies in investments--indicating the need for a structural approach.[3]

In one of the best recent examples of a structural approach, Kaufman explored black-white income inequality after first mapping out the domestic national economy into sixteen industrial sectors.[4] He based the industrial sectorization scheme on a factor analysis of 1970 census and other data, using the following ten measures to categorize the sectors: concentration, size, capital intensity, foreign involvement, government intervention, profit level, autonomy, productivity, level of unionization of workers, and growth.[5] The industrial sectorization approach builds on theories of dual economy.[6]

We used the five-percent 1980 census Public Use Microdata Sample (PUMS) for California (about 1,186,000 individuals) to divide empirically the economy of the state by industrial sector. The sixteen industrial sectors are: (1) oligopoly core manufacturing, (2) core manufacturing, (3) wholesale trade, (4) periphery manufacturing and services, (5) small shops, (6) core utilities and finance, (7) periphery utilities, (8) core transportation, (9) periphery transportation, (10) local monopoly, (11) educational services, (12) agriculture, (13) brokers, (14) real estate, (15) ordnance, and (16) tobacco.[7] The "core" sectors are characterized by their larger size, higher concentration, and greater capital intensity, while "periphery" sectors generally have lower values for these measures.[8] Of these, only four are of the core type: oligopoly core manufacturing, core manufacturing, core utilities, and core transport. Significantly, these four core sectors account for only 21 percent of all employment, evidence of the transformation of the national economy to a mostly service economy since the early 1970s. (Because of the small size of the work force in the ordnance and tobacco sectors, we shall exclude them from our analysis.)

To understand employment inequality in the state, we analyzed the employment level by race/ethnicity, nativity, and gender in four occupational categories within each industrial sector: (1) managers, (2) professionals, (3) technicians, sales, and clerical workers, and (4) blue-collar workers. The four categories are groupings from the

Table 1. Median Income and
Race/Ethnicity, Nativity,

	Median Income	% Labor Force[a]	Sample Size
White US male	1.00 = $17,165	37.7	199,421
White US female	0.47	28.2	149,471
White FB male	1.02	2.7	14,516
White FB female	0.46	2.0	10,735
Black US male	0.69	3.1	16,402
Black US female	0.49	3.0	15,970
Black FB male	0.58	.1	496
Black FB female	0.40	.1	439
Native American male	0.75	.5	2,446
Native American female	0.37	.4	1,910
Japanese US male	0.99	.6	3,132
Japanese US female	0.58	.5	2,594
Japanese FB male	0.93	.2	875
Japanese FB female	0.41	.2	948
Chinese US male	0.99	.3	1,408
Chinese US female	0.58	.2	1,164
Chinese FB male	0.69	.6	2,986
Chinese FB female	0.41	.5	2,459
Filipino US male	0.69	.2	848
Filipino US female	0.46	.1	719
Filipino FB male	0.69	.6	3,227
Filipino FB female	0.52	.7	3,760

Employed Civilian Labor Force by
and Gender in California, 1980.

	Median Income	% Labor Force[a]	Sample Size
Korean US male	0.93	.0	77
Korean US female	0.46	.0	90
Korean FB male	0.69	.2	1,108
Korean FB female	0.40	.2	1,011
Asian Indian US male	0.58	.0	49
Asian Indian US female	0.40	.0	81
Asian Indian FB male	0.93	.2	807
Asian Indian FB female	0.37	.1	378
Vietnamese US male	0.13	.0	8
Vietnamese US female	0.44	.0	10
Vietnamese FB male	0.55	.1	751
Vietnamese FB female	0.40	.1	544
Mexican US male	0.69	3.8	20,275
Mexican US female	0.37	2.8	14,971
Mexican FB male	0.46	4.0	21,142
Mexican FB female	0.29	1.9	9,917
All other males	0.67	2.4	12,524
All other females	0.39	1.9	9,941
Total Population		100.2% [b]	529,610

The median income is relative to U.S.-born white males.

[a] Percentage of the employed civilian labor force.

[b] Percentage does not add up to 100.0 % due to rounding.

Special tabulation from the 1980 census 5-percent Public Use Microdata Sample.

census' broad occupational categories. The first two, managers and professionals, include many who are in the primary labor market, while the latter two, technicians/sales/clerical workers and blue-collar workers, include many in the secondary labor market. However, because our four occupational categories are derived from census data, they do not readily lend themselves to testing traditional formulations of secondary versus primary segmented market theories. The census data also make it difficult for us to test class theories such as those by Wright. However, we are able to explore employment by race/ethnicity, nativity, and gender in the industrial sectors.[9]

Controlling for age and educational level allows us to detect any generational effects, such as a lessening of race and gender discrimination resulting in improvements in employment level for the younger age group. In this initial exploration, the age categories are 25 to 44 and 45 to 65 years of age. In our structural analysis we also test for the importance of educational level as an ascriptive variable (such as race or gender) and not as a human capital variable.[10] The educational attainment level categories are less than four years of college and four or more years of college. Our results indicate that the choice of cut-off at four years of post-secondary education is adequate for testing the importance of a college education with regard to what occupational category workers occupy in the sectorized economy. More detailed educational categories are precluded by the small sample size of some of the populations when stratified by race/ethnicity, nativity, and gender. Our primary statistical analysis is (1) log-linear analysis to verify main-effect variables, and (2) chi-square tests of employment by occupational category, controlling for age group and education.[11]

The analyses were then conducted for each of the seventeen selected key industries that represent the industrial sectors. The sixteen industrial sectors and their composition by industry are shown in Table 2.[12] Plugging 1980 census data into these categories, the table also shows how many percent of the state's employment is provided by each sector. For example, office and accounting machine manufacturing accounts for 4 percent of the employment in the oligopoly manufacturing sector. The key industries we selected for each sector are underlined in the table; most account for a substantial proportion of the employment within the sector. For example, electronic computing equipment manufacturing accounts for 47 percent of the employment in the oligopoly sector, electrical machinery manufacturing for 19 percent of the core manufacturing sector, and eating and drinking places for 30 percent of the small shops sector. The seventeen key industries and the fourteen industrial sectors they represent are shown below:

Industry	**Industrial Sector**
Electronic computing equipment mfg.	oligopoly
Electrical machinery manufacturing	core manufacturing
Wholesale trade of machinery equipment and supplies	wholesale
Department stores	periphery manufacturing and services

Eating and drinking places	small shops
Banking	core utilities and finance
Insurance	core utilities and finance
Water supply	periphery utilities
Sanitary services	periphery utilities
Telephone services	core transport and communications
Trucking services	periphery transport
Building contractors	local monopoly
Elementary and secondary schools	educational services
Colleges and universities	educational services
Agricultural production	agriculture
Security, commodities, and investment brokers	brokers
Real estate	real estate

Data and Analysis

Population and Labor Force Composition by Race/Ethnicity, Nativity, and Gender

It is important to analyze the California labor force not only by race/ethnicity, but also by nativity and gender. Based on the five-percent census sample, the population of California in 1980, as shown in Table 3, was 66.7 percent non-Hispanic white, 15.1 percent Mexican American, 7.6 percent black, 5.2 percent Asian American, 1.0 percent Native American, and 4.4 percent others--reflecting the growing nonwhite population of the state.[13] (Since the sample was 5 percent, the actual total population can be roughly estimated at twenty times 1,186,232, the sample size shown in the table.) Table 3 also shows the composition of the employed civilian labor force--70.6 percent non-Hispanic white, 12.5 percent Mexican American, 6.3 percent black, 5.3 percent Asian American, 0.9 percent Native American, and 4.2 percent others. These figures reveal a proportionately smaller representation of blacks and Mexican Americans in the labor force than in the population, indicating that these groups face problems even in just gaining entry into the labor force.

Foreign-born Californians comprise a major portion of the labor force: 68 percent of Chinese Americans, 82 percent of Filipino Americans, 93 percent of Korean Americans, 99 percent of Vietnamese Americans, 90 percent of Asian Indians, and 47 percent of Mexican Americans are foreign-born--a consequence of large-scale immigration since the passage of the 1965 Amendments to the Immigration and Naturalization Act.

Women also comprise a large part of the California work force. For example, 42 percent of both the U.S.-born whites and Mexican Americans, 49 percent of U.S.-born blacks, 53 percent of foreign-born Filipinos, 47 percent of foreign-born Koreans, and 31 percent of foreign-born Mexican Americans in the labor force are women.

Altogether, our analysis consists of forty populations categorized

Table 2. Composition by Industry of Each Industrial
Force Employed in Each Sector, and in Each

OLIGOPOLY MANUFACTURING (2.2 percent of total employment)	
4%	Office and accounting machine manufacturing
47%	Electronic computing equipment manufacturing[c]
23%	Motor vehicle and equipment manufacturing
5%	Photographic equipment manufacturing
7%	Drug and medicine manufacturing
12%	Petroleum refining
	Miscellaneous petroleum and coal products manufacturing
CORE MANUFACTURING (9.8 percent of total employment)	
3%	Crude petroleum and natural gas extraction
	Glass and glass products
	Cement and plaster products
	Structural clay products
	Pottery and related products
	Miscellaneous stone products
	Blast furnaces, steel works, and mills
	Other primary iron and steel manufacturing
	Primary aluminum manufacturing
	Other primary nonferrous manufacturing
	Cutlery and hardware metal manufacturing
4%	Fabricated structural metal manufacturing
	Metal stamping manufacturing
5%	Miscellaneous fabricated metal manufacturing
	Engines and turbines manufacturing
	Household appliance manufacturing
19%	Electrical machinery manufacturing, not elsewhere classified
	Cycles and miscellaneous transport equipment manufacturing
	Meat products manufacturing
	Dairy products manufacturing
5%	Canning and preserving
	Grain mill products manufacturing
	Bakery products manufacturing
	Confectionery products manufacturing
	Beverage manufacturing
	Miscellaneous food products manufacturing
	Knitting mills
	Dyeing and finishing textile manufacturing
	Floor covering, except hard surface, manufacturing
	Yarn, thread, and fabric mills
10%	Apparel and accessory manufacturing
	Pulp and paper mills
	Miscellaneous paper and pulp products
	Paperboard containers manufacturing

Sector[a] and Percentage of Civilian Work Industry within a Sector, California, 1980[b]	
11%	Printing and publishing, except newspaper
	Industrial chemical manufacturing
	Plastics, synthetics, and resin manufacturing
	Synthetic fiber manufacturing
	Soap and cosmetic manufacturing
	Paints, varnishes, etc., manufacturing
	Agricultural chemical manufacturing
	Miscellaneous chemical manufacturing
	Not specified chemical manufacturing
WHOLESALE MANUFACTURING AND SERVICES (7.5 percent of total employment)	
	Farm machinery manufacturing
	Construction equipment manufacturing
	Metalworking machinery manufacturing
	Railroad locomotive and equipment manufacturing
	Mobile dwellings manufacturing
14%	Legal services
11%	Engineering and architectural services
8%	Accounting and bookkeeping services
3%	Miscellaneous professional and related services
Wholesale trade	
4%	Motor vehicle and equipment
	Drugs and chemicals
	Dry goods and apparel
12%	Food and related products
	Farm products--raw materials
5%	Electrical goods
3%	Hardware, plumbing, heating supplies
	Not specified elec. and hardware products
12%	Machinery equipment and supplies
	Metals and minerals, not elsewhere classified
	Petroleum products
	Scrap and waste materials
	Alcoholic beverages
	Paper and paper products
	Lumber and construction materials
	Wholesalers, not elsewhere classified
4%	Not specified wholesalers
PERIPHERY MANUFACTURING / SERVICES (19.7 percent of total employment)	
	Metal mining
	Coal mining
	Nonmetallic mining

Table 2. Composition by Industry of Each Industrial Force Employed in Each Sector, and in Each

	Logging
	Sawmills
	Miscellaneous wood products
	Screw machine products
4%	Radio, television, communication equipment manufacturing
8%	Aircraft and parts manufacturing
	Ship and boat building
	Scientific instruments manufacturing
	Optical and health service supplies manufacturing
	Watches and clocks manufacturing
	Miscellaneous manufacturing
	Miscellaneous textile products
	Miscellaneous fabricated textile products
	Rubber products
	Miscellaneous plastic products
	Tanned and finished leather manufacturing
	Leather products, except footwear
11%	Department stores
	Limited price variety stores
	Vending machine operators
	Direct selling stores
	Miscellaneous general merchandise stores
	Dairy products retail
	Retail bakeries
	Food retailing not elsewhere classified
	Advertising services
	Services to buildings
	Commercial research and development, and testing services
	Employment agencies
	Business management and consulting services
	Computer programming services
	Detective and protective services
6%	Business services, not elsewhere classified
	Auto services, except repair
5%	Auto repair services
	Electrical repair services
	Miscellaneous repair services
5%	Hotels and motels
	Other lodging places
	Laundering and garment services
3%	Beauty shops
	Barber shops
	Shoe repair shops

Sector[a] and Percentage of Civilian Work	Industry within a Sector, California, 1980[b] (Continued).
	Dressmaking shops
	Miscellaneous personal services
5%	Theaters
	Bowling alleys and pool parlors
4%	Miscellaneous entertainment services
SMALL SHOPS (17.4 percent of total employment)	
3%	Furniture and fixture manufacturing
3%	Newspaper printing and publishing
	Footwear, except rubber, manufacturing
Retail	
	Lumber and building materials
	Hardware and farm equipment
13%	Grocery stores
6%	Motor vehicle dealers
	Tire, battery, and auto accessories
4%	Gas service stations
6%	Miscellaneous vehicle dealers
	Tire, battery, and auto accessories
	Miscellaneous vehicle dealers
5%	Apparel and accessories
	Shoe stores
4%	Furniture and home furnishing
	Household appliances, television and radio
30%	Eating and drinking places
3%	Drug stores
	Liquor stores
	Farm and garden supplies
	Jewelry stores
	Fuel and ice dealers
	Retail florists
4%	Miscellaneous retailing
	Not specified retail
6%	Offices of physicians
3%	Offices of dentists
CORE UTILITIES AND FINANCE (5.7 percent of total employment)	
4%	Radio and television broadcasting
	Electric light and power
6%	Electric and gas utilities
	Gas and steam supply systems
38%	Banking

Table 2. Composition by Industry of Each Industrial Force Employed in Each Sector, and in Each

7%	Credit agencies
37%	Insurance
PERIPHERY UTILITIES (0.5 percent of total employment)	
50%	Water supply
44%	Sanitary services
6%	Other and not specified utilities
CORE TRANSPORT (3.6 percent of total employment)	
	Railroads and railway express
	Street railways and bus lines
6%	Water transport
26%	Air transport
43%	Telephone services
3%	Telegraph and miscellaneous communication services
PERIPHERY TRANSPORT (1.9 percent of total employment)	
63%	Trucking services
13%	Warehousing and storage services
	Pipelines, except natural gas
18%	Services incidental to transport
LOCAL MONOPOLY (13.3 percent of total employment)	
47%	General building contractors, other general contractors, and special trade contractors
	Taxicab services
	Offices of chiropractors
37%	Hospitals
3%	Convalescent institutions
	Offices of health practitioners not elsewhere classified
5%	Health services, not elsewhere classified
EDUCATIONAL AND NON-PROFIT SERVICES (11.9 percent of total employment)	
7%	Private households
51%	Elementary and secondary schools
20%	Colleges and universities
	Libraries
	Educational services, not elsewhere classified
	Not specified educational services
	Museums, art galleries, and zoos
5%	Religious organizations
7%	Welfare services
	Residential welfare facilities
4%	Nonprofit membership organization

Sector[a] and Percentage of Civilian Work
Industry within a Sector, California, 1980[b] (Continued).

AGRICULTURE (3.4 percent of total employment)

52%	Agricultural production, crops
13%	Agricultural production, livestock
14%	Agricultural services
17%	Horticultural services
4%	Forestry
	Fisheries

BROKERS (0.4 percent of total employment)

100%	Security, commodity brokerage, and investment companies

REAL ESTATE (2.5 percent of total employment)

100%	Real estate

[a] From Kaufman, Hodson, and Fligstein (1981).
[b] Shown only for 3 percent or more.
[c] The underlined industries are the key industries we have analyzed.

Table 3. Population and Employed Civilian Labor Force by Race/Ethnicity in California, 1980.

	Population	Employed Civilian Labor Force
Non-Hispanic White American	66.7%	70.6%
Non-Hispanic Black American	7.6	6.3
Native American	1.0	.9
Japanese American	1.1	1.4
Chinese American	1.4	1.5
Filipino American	1.5	1.6
Korean American	.5	.4
Asian Indian American	.3	.2
Vietnamese American	.4	.2
Mexican American	15.1	12.5
All Other Races	4.4	4.2
Total	100.0%	99.8%[a]
	N = 1,186,232	N = 529,802

Special tabulation from the 1980 census 5-percent Public Use Microdata Sample.
[a] Percentage does not add up to 100.0 % due to rounding.

by race/ethnicity, nativity, and gender, as seen in Table 1. For our study, the percentages of the employed civilian labor force shown in Table 1 are used as estimates for employment parity. For example, parity is 37.7 percent for U.S.-born white men, 28.2 percent for U.S.-born white women, 3.1 percent for U.S.-born black men, 0.5 percent for foreign-born Chinese American women, and 3.8 percent for U.S.-born Mexican American men.

Industrial Sector Employment by Race/Ethnicity, Nativity, and Gender

Without analyzing employment by occupational category in each industrial sector in California, the employment patterns do not reveal clearly the effects of race/ethnicity, nativity, and gender. All we see is that U.S.-born white men have high employment levels in the oligopoly, wholesale, periphery utilities, and periphery transport sectors, whereas U.S.-born white women have high employment levels in the educational services, real estate, and small shops sectors. U.S.-born black men have high employment levels in the periphery utilities and core and periphery transport sectors; foreign-born Chinese men in the small shops sector; U.S.-born Japanese American and foreign-born Filipino men in the agriculture sector; foreign-born Filipino women in the core utilities and local monopoly sectors; foreign-born Korean women and foreign-born Vietnamese men and women in the core manufacturing sector; U.S.-born Mexican American men in the periphery utilities, periphery transport, and agriculture sectors; U.S.-born Mexican American women in the core manufacturing and educational services sectors; foreign-born Mexican

American men in the agriculture sector; and foreign-born Mexican American women in the core manufacturing and agriculture sectors. When we analyze the employment by occupational categories, however, we see more of the differentials in employment level associated with race/ethnicity, nativity, and gender.

Employment in the Six Dominant Industrial Sectors in California

Census data from 1980 show that six of the fourteen industrial sectors provide the bulk of the employment in the California economy. The core manufacturing, periphery manufacturing and services, wholesale trade, small shops, local monopoly, and educational services sectors combined account for 80 percent of the employment in the state.

(1) The core manufacturing sector in California is comprised mostly of the electrical machinery, apparel and accessories, and printing and publishing (except newspapers) industries. The employment distribution in this sector by race/ethnicity, nativity, and gender is as follows: U.S.-born and foreign-born white men as managers and professionals; U.S.-born and foreign-born Japanese and Chinese American men as professionals; foreign-born Korean American men as managers; and foreign-born Asian Indian men as professionals. U.S.-born women, on the other hand--mostly white, black, Native American, Japanese American, Chinese American, and Filipino American--are represented mainly in the technician, sales, and clerical ranks, which we shall refer to as "clerical" from here on.[14] Most U.S.-born black, Native American, and Mexican American men are in the blue-collar ranks. However, foreign-born women--Japanese,

Chinese, Filipino, Korean, Vietnamese, and Mexican--are also mostly in the blue-collar ranks. Thus, employment in this sector shows white men as mostly managers and professionals; Asian men as mostly professionals; U.S.-born women as clerks; and foreign-born Asian and Mexican American women and U.S.-born black and Mexican American men predominantly as blue-collar workers--showing gender differences in the white-collar ranks, and both gender and race/ethnicity differences in the blue-collar ranks.

(2) The periphery manufacturing and services sector is comprised mostly of industries such as aircraft and communications parts manufacturing, department stores, hotels and motels, and business services. The pattern of employment by race/ethnicity, nativity, and gender is much like that in the core manufacturing sector, except that here we have more clerical workers and fewer blue-collar workers.

(3) The wholesale trade sector is comprised mostly of the machinery equipment and supplies and food products wholesale industries, but it also includes professional services such as legal, engineering, architectural, and accounting services. In this sector, white and Asian men again are mostly managers and professionals, while U.S.-born women of all races, comprising 40 percent of the employment in this sector, are mostly sales and clerical workers. This sector also shows a labor force in which most managers and professionals are men, while most clerical workers are women.

(4) The small shops sector is a periphery type of sector consisting mostly of retail industries such as eating and drinking places, grocery stores, motor vehicle dealers, gasoline service stations, apparel

and accessory stores, and offices of physicians and dentists. It also includes furniture manufacturing and newspaper printing and publishing. Clerical and blue-collar employment predominate in this sector, accounting for 85 percent of all workers. U.S.-born women of all races and foreign-born Filipino women are mostly clerical workers, while other foreign-born Asian and Mexican women are mostly blue-collar workers. U.S.-born black, Native American, Filipino, and Mexican American men are mostly blue-collar workers, as are foreign-born Chinese, Japanese, Korean, Asian Indian, and Vietnamese men.

(5) The local monopoly sector is dominated by the building contractors industry which will be discussed in the analyses of selected key industries.

(6) The educational services sector is made up mostly of elementary and secondary schools, and colleges and universities, which respectively account for 51 percent and 20 percent of the employment in the sector. Professionals dominate this sector, accounting for 45 percent of the employment. In this sector, white men and women and Japanese American men are mostly professionals, Asian American women are mostly clerical workers, while black men and women, Filipino American men (both U.S.- and foreign-born), and Mexican Americans (both men and women and both U.S.- and foreign-born) are mostly blue-collar workers.

Employment in Key Industries by Race/Ethnicity, Nativity, and Gender

To further understand the employment in the industrial sectors, we focus on the seventeen key industries which account for the largest percentage of employment in the sectors within which they are located. The employment patterns observed are as follows:

(1) The electrical machinery manufacturing industry in the core manufacturing sector and electronic computing equipment manufacturing industry in the oligopoly manufacturing sector show the same general pattern:

(a) College-educated (with four or more years of college) U.S.- and foreign-born white men in both age groups (25-44 years old and 45-65 years old) dominate the employment in both the managerial and professional ranks. In the younger and college-educated professional ranks, foreign-born Chinese American and Asian Indian men also are found in sizable numbers. Younger and college-educated foreign-born Filipino men and women, on the other hand, are employed mostly as technicians and clerical workers.

(b) In the clerical ranks, less-educated white women, both U.S.- and foreign-born and both younger and older, are employed at or above parity.

(c) In the blue-collar ranks of less-educated workers (less than four years of college), we find a different population: younger U.S.-born black and Mexican American women, and foreign-born Chinese, Filipino, Korean, Vietnamese, and Mexican American women. In these ranks, as Table 4 for electrical machinery manufacturing shows, these foreign-born nonwhite women are employed at two to eight times parity. (In electronic computing equipment manufacturing, their employment levels are two to six times

Table 4. Number and Employment Level Relative to Civilian Labor Force Parity by Race, Nativity, and Gender in Electrical Machinery Manufacturing for Younger[a] and Less-Educated Groups.

	Manager	Profess-ional	Tech/Sales/ Clerk	Blue Collar
	Ratio[b] (N)	Ratio (N)	Ratio (N)	Ratio (N)
White US[c] male	1.2 (135)	1.6 (131)	0.8 (286)	0.5 (358)
White US female	1.1 (91)	0.6 (37)	1.3 (373)	0.7 (380)
White FB male	1.6 (12)	2.0 (12)	0.6 (15)	0.5 (25)
White FB female	--[d] (3)	-- (3)	1.3 (26)	1.0 (41)
Black US male	-- (2)	0.9 (6)	0.7 (21)	1.0 (61)
Black US female	0.7 (6)	-- (4)	1.2 (36)	1.3 (80)
Native American male	-- (2)	-- (2)	1.6 (16)	
Japanese FB female	-- (3)	3.5 (14)		
Chinese FB female	-- (3)	-- (2)	1.6 (15)	
Filipino FB male	-- (1)	1.3 (8)	2.7 (31)	
Filipino FB female	-- (1)	-- (1)	1.3 (9)	6.7 (94)
Korean FB female	-- (3)	5.5 (21)		
Vietnamese FB male	-- (1)	0.2 (25)	8.0 (16)	
Vietnamese FB female	-- (1)	10.0 (10)	13.0 (25)	
Mexican US male	0.4 (5)	-- (4)	1.2 (20)	0.9 (91)
Mexican US female	0.8 (7)	0.8 (5)	1.8 (52)	2.8 (159)
Mexican FB male	-- (2)	-- (2)	0.4 (14)	2.0 (162)
Mexican FB female	-- (1)	-- (3)	0.8 (16)	4.7 (178)
N	(289)	(221)	(1,007)	(1,988)
Occupational Distribution	8.2%	6.3%	28.7%	56.7%

[a]Younger = 25-44 years old. Less-educated = less than 4 years of college.
[b]Ratio = % employment divided by % in employed civilian labor force.
[c]US = U.S.-born FB = Foreign-born
[d]"--" Ratio not calculated because cell count less than five.
Chi-square = 719.2 df = 105 Significance = 0.0001
Population samples with less than 20 are deleted from tables; however, column totals are summed from all populations.

parity.) Also employed at higher than parity are younger foreign-born Filipino, Vietnamese, and Mexican American men as well as older foreign-born Filipino and Vietnamese men and women. Overall, the pattern in the electrical machinery manufacturing and the electronic computing equipment manufacturing industries is one of mostly college-educated white men as professionals and managers compared to mostly less-educated and foreign-born women of color as blue-collar workers.

(2) In the wholesale trade of machinery equipment and supplies industry of the wholesale sector, managers and clerical workers account for 72 percent of the employment. Regardless of educational level or age group, U.S.-born white men dominate these ranks with employment levels at about 1.9 times (employed civilian labor force) parity in the managerial ranks and 1.5 times parity in the clerical ranks. The only other workers found in the industry are U.S.-born white women near parity as clerical workers and foreign-born Mexican American men at about twice parity as blue-collar workers, both in the less-educated ranks.

(3) The security, commodities, and investment brokers industry of the brokers sector and the real estate industry of the real estate sector have similar employment patterns. Most jobs in these industries are managerial or clerical. In the college-educated ranks of both age groups, U.S.-born white men dominate the employment (at about twice parity) in both the managerial and clerical ranks. By contrast, in the less-educated ranks of both age groups, U.S.-born white women are employed at levels higher than parity as both managers and clerical

workers. The pattern of white men as college-educated managers and white women as less-educated managers suggests lower-level management jobs for women in these industries. The only other workers found in significant numbers are U.S.-born Mexican American men employed at about two to three times parity in the less-educated blue-collar ranks of the real estate industry.

(4) In the college-educated ranks of the colleges and universities industry of the educational services sector, about two-thirds of employees of both age groups are professionals; about 14 percent are managers. U.S.-born and foreign-born white men, at about 1.4 times parity, dominate the employment in the professional ranks; within the older group, they also dominate the managerial ranks. U.S.- and foreign-born white women are at about parity in the professional ranks. U.S.-born black men are employed at about one-half of parity, while U.S.-born black women are found only in the younger group at about two-thirds of parity. The only other nonwhite workers employed in the professional ranks are younger, college-educated, U.S.-born Japanese American women (at about 1.5 times parity), foreign-born Chinese American men and women (at about 1.5 to 2 times parity), and foreign-born Asian Indian men (at about 3.5 times parity). (The employment pattern for the younger and college-educated is shown in Table 5.) Younger, college-educated, and foreign-born Filipino men and women are employed at nearly twice parity but as clerical workers. Similarly, college-educated white women of both age groups, both U.S.- and foreign-born, are employed at nearly twice parity as clerical workers. Younger, college-educated,

Table 5. Number and Employment Level Relative to Civilian Labor Force Parity by Race, Nativity, and Gender in Colleges and Universities for Younger[a] and College-Educated Groups.

	Manager	Profess-ional	Tech/Sales/ Clerk	Blue Collar
	Ratio[b] (N)	Ratio (N)	Ratio (N)	Ratio (N)
White US[c] male	1.0 (172)	1.2 (1,112)	0.8 (273)	1.3 (73)
White US female	1.2 (153)	1.1 (731)	1.4 (377)	0.7 (29)
White FB male	1.2 (15)	2.0 (133)	2.3 (57)	1.6 (6)
White FB female	1.0 (9)	1.2 (61)	1.1 (20)	--[d] (4)
Black US male	0.8 (11)	0.4 (31)	0.2 (5)	-- (2)
Black US female	0.7 (9)	0.7 (52)	0.6 (16)	-- (1)
Japanese US female	-- (4)	1.6 (19)	2.4 (11)	
Chinese FB male	-- (2)	2.2 (32)	3.0 (17)	-- (4)
Chinese FB female	-- (3)	1.4 (18)	3.6 (17)	
Filipino FB male	-- (2)	1.7 (9)	-- (1)	
Filipino FB female	2.0 (6)	-- (2)	1.8 (12)	
Asian Indian FB male	3.5 (16)	5.5 (10)	-- (1)	
Mexican US male	1.0 (17)	0.4 (38)	0.4 (15)	1.3 (7)
Mexican US female	0.5 (6)	0.4 (23)	0.4 (11)	-- (1)
N	(442)	(2,413)	(926)	(144)
Occup. Distribution	11.3%	61.5%	23.6%	3.7%

[a]Younger = 25-44 years old. College-educated = 4 or more years of college.

[b]Ratio = % employment divided by % in employed civilian labor force.

[c]US = U.S.-born FB = Foreign-born

[d]"--" Ratio not calculated because cell count less than five.

Chi-square = 263.6 df = 99 Significance = 0.0001

Population samples with less than 20 are deleted from tables; however, column totals are summed from all populations.

U.S.-born Japanese American women and foreign-born Chinese American men and women are also employed at about three times parity as clerical workers. In the less-educated ranks, we find U.S.-born white women as managers (similar to the pattern seen before in the security, commodities, and investment brokers industry and the real estate industry). In these less-educated ranks, most of the clerical workers are U.S.-born white, black, and Mexican American women, while U.S.-born black men and women and foreign-born Mexican American men and women are blue-collar workers.

The larger pattern in the colleges and universities industry is one of white men and, to a lesser degree, white women, as managers and professionals; younger U.S.-born Japanese American men and women and younger foreign-born Chinese American men as professionals; white, black, Asian American, and Mexican American women as clerical workers; and black and Mexican American men and women as blue-collar workers.

(5) In the following four key industries--building contractors of the local monopoly sector, trucking services of the periphery transport sector, and both sanitary and water supply services of the periphery utilities sector--blue-collar workers of both age groups who are U.S.-born white, black and Mexican American men dominate the employment. The pattern is also true for Native American men in building contractors and trucking services. Blue-collar workers are highly organized into unions in these industries.[15] Although the pattern shows the traditional domination of blue-collar ranks by men, it now includes both white and nonwhite men in these ranks--very

likely the result of affirmative action programs over the last decade. Table 6 for the building contractors industry is typical of the employment pattern. In the blue-collar ranks, which account for 82 percent of the employment in this industry, U.S.-born white, black, Native American, Filipino, and Mexican American men are all at or above parity. On the other hand, the groups traditionally excluded from these blue-collar ranks--foreign-born Chinese, Filipino, and Korean men--are below parity.

(6) In the elementary and secondary schools industry of the educational services sector, of the college-educated workers, 86 percent are professionals. Both age groups of the professional ranks (predominantly teachers) are mostly women: U.S.-born white, black, Japanese American, Chinese American, and (to some extent) Mexican American women. While U.S.-born white men are at about 0.8 times parity as professionals, they are at about 1.5 times parity as managers. U.S.-born black men and women, especially the younger ones, are also found in the managerial ranks. Table 7 for younger and college-educated workers shows the typical employment pattern in the industry.

In the less-educated ranks, clerical and blue-collar workers account for most of the employment. The clerical workers are mostly U.S.-born women--white, black, and Mexican American--plus some older foreign-born white women. The blue-collar workers are mostly U.S.-born white women, black men and women, and Mexican American men and women. An analysis of the detailed occupational distribution in the industry reveals that women in these ranks are

Table 6. Number and Employment Level Relative to Civilian Labor Force Parity by Race, Nativity, and Gender in Building Contractors for Younger[a] and Less-Educated Groups.

	Manager	Profess-ional	Tech/Sales/ Clerk	Blue Collar
	Ratio[b] (N)	Ratio (N)	Ratio (N)	Ratio (N)
White US male[c]	1.7 (503)	1.6 (102)	0.6 (311)	1.8 (7122)
White US female	0.6 (121)	0.4 (21)	2.0 (714)	0.1 (153)
White FB male	1.4 (29)	2.8 (13)	0.4 (15)	1.4 (404)
White FB female	0.4 (5)	--[d] (1)	1.6 (42)	0.1 (12)
Black US male	0.2 (5)	1.2 (6)	0.4 (18)	1.1 (355)
Black US female	-- (4)	-- (1)	0.7 (27)	0.0 (8)
Native Amer. male	-- (4)	-- (1)	0.8 (5)	2.6 (133)
Japanese US male	-- (4)	-- (4)	0.3 (22)	
Chinese FB male	-- (1)	-- (4)	-- (2)	0.3 (26)
Filipino US male	-- (1)	-- (1)	-- (1)	1.0 (24)
Filipino FB male	-- (1)	-- (4)	0.3 (19)	
Korean FB male	-- (1)	1.0 (18)		
Mexican US male	1.4 (40)	0.8 (5)	0.3 (16)	2.2 (870)
Mexican US female	-- (3)	-- (2)	0.8 (29)	0.0 (10)
Mexican FB male	0.4 (11)	-- (2)	0.2 (11)	2.0 (853)
Mexican FB female	-- (1)	-- (1)	0.5 (8)	0.1 (16)
N	(763)	(169)	(1,295)	(10,505)
Occup. Distribution	6.0%	1.3%	10.2%	82.5%

[a]Younger = 25-44 years old. Less-educated = less than 4 years of college.
[b]Ratio = % employment divided by % in employed civilian labor force.
[c]US = U.S.-born FB = Foreign-born
[d]"--" Ratio not calculated because cell count less than five.
Chi-square = 6042.3 df = 96 Significance = 0.0001
Population samples with less than 20 are deleted from tables; however, column totals are summed from all populations.

Table 7. Number and Employment Level Relative to Civilian Labor Force Parity by Race, Nativity, and Gender in Secondary and Elementary Schools for Younger[a] and College-Educated Groups.

	Manager	Profess-ional	Tech/Sales/Clerk	Blue Collar
	Ratio[b] (N)	Ratio (N)	Ratio (N)	Ratio (N)
White US[c] male	1.2 (233)	0.7 (2,297)	0.4 (46)	0.5 (65)
White US female	1.0 (148)	1.9 (4,593)	1.9 (167)	1.8 (174)
White FB male	1.0 (14)	0.3 (74)	--[d] (3)	-- (2)
White FB female	0.6 (6)	0.9 (159)	1.2 (7)	1.2 (8)
Black US male	1.2 (19)	0.4 (125)	0.6 (6)	0.8 (9)
Black US female	1.6 (24)	1.4 (371)	2.0 (19)	1.4 (14)
Native Amer. male	-- (10)	0.4 (19)	-- (4)	
Native Amer. female	-- (1)	0.8 (26)	-- (2)	-- (1)
Japanese US male	-- (1)	0.8 (38)	-- (1)	
Japanese US female	-- (2)	2.8 (120)	3.8 (6)	4.6 (8)
Chinese US male	-- (2)	1.0 (24)	-- (1)	-- (1)
Chinese US female	-- (4)	4.0 (68)	-- (2)	
Filipino FB female	-- (3)	0.6 (31)	3.7 (8)	-- (4)
Mexican US male	0.8 (16)	0.4 (146)	0.4 (5)	0.8 (10)
Mexican US female	0.6 (9)	0.8 (189)	0.8 (7)	0.8 (8)
Mexican FB male	0.3 (6)	0.1 (34)	-- (4)	
Mexican FB female	-- (4)	0.2 (36)	0.8 (5)	-- (4)
N	(512)	(8,632)	(310)	(342)
Occup. Distribution	5.2%	88.1%	3.2%	3.5%

[a]Younger = 25-44 years old. College-educated = more than 4 years of college.
[b]Ratio = % employment divided by % in employed civilian labor force.
[c]US = U.S.-born FB = Foreign-born
[d]"--" Ratio not calculated because cell count less than five.
Chi-square = 450.8 df = 108 Significance = 0.0001
Population samples with less than 20 are deleted from tables; however, column totals are summed from all populations.

mostly childcare and food service workers, while men are mostly janitors, groundskeepers, bus drivers, and building maintenance workers.

(7) The banking and insurance industries of the core utilities and finance sector and the department stores industry of the periphery manufacturing and services sector have a similar employment pattern, typified by the banking industry, as shown in Table 8. Managers and clerical workers dominate the employment in these industries. In the college-educated ranks, the managers are predominantly U.S.-born white men, while U.S.-born black men and women are mostly clerical workers, as are foreign-born Chinese and Filipino American men and women.

In the less-educated ranks, clerical workers are heavily represented. They are mostly women: U.S.- and foreign-born white and Filipino; U.S.-born black and Mexican American; and foreign-born Chinese. U.S.-born white, black, and Mexican American women are also employed at high levels as managers who, since they are less educated, are probably in managerial categories different from those held by college-educated white men. The census occupational categories for managers in these industries do not supply enough detail to differentiate between those occupations that require more education from those that require less.

The general pattern in the banking, insurance, and department stores industries reveals college-educated U.S.-born white men in the managerial ranks and both college-educated and less-educated U.S.-born women, white and nonwhite, in the clerical ranks.

(8) In the telephone services industry of the core transport and

Table 8. Number and Employment Level Relative to Civilian Labor Force Parity by Race, Nativity, and Gender in Banking for Younger[a] and Less-Educated Groups.

	Manager	Profess-ional	Tech/Sales/ Clerk	Blue Collar
	Ratio[b] (N)	Ratio (N)	Ratio (N)	Ratio (N)
White US[c] male	0.5 (196)	0.7 (11)	0.1 (127)	0.8(23)
White US female	1.8 (512)	1.4 (17)	1.8(1301)	0.5(10)
White FB male	0.7 (20)	0.1 (11)	--[d] (1)	
White FB female	1.8 (37)	-- (2)	2.4 (120)	-- (1)
Black US male	0.6 (20)	-- (2)	0.5 (41)	2.1 (5)
Black US female	1.7 (53)	-- (1)	3.3 (253)	-- (3)
Chinese FB female	2.2 (11)	-- (1)	4.8 (62)	
Filipino US female	-- (3)	7.0 (17)		
Filipino FB male	-- (2)	-- (1)	1.2 (17)	-- (4)
Filipino FB female	1.1 (8)	3.8 (70)	-- (1)	
Mexican US male	0.5 (19)	0.3 (25)	2.0 (6)	
Mexican US female	1.6 (48)	-- (3)	2.3 (165)	-- (1)
Mexican FB female	0.3 (6)	1.0 (52)	-- (2)	
N	(1,034)	(44)	(2,550)	(77)
Occup. Distribution	27.9%	1.2%	68.8%	2.1%

[a]Younger = 25-44 years old. Less-educated = less than 4 years of college.

[b]Ratio = % employment divided by % in employed civilian labor force.

[c]US = U.S.-born FB = Foreign-born

[d]"--" Ratio not calculated because cell count less than five.

Chi-square = 564.7 df = 105 Significance = 0.0001

Population samples with less than 20 are deleted from tables; however, column totals are summed from all populations.

communications sector, those in the ranks of college-educated managers and professionals are mostly U.S.-born white men and, to some extent, white women. In these college-educated ranks, however, we also find clerical workers: telephone operators and office clerks, who are mostly U.S.-born white men and women, black women, and foreign-born Filipino women. The less educated ranks are mainly comprised of clerks and blue-collar workers. The clerical workers are mostly women: U.S.-born white, black, Native American, Japanese American, and Mexican American. The blue-collar workers are predominantly younger U.S.-born white, black, and Mexican American men as well as older white men. Most blue-collar workers in the industry are telephone installers, with a few mechanics and repairs supervisors.

The general pattern in the telephone services industry is white males as managers and professionals, both white and nonwhite women as clerical workers, and both white and nonwhite men as blue-collar workers. Also, except for foreign-born white women, few foreign-born workers are employed in the industry.

(9) In the agricultural production industry of the agriculture sector, less-educated and blue-collar workers of both age groups account for 85 percent of the employment. In the younger age group, employment in the blue-collar ranks is dominated by U.S.-born Mexican American and Native American men and by foreign-born Asian Indian men and Mexican American men and women. In the older age group, work is done mostly by both U.S.-born and foreign-born Mexican American men and women; we also find foreign-born Filipino

men and U.S.-born Japanese American men and women in this industry. Table 9 shows these latter groups to be at more than twice parity, with U.S-born Japanese American men and foreign-born Mexican men at about seven times parity. This is a continuation of the historical employment pattern in the state, with men of color being recruited to supply the labor for the agricultural industry.

(10) In the eating and drinking places industry of the small shops sector, younger and less-educated workers account for 58 percent of the employment; the employment distribution of these workers is given in Table 10, which shows that the blue-collar workers, who account for 76 percent of the employment, are predominantly foreign-born Japanese American, Chinese American, and Mexican American men and women--all employed at three to five times parity. These same populations also dominate the blue-collar ranks within the older group. From Table 10 we see that the younger group also includes foreign-born Korean and Vietnamese women employed at three to four times parity. Both U.S.- and foreign-born white women are in the blue-collar ranks at about 1.5 times parity. U.S.- and foreign-born white men and foreign-born Chinese American men dominate the employment in the managerial ranks. We also see the traditional high employment level of foreign-born Chinese Americans in this labor-intensive industry. With the exception of blacks, the larger pattern in this industry is a higher-than-parity level of employment for foreign-born men and women of color in the blue-collar ranks.

Table 9. Number and Employment Level Relative to Civilian Labor Force Parity by Race, Nativity, and Gender in Agricultural Production for Older[a] and Less-Educated Groups.

	Manager	Profess-ional	Tech/Sales/ Clerk	Blue Collar
	Ratio[b] (N)	Ratio (N)	Ratio (N)	Ratio (N)
White US[c] male	1.2 (19)	--[d] (2)	0.3 (8)	0.9 (761)
White US female	0.9 (11)	-- (1)	2.3 (45)	0.2 (106)
White FB male	-- (1)	0.7 (40)		
White FB female	-- (1)	-- (3)	0.4 (19)	
Black US male	0.5 (32)			
Japanese US male	-- (3)	6.8 (90)		
Japanese US female	-- (3)	2.0 (22)		
Filipino FB male	2.5 (33)			
Filipino FB female	0.8 (14)			
Mexican US male	-- (1)	-- (1)	2.4 (198)	
Mexican US female	-- (3)	1.2 (73)		
Mexican FB male	-- (4)	-- (1)	-- (3)	6.7 (579)
Mexican FB female	-- (1)	2.3 (95)		
N	(42)	(6)	(69)	(2,191)
Occup. Distribution	1.8%	0.3%	3.0%	94.9%

[a]Older = 45-65 years old. Less-educated = less than 4 years of college.
[b]Ratio = % employment divided by % in employed civilian labor force.
[c]US = U.S.-born FB = Foreign-born
[d]"--" Ratio not calculated because cell count less than five.
Chi-square = 515.1 df = 93 Significance = 0.0001
Population samples with less than 20 are deleted from tables; however, column totals are summed from all populations.

Table 10. Number and Employment Level Relative to Civilian Labor Force Parity by Race, Nativity, and Gender in Eating and Drinking Places for Younger[a] and Less-Educated Groups.

	Manager	Profess-ional	Tech/Sales/ Clerk	Blue Collar
	Ratio[b] (N)	Ratio (N)	Ratio (N)	Ratio (N)
White US[c] male	1.0 (439)	1.5 (51)	0.2 (43)	0.4 (752)
White US female	0.8 (273)	0.5 (12)	1.7 (239)	1.3 (2071)
White FB male	2.5 (82)	--[d] (3)	0.4 (6)	0.9 (134)
White FB female	1.5 (36)	2.6 (25)	1.6 (173)	
Black US male	0.9 (32)	1.8 (5)	-- (3)	0.6 (103)
Black US female	0.3 (9)	-- (1)	1.2 (18)	0.5 (78)
Native American male	-- (3)	-- (2)	0.6 (14)	
Native American female	1.0 (5)	4.8 (9)	1.8 (37)	
Japanese FB male	4.0 (10)	3.0 (33)		
Japanese FB female	-- (2)	-- (1)	4.5 (48)	
Chinese FB male	3.0 (22)	-- (3)	5.5 (182)	
Chinese FB female	2.2 (13)	5.0 (12)	2.8 (78)	
Filipino FB male	1.0 (6)	0.8 (28)		
Filipino FB female	-- (1)	-- (2)	2.7 (9)	0.7 (26)
Korean FB male	-- (3)	-- (1)	1.5 (16)	
Korean FB female	1.5 (9)	-- (3)	4.0 (45)	
Vietnamese FB female	-- (1)	3.0 (17)		
Mexican US male	0.9 (43)	1.4 (5)	0.3 (5)	0.6 (128)
Mexican US female	0.6 (22)	2.3 (31)	1.0 (146)	
Mexican FB male	1.4 (69)	2.2 (8)	0.4 (8)	3.4 (746)
Mexican FB female	0.7 (16)	2.6 (24)	1.8 (193)	
N	(1,194)	(91)	(485)	(5,498)
Occup. Distribution	16.4%	1.3%	6.7%	75.6%

[a]Younger = 25-44 years old. Less-educated = less than 4 years of college.

[b]Ratio = % employment divided by % in employed civilian labor force.

[c]US = U.S.-born FB = Foreign-born

[d]"--" Ratio not calculated because cell count less than five.

Chi-square = 915.0 df = 105 Significance = 0.0001

Population samples with less than 20 are deleted from tables; however, column totals are summed from all populations.

Discussion

This analysis has focused on the six major sectors that account for 80 percent of the employment in California: core manufacturing, wholesale trade, periphery manufacturing and services, small shops, local monopoly, and educational services. Our findings for the industrial sectors and seventeen selected key industries that dominate employment reveal the following patterns for the population by race/ethnicity, nativity, and gender:

(a) *Continuing predomination of white men, both U.S.- and foreign-born, as managers and professionals.* White men and, to a lesser extent, Asian American men, have high levels of employment as managers and professionals in the core manufacturing and wholesale sectors. College-educated white men, both U.S.- and foreign-born, dominate the managerial ranks in electronic computing equipment manufacturing, electrical machinery manufacturing, wholesale trade of machinery equipment and supplies, securities, commodities, and investment brokers, real estate, colleges and universities, elementary and secondary schools, banking, insurance, and telephone services. White women, on the other hand, work as less-educated managers, in contrast to white men, who serve as college-educated managers in the brokerage, real estate, banking, insurance, and department stores, colleges and universities, elementary and secondary schools, and telephone services industries.

(b) *Domination of union-organized blue-collar employment by U.S.-born men, both white and nonwhite.* U.S.-born men, both white and nonwhite, and to a far lesser extent, foreign-born men, are in the blue-collar ranks of the local monopoly, periphery utilities, core transport and communications, and periphery transport sectors. The blue-collar ranks traditionally dominated by union-organized workers include mostly less-educated U.S.-born white, black, Native American, and Mexican American men in the building contractors, trucking, sanitary services, water supply, and telephone services industries. In contrast, there is a low employment level of foreign-born men of color in these industries, which is a reflection of the widespread perception that foreign-born workers drive down wages for organized domestic labor.[16] On the other hand, foreign-born blue-collar men of color are employed in industries with less union organization. Foreign-born Mexican American men are employed at high levels as assemblers and packagers in the wholesale trade of machinery equipment and supplies industry; they are also employed as janitors and gardeners in the real estate industry.

(c) *Continuing gender segregation and underemployment of women, both white and nonwhite.* Both white and nonwhite women, particularly the U.S.-born, have high employment levels as clerical workers in the core manufacturing, periphery manufacturing and services, small shops, and educational services sectors. In analyzing the key industries, we see this pattern in colleges and universities, elementary and secondary schools, and telephone services industries. The high employment level of college-educated white and nonwhite women in the clerical ranks of industries such as banking, insurance, department stores, and colleges and universities, provides strong evidence of underemployment; these ranks also include younger college-educated U.S.-born Japanese American women and foreign-born Filipino and Chinese American men and women.

(d) *Concentration of foreign-born men and women of color in assembly-line jobs and U.S.-born men of color in cleaning service jobs*. Foreign-born men and women of color and U.S.-born men of color are employed at high levels as blue-collar workers (mostly assembly line workers) in the core manufacturing, small shops, and educational services sectors. These include less-educated U.S.-born black and Mexican American women and foreign-born Chinese, Filipino, Korean, Vietnamese, and Mexican American women in the electrical machinery and electronic computing equipment manufacturing industries, as well as less-educated black and Mexican American men and women in the blue-collar ranks of elementary and secondary school and college and universities industries.

(e) *Concentration of foreign-born men and women of color in low-wage blue-collar jobs*. Foreign-born men and women of color and U.S.-born Japanese Americans and Mexican Americans are concentrated as less-educated and low-wage blue-collar workers in the eating and drinking places and agricultural production industries. In the eating and drinking places industries, most of the blue-collar workers are less-educated foreign-born men and women of color: Japanese, Chinese, Korean, Vietnamese, and Mexican American. Also employed in these blue-collar ranks are both U.S.- and foreign-born white women and foreign-born college-educated Chinese American men. The managers in the industry are mostly foreign-born Chinese men and college-educated white men, both U.S.- and foreign-born. The high representation of foreign-born Chinese men in the industry is indicative of their underemployment in an "economic niche" that this population has carved out for itself.

In the agricultural production industry, most workers are less-educated, younger, blue-collar men and women of color, including mostly foreign-born Filipino and Asian Indian men, foreign-born Mexican American men and women, and U.S.-born Mexican American men. Also included are older U.S.-born Japanese American men and women, with the men mostly farmers and farm managers, and the women mostly farm laborers.

Conclusions

Based on our analysis of the employed civilian labor force in California in 1980, the overall pattern we see across industrial sectors and key industries consists of:

(1) race segregation, with white men (U.S.-and foreign-born) in the managerial and professional ranks, and U.S.-born men of color (black and Mexican American) and foreign-born men and women of color (Filipino, Chinese, Korean, Vietnamese, and Mexican American) in the low-wage blue-collar ranks;

(2) gender segregation, with both white and nonwhite (black, Asian American, and Mexican American) women in the clerical ranks, with underemployment evident from the presence of many who are college-educated;[17]

(3) control of the union-organized ranks by U.S.-born men, both white and nonwhite (black, Native American, and Mexican American),

with continuing exclusion of women and foreign-born workers; and

(4) bias against foreign-born men and women of color as revealed by race segregation and exclusion from union-dominated ranks.

Thus, overall, race, gender, and nativity systematically segregate and stratify workers in the state. Educational attainment level, used as a variable in the study, has not greatly affected the segregation patterns by race and gender. Similarly, there are no significant differences between the patterns of the two age groups. The theoretical implication of these empirical patterns is that race, gender, and nativity seem more important than class (as it is defined by occupational and industrial sector divisions in the state) as determinants of socioeconomic stratification.

Further studies should investigate the race, gender, and nativity employment patterns for other states, such as Illinois and New York, which contain major metropolitan areas, important centers of commerce and industry, and large populations of racial and ethnic minorities, both U.S.- and foreign-born. Future studies can also focus on particular populations and their occupational distribution within industries selected on the basis of the severity of the employment disparities found therein. Industries with a large multiracial work force, as well as those with few minorities, can be the focus of such studies. Some studies can use methodologies such as ethnographic, internal labor market, and employer case studies, while others can investigate the likely connection of the employment patterns to the global economy and the international division of labor.

The present study also has policy implications. The employment patterns observed should be addressed by employers in their affirmative action programs, which can set targets for the hiring and promotion of racial minorities and women in the ranks from which they are presently absent or poorly represented. Together with employers, employee groups can look into restrictive promotion practices and other barriers to upward mobility. State and federal contract compliance agencies, the U.S. Equal Employment Opportunity Commission, and attorneys in private practice can all be alerted to the existing employment disparities. Affirmative action efforts should continue in trade apprenticeship programs and referral unions that control the flow of labor in the higher-paying blue-collar ranks. Studies of economic inequality in the American workplace must continue to investigate the effects of race/ethnicity, gender, and nativity on workers.

Notes

1. Robert L. Kaufman, Randy Hodson, and Neil D. Fligstein, "Defrocking Dualism: A New Approach to Defining Industrial Sectors," *Social Science Research* 10 (1981):1-31.

2. Amado Cabezas and Gary Kawaguchi, "Preliminary Structural Analysis of Economic Inequality for Asian and Pacific Americans in California," unpublished paper presented at the 82nd Annual Meeting of the American Sociological Association, Chicago, Illinois, August, 1987; Barry Chiswick,"An Analysis of the Earnings and Employment of Asian-American Men," *Journal of Labor Economics* 1 (1983):197-214; Victor Nee and Jimy Sanders, "The Road to Parity: Determinants of the Socioeconomic Achievement of Asian Americans," *Ethnic and Racial Studies* 8 (January 1985):75-93; Morrison G. Wong, "The Cost of Being Chinese, Japanese, and Filipino in the United States, 1960, 1970, 1976," *Pacific Sociological Review* 25 (January 1982):59-78.

3. Cabezas and Kawaguchi, "Preliminary Structural Analysis."

4. Kaufman, Hodson, and Fligstein, "Defrocking Dualism"; Robert L. Kaufman, "A Structural Decomposition of Black-White Earnings Differentials," *American Journal of Sociology* 89 (1983):585, finds that black-white earnings differentials result from (1) differential earnings between blacks and whites within labor market divisions and (2) differential earnings across labor market divisions for all workers combined with differential employment levels for blacks and whites across labor market divisions. Because the second factor contributes at least 14 percent of the black-white earnings gap, Kaufman states that "eliminating all black-white differences within labor market divisions would still leave a significant earnings gap between blacks and whites due to the structure of the labor market."

5. We assume that changes in the economy between 1970 and 1980 have not been so large as to invalidate the sectorization results obtained

using 1970 census and other data.

6. A good discussion of dual economy theory is found in Randy Hodson and Robert L. Kaufman, "Economic Dualism: A Critical Review," *American Sociological Review* 47 (December 1982):727-739.

7. Kaufman, Hodson, and Fligstein, "Defrocking Dualism."

8. Ibid. In general, the size of an industrial sector is its share of total economic activity, concentration is domination by a small number of companies, and capital intensity is level of technology employed. The values of the summary measures by sector are shown in Table 4, page 17 of Ibid. It should be noted that the names of the industrial sectors are not necessarily descriptive of the set of summary measures that characterize each sector.

9. Richard Edwards, *Contested Terrain: The Transformation of the Workplace in the Twentieth Century* (New York: Basic Books, 1979); David M. Gordon, Richard Edwards and Michael Reich, *Segmented Work: Divided Workers* (London: Cambridge University Press, 1982); Robert L. Kaufman, "Racial Discrimination and Labor Market Segmentation" (Ph.D. diss., University of Wisconsin, Madison, 1981). To empirically test Wright's latest class theory, data would be needed by race, nativity, and gender for the capital, credentials, and organizational assets of workers. Erik Olin Wright, *Classes* (London: Verso Editions, 1985).

10. In an earlier study, Wright and Perrone had seen differences in the returns of education between race and gender groups within classes of workers, managers, and employers. Erik Olin Wright, and Luca Perrone, "Marxist Class Categories and Income Inequality," *American Sociological Review* 42 (February 1977):32-55.

11. The chi-square statistic tests for the statistical significance of a possible relationship between two variables. The log-linear analysis verifies age group, educational level, population by race/ethnicity, nativity, and gender, and employment level by occupational category to be main-effect variables. All interactions between any two of the

variables are statistically significant at at least the 0.0001 level. For discussions of the log-linear analysis, see Y. M. M. Bishop, S. E. Feinberg, and P. W. Holland, *Discrete Multivariate Analysis* (Cambridge, Mass.: The MIT Press, 1975); Leo A. Goodman, *Analyzing Qualitative/Categorical Data: Log-Linear Models and Latent Structure Analysis* (Cambridge, Mass.: Abt, 1978); SPSS Inc., *SPSSX User's Guide*, 2nd ed. (Chicago, Ill.: SPSS Inc., 1986).

12. From Kaufman, Hodson, and Fligstein, "Defrocking Dualism"; the sectorization analysis by Kaufman et al. used 1970 census and other data. In our analysis using 1980 census data, we found only a few of the industrial categories to be different between the two censuses.

13. 1980 Census five-percent Public Use Microdata Sample.

14. For the state, managers account for about 12 percent of all workers, professionals for about 13 percent, technicians for about 3 percent, sales workers for about 9 percent, clerical workers for about 20 percent, and blue collar workers for about 43 percent. Thus, those in our "clerical" ranks are mostly clerical workers.

15. This can be seen from Table 4, page 17, of Kaufman, Hodson, and Fligstein, "Defrocking Dualism," from the high values of the summary measure of unionization for the industrial sectors to which these four industries belong.

16. Edna Bonacich, "Advanced Capitalism and Black/White Race Relations in the United States: A Split Labor Market Interpretation" *American Sociological Review* 41 (February 1976):34-51; Lucie Cheng and Edna Bonacich, *Labor Immigration Under Capitalism: Asian Workers in the United States Before World War II* (Berkeley and Los Angeles: University of California Press, 1984).

17. Barbara F. Reskin and Heidi I. Hartmann, *Women's Work, Men's Work: Sex Segregation on the Job* (Washington, D.C.: National Academy Press, 1986).

Poverty in the United States: Race, Ethnic, and Gender Differentials

Adalberto Aguirre, Jr.

More than twenty years ago, Michael Harrington argued that poverty must be eliminated in America: "In a nation with a technology that could provide every citizen with a decent life, it is an outrage and a scandal that there should be such misery."[1] Perhaps in response to his challenge, the federal government escalated the "War on Poverty" and introduced more programs to involve the poor in economic activities. Despite the victory in several battles against poverty, the "War on Poverty" was never won because as federal money targeted for poverty programs dwindled, poor people became unemployed once again in large numbers.[2] However, the "War On Poverty" created the image that poverty had been removed from American society. Consequently, Edward Gramlich has observed: "Both politicians and funding agencies sometimes appear to consider poverty research passé--an issue of the 1960s but not of the 1970s."[3]

Does poverty still exist in the United States in the late 1980s? According to the Reagan administration, people are poor because they do not know any better. The Reagan administration asks why the government should bother with people who have simply neglected themselves and depicts poverty simply as something created by temporary fluctuations in our economy. According to this line of thinking, some people are poor by choice while others are poor by force of circumstance. In any case, poverty seems to be only a temporary phenomenon.

This essay maintains that poverty is a persistent feature in U.S. society and is a structural arrangement which is most noticeable among racial/ethnic minorities and women. According to the 1980 census, only 8 percent of white households were below the poverty level in 1980, compared to 29 percent of black, 23 percent of Hispanic, and 33 percent of female-headed households.[4]

Poverty in the U.S. after 1970

While a relatively stable number of people earned incomes below the poverty level in the 1970s, by the early 1980s there was a substantial increase in the absolute number of people, as well as a rise in the percentage of the total population with incomes below the poverty level. Table 1 shows that for every group, the greatest increase in the poverty rate occurred between 1980 and 1983, so that by 1983, there were 24 million white persons, over 4 million Hispanic persons, and 10 million black persons below the poverty level. The poverty rate in the country increased from 11.1 percent to 13.0 percent between 1970 and 1980, but during the 1980-82 recessionary period, it increased from 13.0 percent to 15.2 percent.

Table 1
Persons in Poverty

	All Persons	White	Hispanic	Black
1970	27,398*	17,484	2,366	7,548
1980	31,769	19,699	3,491	18,579
1983	38,108	23,974	4,249	9,885
1970	11.1%	9.9%	21.9%	33.5%
1980	13.0%	10.2%	25.7%	32.5%
1983	15.2%	12.1%	28.4%	35.7%

*numbers are in thousands
Source: U.S. Bureau of the Census, 1981, 1984.

An examination of the poverty rate among families produces an interesting contrast with the poverty rate for persons. On the one hand, the proportion of persons in poverty within the Hispanic and black populations (see Table 1) is similar to the proportion of families in poverty within each population (see Table 2). The poverty rate for persons as well as for families in the Hispanic and black populations is more than two times larger than the poverty rate for white persons and white families. On the other hand, while the poverty rate for white families increased steadily between 1970 and 1980, the poverty rate for Hispanic and black families between 1970 and 1980 fluctuated. For example, the poverty rate for Hispanic families increased between 1970-1975, but decreased between 1975-1980. In contrast, the poverty rate for black families decreased between 1970-1975, but increased between 1975-1980. As a result, between 1970 and 1980 there was an overall increase in the poverty rate for Hispanic families and for white families, but a decrease in the poverty rate for black families.

Table 2
Families in Poverty

	White	Hispanic	Black
1970	3,708*	468	1,481
1975	3,838	627	1,513
1980	4,195	751	1,826
1983	5,223	933	2,162
1970	8.1%	21.5%	32.2%
1975	8.3%	26.3%	30.1%
1980	8.6%	25.1%	31.1%
1983	10.7%	27.8%	34.7%

*numbers are in thousands
Source: U.S. Bureau of the Census, 1981, 1984.

The substantial increase in the poverty rate for both persons and families between 1980-1983, in comparison with changes in the poverty rate between 1970-1980, suggests that, contrary to conventional wisdom, the rate of poverty in American society is increasing, and poverty is a persistent phenomemon. While a large majority of the total U.S. is victimized by social forces that promote poverty, the larger proportions of poor persons and families within the Hispanic and black populations suggest that a decline into poverty may be a structural feature that entraps the Hispanic and black populations to such an extent that it becomes a fact of life in their communities.

Table 3 reveals a paradox: between 1970 and 1980 the poverty rate for all families increased despite an increase in the median family income for all groups. As the number of female householder families increased by 2.1 percent between 1970 and 1980, and their poverty rate also increased, the proportion of female householder families among the population of poor families increased significantly during this period.

Between 1980 and 1983, however, the poverty rate for all families increased and the median family income for all groups decreased. In particular, the poverty rate for female householder families increased more than twice the increase in poverty rate for all families, and the decrease in family median income was 65 percent greater for female householder families than for all families. Since there was an increase of only 0.8 percent in the number of female householder families between 1980 and 1983, one can conclude that such an increase came from the existing pool of female householder families rather than from new female-headed households entering the pool.

Based on the information presented in Table 3 one can see that:

(a) there does not appear to be a clear association between poverty rates for families and median family income; that is, the poverty rate can increase regardless of whether there is an increase or decrease in family median income;

(b) between 1970 and 1983, the increase in the poverty rate for female householder families outpaced the rise in the poverty rate for all families; and

(c) since the increase in the poverty rate of female householder families has exceeded the increase in their numbers, this suggests that female householder families are becoming poorer more quickly than other families.

Table 3
Factors Associated with Poverty Indicators

	1970-1979	1980-1983
Changes in the Percentage of Families below the Poverty Level		
1. All Families	+0.5%	+2.1%
2. Female householder families	+8.4%	+4.9%
Changes in Median Family Income		
1. All Families	+4.9%	-8.6%
2. Married Couple Families	+8.2%	-7.2%
3. Female Householder Families	+3.5%	-13.1%
Increase in Female Householder Families	+2.1%	0.8%

Source: U.S. Bureau of the Census, 1981, 1984, 1985.

Female Householder Families

One of the most important changes in the composition of the family during the 1970s was an increase in the number of families maintained by women with no husbands present.[5] These families constituted 15 percent of all families in 1980, up from 11 percent in 1970. In 1980, they made up 48 percent of all families below the poverty level that year, compared with 36 percent in 1969.[6] By 1983 about one out of three persons below the poverty level belonged to a family maintained by a woman with no husband present.[7] Fully 36 percent of these families had incomes below the poverty level in 1983, which was significantly higher than the 12.3 percent for all families. About two-fifths of the overall increase in the number of poor families since 1980 is attributable to an increase in the number of families maintained by women.[8]

According to Table 4, some of the more salient features of female householder families in poverty in terms of race and ethnic background are:

1. Almost three times as many Hispanic and almost four times as many black female householder families live in poverty as white female householder families.

2. The largest number of Hispanic and black female householder families in poverty (46.6 percent and 66.4 percent, respectively) are those in which the age of the householder is between fifteen and twenty-four years. In comparison, only 23.3 percent of white female householder families in poverty are in this age group.

3. Hispanic and black female householder families are larger and

Table 4
Female Householder Families in Poverty, 1982

	Total	White	Hispanic	Black
All families	12.3%	9.7%	26.1%	32.4%
Age of Householder				
15-24 years	29.5%	23.3%	46.6%	66.4%
25-34	16.2%	13.0%	30.2%	37.2%
35-44	12.0%	9.5%	25.3%	30.1%
45-54	8.8%	6.8%	18.5%	24.9%
55-59	8.5%	6.7%	17.6%	24.6%
60-64	8.7%	7.2%	16.3%	22.7%
65 +	8.7%	6.6%	19.1%	27.2%
Mean Size of Family	3.64	3.50	4.11	3.87
Mean Number of Children	2.28	2.21	2.56	2.37
% H. S. Graduates	48.4	50.8	26.7	42.4
Number of Workers				
0	33.2%	24.4%	71.9%	75.4%
1	16.1%	13.5%	30.3%	33.5%
2	5.0%	4.4%	11.6%	11.0%
3 +	3.6%	3.1%	6.8%	8.7%
Employment Status				
Employed	7.2%	6.2%	15.8%	16.1%
Unemployed	36.2%	30.4%	42.5%	57.5%
Did not Work Last Year	27.0%	20.1%	57.1%	60.2%
Median Income	-	-	59.0%	62.0%
Free School Lunch	-	43.6%	59.7%	51.7%
Food Stamps	-	72.3%	74.8%	76.4%

Source: U.S. Bureau of the Census, 1983; Select Committee on Hunger, 1986.

have more children living at home than white female householder families.

4. Almost three-fourths of both Hispanic and black female householder families do not have any workers in the family. But for those households with workers, the largest subgroup contains three or more workers.

5. Hispanic and black female houshold heads are less likely to have worked last year than white female household heads.

6. In those households where the head was employed full-time last year, Hispanics earned 59 percent and blacks earned 62 percent of the median income of white female household heads.

7. In households with children 5-18 years old, black and Hispanic children are more likely to receive a reduced-cost or free school lunch than white children: 59.7 percent and 51.7 percent respectively, compared to 43.6 percent for white children.

8. Almost three-fourths of white, Hispanic, and black female-headed households receive food stamps.

One can thus observe that differences by race and ethnicity exist in the population of poor female householder families. In particular, Hispanic and black female householder families in poverty consist of more members and are headed by younger persons. More of these families have no workers, but of those that do, there are a larger number of workers. Hispanic and black female heads of household are less educated than are white female heads of household. Not only do more Hispanic and black female householder families live in poverty than white female householder families, but they appear to be much poorer than their white counterparts.

Implications

Poverty is a persistent feature of American society and it appears to be increasing among minorities and women, when compared with the white population as a whole. These facts underscore the vulnerability of minorities and of women, who comprise a highly visible pool of labor that can be paid low wages and who can be easily ignored during times of economic hardship.[9] There are also distinct intergroup differences among the poor: some are "poorer" than others. Different status characteristics--race, ethnicity, and gender--all contribute to the stratification of poor people and poor families in American society. From the data we have examined, it appears that the "poorer of the poor" are increasing in number, and are becoming an increasingly entrapped segment of society. That is to say, the close association between the growth of female householder families and their poverty status suggests that these households may be perpetuating themselves. As young members of such households leave home, they may simply be starting new households that resemble the ones they have left.

Conclusion

We have observed that in the 1980s poverty is not only still prevalent in American society, but it appears to be on the rise. In particular, poverty among minorities and women is a visible measure of their unequal position in the structure of American society. The rapid increase in the rate of poverty among minority and female-headed households in general eclipses any likelihood of intergenerational improvement in particular households. The distressing fact is that children growing up in households in poverty may never have the opportunity to enjoy the full benefits of being members of American society.

Notes

1. M. Harrington, *The Other America: Poverty in the United States* (Baltimore: Penguin Books, 1963), 24.

2. J. Berry, *Feeding Hungry People: Rulemaking in the Food Stamp Program* (New Brunswich, N.J.: Rutgers University Press, 1984).

3. E. Gramlich, "Future Research on Poverty and Income Maintenance," *Poverty and Public Policy,* ed. V. Covello (Cambridge, Mass.: Schenkman Pub. Co., 1980), 15.

4. U.S. Bureau of the Census, *Consumer Income*, Series P-60, no. 127 (Washington, D.C.: Government Printing Office, 1981).

5. National Advisory Council on Economic Opportunity, *Women and Children: Alone and in Poverty*, Washington, D.C., September, 1981; U.S. Bureau of the Census, *Population Profile of the United States: 1981*, Series P-20, no. 374 (Washington, D.C.: Government Printing Office, 1982).

6. U.S. Bureau of the Census, *Consumer Income*, Series P-60, no. 130 (Washington, D.C.: Government Printing Office, 1981).

7. U.S. Bureau of the Census, *Population Profile of the United States 1983/84*, Series P-23, no. 145 (Washington, D.C.: Government Printing Office, 1985).

8. Committee on Labor and Human Resources, *Women in Transition, 1983* (Washington, D.C.: Government Printing Office, 1984).

9. G. Carliner, "Female Labor Force Participation Rates for Nine Ethnic Groups," *Journal of Human Resources* 16, no. 2 (1981):49-52; N. Rytina, "Occupational Segregation and Earnings Differences by Sex," *Monthly Labor Review* 104 (1981):49-52; F. Piven and R. Cloward, *Regulating the Poor: The Functions of Public Welfare* (New York: Pantheon Books, 1971).

The Socioeconomic Status of the Hispanic Population in the United States

Refugio I. Rochin

The Hispanic population in the United States, far from being homogeneous, is composed of different racial as well as cultural groups. There are Spanish-speaking blacks, whites, and Native Americans. People of Hispanic origin have also immigrated from different countries, each with its own culture. Furthermore, each of these groups is concentrated in a different region of the United States and casts a distinct social and economic profile. Various public policy issues are not equally important to the many groups: Chicanos are more concerned about immigration than Puerto Ricans, who are United States citizens by birth; Cubans are more concerned about Fidel Castro and Communism than other Hispanics; while the political status of Puerto Rico is of far more interest to Puerto Ricans than to others. Geographic distance between the groups also works against the political and economic unification of the Hispanic population. Nonetheless, as a whole, Hispanics are seriously disadvantaged and are found concentrated in self-contained barrios which are often separated from mainstream society. Many live in poverty and experience high rates of un- and underemployment. Because of their increasing numbers, along with their low rates of educational attainment, need for public support, limited English, lack of political participation, and cultural uniqueness, they are no longer an "invisible" minority but are, rather, a growing source of controversy and, at times, of apprehension among non-Hispanics.

In this article, I shall review literature from scholarly journals, news accounts, and government documents in order to identify pertinent facts and findings regarding the socioeconomic status of Hispanics in the United States. Working with diverse literature reflects two premises on which this article is based: (1) there is a need to collect, select, organize, and condense existing knowledge about Hispanics; and (2) the utility of such a synthesis is enhanced by focusing on major issues and research in a manner that does not rely solely on any particular school of thought or method of analysis. The paper focuses on five sets of indicators about Hispanics: demographic statistics; income and poverty; education, language and assimilation; employment, wages and occupation; and entrepreneurial activities. There is no clear-cut dividing line among these sets, and I shall attempt to derive significant generalizations about differences between Hispanics and non-Hispanics. The paper ends with some suggestions for further research and policy-making.

Hispanics are identified here as persons in the United States whose origin is Mexican, Puerto Rican, Central or South American, or are identified by some other Spanish designation such as Spanish, Latino, Chicano, etc. The ongoing debate about the use of the term

"Hispanics" is not at issue here; rather, what I shall do is paint a comprehensive picture of socioeconomic issues confronting this major group in America.

Demographics

Hardly a report is written without depictions of Hispanics in terms of their growing numbers, concentrations, composition, and age/sex/ethnic distributions. Such numbers can provide several insights for understanding Hispanics. From 1980 to 1987, the Hispanic population increased by 30.0 percent (from 14,458,000 to 18,790,000), while the nation's total population increased by 7.3 percent (from 222,461,000 to 238,789,000). When we subtract the growth of the Hispanic population from the total population growth, the non-Hispanic United States population increased by only 5.8 percent (from about 208 million to 220 million). The rate of growth of the Hispanic population was thus five times greater than the growth of the non-Hispanic population.

These rather different rates of population growth are due in part to the relative youthfulness, higher fertility rates, and higher net migration rates of Hispanics. More than one-third (36 percent) of Hispanics are less than eighteen years old, compared to about one-quarter (26 percent) of non-Hispanics. The median age for Hispanics in 1987 was 25 years, compared to 26.3 for blacks and 32.2 for whites, which means that Hispanics have relatively more people at childbearing age than non-Hispanics. Furthermore, Hispanics have relatively high fertility rates. Hispanic women 18-44 years of age had an average of 86.1 births per 1,000 in 1986, compared to black women with 72.2, and white women with 64.6. Hispanics tend to marry at a younger age than other Americans do, and Hispanic women are more likely than women of other ethnic backgrounds to marry while in their teens. In 1980, 7.3 percent of Hispanic women 15-19 years old had babies, compared to 10.2 percent of black women and 4.5 percent of white non-Hispanics of the same age group.[1] Although the majority of Hispanic teenage mothers are married when they have children, most have not finished high school. The net result of high fertility and teenage marriage is a relatively high dependent-to-workforce ratio for Hispanics, about 0.65 as compared to 0.40 for non-Hispanics. In other words, Hispanic parents have more young people to care for per income earner than non-Hispanic parents. Moreover, Hispanic teenage pregnancy is increasing.

Hispanic family size has declined somewhat since 1970. However, the mean number of persons per Hispanic family in 1986 was still high at 3.87, compared to 3.21 persons in the non-Hispanic family. Currently, 52.0 percent of Hispanic families contain four or more persons and 12.5 percent have six or more. Among non-Hispanics, on the other hand, only 36.0 percent of the families have four or more persons and only 5.0 percent have six or more. Fertility rates partially explain these differences in family size, but Hispanics are also more likely than other Americans to live in multigenerational households. Hispanic elderly, a small but rapidly growing group, are less likely than white or black elderly to be placed in institutions away from their families, which adds to the dependency ratio of Hispanic families.[2]

The number of Hispanic single-parent households is increasing, as is the percentage of Hispanic children under eighteen living with one rather than both parents. In 1988, 23.4 percent of Hispanic households were headed by a female with no male present, compared to 15.8 percent for non-Hispanic households; 6.8 percent were headed by a male with no female present, compared to 4.0 percent for non-Hispanics; and 69.8 percent were headed by a married couple, compared to 80.3 percent for non-Hispanics.[3] Despite the rise in single-parent households, Hispanics remain less likely than the general population to be divorced, and because of multigenerational clustering, they are also more likely than the overall population to live in larger households.[4]

Relatively large families, high fertility rates, and youthful parents assure a rapidly growing Hispanic population, even without positive net in-migration, but Hispanic population growth is also due to high rates of both legal and undocumented immigration. Though the numbers are unreliable, total undocumented United States immigration is generally estimated to account for an annual inflow of a half million aliens, the majority of whom are Hispanics from Mexico and Central America.[5] Moreover, in response to the Immigration Reform and Control Act of 1986, as of May 1988, news releases from the Immigration and Naturalization Service reported that a total of 1.6 million people applied for amnesty. Another 470,000 immigrant farmworkers registered for legal residence under a separate program, which raises the total applicants to 2.1 million. Over 910,000 applications were filed in Los Angeles alone and more than 70 percent of all applications were from Mexicans (the future "Chicanos" of the U.S.).[6]

The Hispanic population includes large numbers of recent immigrants and first-generation offspring, who not only experience new economic and cultural surroundings but also often speak Spanish as their first and only language. About one-fourth of Mexican-origin Hispanics are born in Mexico, while three-fourths of Cuban-origin individuals and two-thirds of the Central and South American-origin populations are foreign-born, adding to the cultural diversity among Hispanics.

The size of the various sub-groups of Hispanics is shown in Table 1.

Table 1

Number of Hispanics by Ethnic Origin, 1987

	Number	Percent of Total
Mexican origin	11.8 million	62.8
Puerto Rican origin	2.3 million	12.2
Cuban origin	1.0 million	5.3
Central and S. Amer.	2.1 million	11.2
Other Hispanic	1.6 million	8.5
Total	18.8 million	100.0

Hispanic subgroups are concentrated in particular regions, i.e., Mexican-origin Hispanics or Chicanos are located mainly in the Southwest; Puerto Rican-origin Hispanics in New York, New Jersey, and Puerto Rico; and Cuban-origin Hispanics in Florida. Central and South American-origin Hispanics live mostly in the mid-Atlantic states.[7] Nearly one-third of Hispanics live in California, most of whom are Chicanos, representing nearly 22 percent of the state's population. In the Los Angeles basin, Hispanics make up 27 percent of the area's population. California, Texas, and the metropolitan areas of New York, Miami, and Chicago account for 70 percent of the Hispanic population. Hispanics are more likely to live in metropolitan areas than non-Hispanics: 87 percent reside within metropolitan areas compared to 74 percent of non-Hispanics. However, Mexican-Americans are relatively less urbanized than other Hispanics, and many live and work in rural areas.

Because the economic and labor market conditions of major metropolitan areas to a large extent determine the political and socioeconomic position of Hispanics, and because there has been and will continue to be growth in the Hispanic school-age population, the subgroups of Hispanics will continue to be particularly concerned about education, social welfare, employment, and economic opportunities in the areas where they are settled.

United States Census Bureau projections of the Hispanic population indicate a doubling in thirty years and a possible tripling in sixty years.[8] Most of the Hispanic population growth will occur among those aged thirty-five and older. The number of Hispanics sixty-five years and older may quadruple by 2015. Meanwhile, the white population may peak in size by 2020 at 204 million, along with 44 million blacks and 13.7 million others. Thus, in the approaching decades the importance of Hispanics is bound to increase if only because of their numbers.

Income and Poverty

Having seen the differences between Hispanics and non-Hispanics in terms of several sociodemographic features, it is not surprising to find that Hispanics also differ in income and purchasing power from non-Hispanics. In fact, the 1980 Census of Population revealed only two major groups with annual family incomes below the national average of $23,092--Hispanic families, with $17,263 (75 percent of the national average) and black families with $15,711 (68 percent of the national average). Whites of European ancestry and Asian/Pacific Islanders had mean family incomes at or above the national average in 1980, $24,385 and $26,575, respectively. Although the mean family income of Hispanics increased to $22,566 in 1985 ($21,651 for blacks) this was an almost negligible improvement compared to the increase in white income to $30,258. These statistics show that the economic position of Hispanics relative to the general population is, and has long been, markedly low. Many of the nation's 64 million families are economically deprived, but the fact of the matter is that on the average, Hispanic and black families are the most likely of all to be poor in the United States.

In 1986, the most recent year with official poverty data, 1.1

million Hispanic families were living in poverty. The poverty rate for Hispanic families was nearly 25 percent, which is two and a half times more than the 10 percent poverty rate for non-Hispanic families. In addition, because of the growth of the Hispanic population, about 210,000 more Hispanic families were living in poverty in 1986 than in 1980.[9]

Since the Census Bureau began collecting poverty data on Hispanics in 1972, there have been relatively few studies following the trends and correlates of Hispanic poverty. However, the number of Hispanics living in poverty and the number and percentage of Hispanic children living in poverty hit record highs in 1985, according to the Center on Budget and Policy Priorities.[10] The Center reported that the Hispanic poverty rate (the percentage of Hispanics who are poor) hit 29 percent, with 5.2 million Hispanics living in poverty. For the population as a whole, the poverty rate declined from 14.4 percent in 1984 to 14.0 percent in 1985. Since 1973, the typical Hispanic family's income, adjusted for inflation, has fallen more than $2,000, a drop of 10 percent, and since 1982, the average per-person income for Hispanics has gone lower than the per-person income for blacks. The Center reported that

> . . . while 12.2 percent of black married couple families are poor (about one in every eight) and 6.1 percent of white married couple families are poor (one in every sixteen), some 17 percent of Hispanic married couples are poor (more than one in every six). In addition, 50.5 percent of black female-headed families are poor, but 53.1 percent of Hispanic female-headed families are poor.[11]

The Center also indicated that 66.9 percent of black children living in female-headed families are poor, but that an even higher percentage--72.4 percent--of Hispanic children in such families are poor.

Low income and poverty pose serious and damaging consequences for Hispanics. Low income accentuates the need for family members to work at an early age and often leaves problems like poor health and housing uncorrected. Absolute poverty prevents many Hispanics from making critical investments in education, the backbone of human capital formation, as well as of employment and earnings. Bearing the heaviest burdens of poverty are Chicanos of the Southwest and Puerto Ricans of the East Coast.

Relatively less inclined to poverty are members of the Cuban communities of Florida, where self-employment is relatively prevalent and where the Cuban immigrants tend to have above average success in the labor market.[12] Even with the 1980 influx of Cuban refugees of impoverished roots, Cubans of South Florida have made impressive progress in the United States.[13] Perez attributes the Cuban success story to the high degree of economic cooperation within the family:

> It is a family with characteristics tailored to facilitate upward mobility: a relatively large number of workers, high rates of female employment, the presence of an elderly generation that contributes directly and indirectly to the household's economic welfare, low fertility, and high levels of school enrollment.[14]

In short, the Cuban household, according to Perez, combines family numbers, earnings, and motivation into a self-sustaining mechanism for upward mobility.

By contrast, the accounts written in the 1960s by anthropologists Oscar Lewis, William Madsen, Arthur Rubel, Munro Edmonson, and Margaret Clark, of strong family networks in Puerto Rican and Mexican communities, are far from positive.[15] Their studies tend towards a pathological analysis of Mexican-Americans and Puerto Ricans, strongly suggesting that Hispanics are their own worst enemies in causing economic deprivation. These early anthropological writings have since been challenged and strongly criticized, mainly by Hispanic scholars of the 1970s.[16]

More recently, research by Mines and Nuckton has shown that Mexican immigrants tend to set up "beachhead communities" which assist future immigrants from Mexico with settlement in the United States, especially in California. Tienda found that U.S. family connections are important for the immigration of Mexicans into the country and for their social and emotional adjustment, but that the Mexican experience differs from that of Cubans, for whom the maintenance of ascriptive relations gives the immigrants an advantaged position vis-à-vis those who do not have such connections. In short, the research to date would lead us to infer that in the Mexican settlement process, immigrant poverty begets continued poverty of Mexican-Americans or Chicanos, while in the Cuban case, relatively higher immigrant wealth abets their ability to succeed in the United States.[17]

Education, Language and Assimilation

Despite the important role that family can play in alleviating poverty among some groups of Hispanics, what seems to count more for future economic gain is education. In many studies of Hispanics, relatively low rates of high school completion are highly correlated with economic deprivation. According to the Center on Budget and Policy Priorities, in 1985 62 percent of the Hispanic families below the poverty level contained adults who had less than four years of high school.[18] Nearly 30 percent of the impoverished Hispanics up to thirty-four years of age did not have a high school diploma. Only 12.3 percent of whites and 16.7 percent of blacks among the same age groups did not have a high school diploma.

Most alarming is the growing number of functionally illiterate among Hispanics, reading at a fourth grade level or less. Out of approximately twenty-three million functionally illiterate people in the United States today, approximately one-half, twelve million, are Hispanics age sixteen or older. Moreover, according to a recent study by SER, Jobs for Progress, Inc., a Hispanic-oriented organization based in Dallas, more than one-third of Hispanic mothers on public assistance are illiterate.[19] School achievement, though slowly improving overall, is a serious problem for all Hispanics but is most troublesome for Chicanos and Puerto Ricans. In the Los Angeles Unified School District, Chicanos have the highest high-school dropout rate of any minority group--at least 45 percent leave school between the 10th and 12th grades. Of California's Chicanos who do graduate from high school, only about 5 percent are academically qualified--under existing guidelines based on grade-point averages and test scores--to enter the University of California. The rates of eligibility for whites and Asians are three and four times higher, respectively. As a result, Chicanos are nearly twice as likely as whites to attend two-year colleges and half as likely to attend universities. Data from the California Commission on Postsecondary Education show that, based on past performance, fewer than 20 of every 1,000 Hispanic or black ninth graders today are likely to ever graduate from a four-year college or university. The comparable graduation rates for white and Asian ninth graders are 60 and 175 per 1,000.[20] In short, the educational pipeline from elementary grades through college is hemorrhaging and Hispanics are losing out. Rapid growth in the Hispanic population coupled with increasing poverty and a dismal picture of their educational situation are affecting the prosperity and well-being not only of Hispanics, but of the society as a whole.[21]

Recognizing the important role of education, Chicano parents in Los Angeles, as well as in other areas, filed a lawsuit alleging that for decades the school district spent hundreds of dollars less per pupil in minority areas, forcing Chicano students to attend overcrowded schools with less experienced teachers, fewer supplies, and poorer equipment. The common lack of "educational equity" and the failure of school leaders throughout the state to respond to the charges is considered a primary cause of poor educational attainment of Hispanics.

Another explanation for the poor schooling record of Hispanics is a lack of English skills, or "limited English proficiency." Birthplace, language spoken at home and at work, and training in school all affect the facility for English. In 1980, Spanish speakers accounted for 46 percent of the language-minority population of about 23 million persons. Thus, for over 10 million people, English is second to Spanish; this has been particularly true for recent immigrants but less true for second- and third-generation Hispanics. How important English is and how best to address the limited English proficiency of different generations of Hispanics are questions often asked by the educational community.

Some researchers have suggested that English proficiency is more important and has greater effects on the employment and earnings of Hispanics than general schooling.[22] McManus presents the argument this way:

> Since English skills provide substantial wage gains, assimilation of minority-language immigrants will be facilitated by English language training. To the extent that 'bilingual education' interferes with rapid integration into the U.S. language mainstream, it ought to be discouraged.[23]

According to this view, proficiency in English is synonymous with assimilation.

A particularly interesting article by Koch partially corroborates this argument.[24] He examined the incomes earned by eighteen groups of immigrants, who comprised two-thirds of all immigrants during the 1970s, using census data for 1970 and 1980. Koch found considerable disparity in the family incomes earned by the various groups of settled immigrants, from a low of $9,569 to a high of $25,431.[25] The families of four immigrant groups (from the United Kingdom, the Philippines,

India, and Canada) earned incomes higher than the median income of native U.S. families. The lowest family incomes were earned by immigrants from three non-English speaking countries: the Dominican Republic, Mexico, and Haiti. Koch went on to examine the effects that education and mastery of the English language had upon these immigrants' incomes. As expected, education was a significant predictor of settled immigrants' incomes. But Koch also found a substantial payoff to the acquisition of English language skills by immigrants. He added that

> . . . this implies that public policy should be directed at increasing the English language facility of immigrants as quickly as possible. While this result does not constitute an endorsement of either "immersion" or the "bilingual" approaches to the English language education of immigrants, it does supply impetus for studies that are directed at determining which method is superior in increasing immigrants' facility with the English language.[26]

Several other studies corroborate the importance of English and formal education for better income and employment.[27] Whereas Koch used data on groups, these other studies rely mostly on data on individuals. For example, Grenier utilized data from the 1976 Survey of Income and Education for 2,428 Hispanic males and 5,970 non-Hispanic males and found that lack of English language proficiency could lower Hispanic immigrants' incomes by as much as 23 percent.[28] Similar research by McManus, Gould, and Welch and Reimers suggest a smaller but still substantial penalty for family earnings.[29] McManus calculated that the costs of deficiency in English are more than $1000 per year among most non-English speaking male immigrants for eight of eleven language groups that he studied, also based on 1976 SIE data.[30] Interestingly, two groups of immigrant men stand to lose over $6000 per annum for deficiencies in English: Chinese immigrants would lose $6322 and Russian immigrants $6043. Hispanic male immigrants would lose $2567 per year by not raising their English proficiency to levels attained by "native" Hispanics who speak only English. Regardless of ethnic origin, lost earnings from an inability to communicate in English are substantial. Over a working lifetime of twenty to forty years, the opportunity costs would rise to tens of thousands of "lost" dollars. Reimers also pointed out that:

> The Puerto Ricans would be helped about equally [from education and English] by converting their English deficiencies and by attaining the same level of education as white non-Hispanics. Mexican-Americans would benefit much more from increased education than from language programs alone. . . . Cubans, on the other hand, stand to gain more from language programs, as their education level is already high.[31]

Similarly, McManus, Gould and Welch asserted that "differences associated with English language skills explain virtually all of the Hispanic wage differences usually attributed to ethnicity, national origin, and time in the United States."[32]

One other question remains on this issue: if English acquisition has high payoffs for Hispanic subgroups, then why don't they make more personal investment in it? The simplest answer given by McManus is that the costs of acquiring English fluency are greater than the benefits they would derive from it.[33] If there is validity to this statement, then finding ways to speed up the process of improving fluency by assuring Hispanics low-cost access to English training may be worthwhile.

A related but controversial topic is the importance of "assimilation" for Hispanic betterment. It has been the subject of numerous studies.[34] Assimilation, a term widely used in American sociology to explain immigrant success, occurs when persons of diverse ethnic and racial backgrounds interact in, and accept the lifestyle of, the larger community. Thus, according to typical sociology textbooks, complete assimilation implies the absence of discrimination, prejudice, value and power conflicts, and separate social structures based on racial or ethnic concepts. As used by Borjas and Tienda,

> . . . assimilation refers to a process whereby immigrants acquire skills, including English proficiency and knowledge about the U.S. labor market and other social institutions which ultimately will enhance their socioeconomic success and their earnings in particular.[35]

Thus, assimilation takes on different interpretations. The concept, nonetheless, raises the issue of the receptiveness of the dominant community toward Hispanics, as well as the skills required by immigrants themselves to learn about labor markets and social institutions in a different ethnic setting. How critical is assimilation for Hispanics?

According to a Rand study by McCarthy and Valdez, the complete assimilation of Hispanics takes three generations.[36] As they argued, new immigrants take the lowest-level jobs, while their children move into more skilled positions, becoming machinists, drill-press operators, or highly trained craftsmen such as carpenters, plumbers, and masons. The grandchildren of the immigrants, the second native-born generation, are found in professional, management, and technical positions, as nurses, teachers, lawyers, and accountants. Furthermore, the Rand study noted that by the third generation, the vast majority of Hispanics are English-dominant and that "the transition to English begins almost immediately and proceeds very rapidly." This fact, however, is not always obvious, according to the authors, because there is significant new immigration of Spanish speakers into communities with large Hispanic populations.

Another study on assimilation by Miller and Valdez examined the issue of the life-satisfaction of recent Mexican immigrants and later generations.[37] According to conventional wisdom, the recent immigrant is likely to be more content with his/her present state, given the comparison with circumstances he/she experienced before immigration from Mexico. This argument implies that conditions are much worse in Mexico and that the immigrants are similar to those who remain in Mexico. Furthermore, arguments based on assimilation stipulate that the immigrants' frames of reference shift from Mexico to the United States over time with progressive acculturation, causing dissatisfaction if conditions do not substantially improve. Contrary to these arguments, Miller and Valdez found that recent male immigrants on the whole do not define their present economic status more favorably, mainly because they are still very poor in the United States. Although they found that immigrants who have been in the United States longer consider their income to be more adequate than recent immigrants, this is seen as a function of the greater actual income of the former. In the final analysis, Miller and Valdez conclude that

> . . . it appears invalid to maintain that poverty among Mexican immigrants is less objectionable since they do not perceive themselves as deprived. Poor immigrants differ little from the poor of other generations in evaluating their economic plight.[38]

In another quantitative analysis of assimilation and its relation to Chicano workers' well-being, Arce and Torres determined that education is highly correlated not only with use of English, but with discouraged use of Spanish. In other words, the use of English over Spanish by later generations "may be dictated by the environment and not by whether one prefers to use one or the other language." Accordingly, although cultural assimilation factors are useful for examining status attainment among Chicanos, such factors may be a reflection of other, more critical and determinant forces. Consequently, the authors suggest that "the study of labor market environments, and entrance into these environments, might add greater insight into the nature of inequality than studying individual orientations to specific cultures."[39]

Whether or not Hispanics are assimilated more or less quickly than other ethnic groups, they do seem to retain a sense of their cultural identity more tenaciously, possibly because of their proclivity for Spanish and ties to Latino culture. Perhaps newer models that stress acculturation, as opposed to assimilation--models that work through processes of mass culture--should be emphasized in dealing with issues of Hispanics in the United States; for example, ethnic studies in educational systems, awareness training in public service, etc. In this way, ethnic identity may be preserved through language, cultural expression, and ethnic ties, while simultaneously values, beliefs, norms, and attitudes are brought close to those of the dominant culture.

Despite the process of assimilation, income inequality is increasing within the Hispanic population. Chiswick, Borjas, and others have documented substantial differences in earnings for different Hispanic groups as well as between U.S.-born and immigrant Hispanic workers.[40] Although assimilation might close the gap between Hispanics and non-Hispanics, attention should be paid to current and growing inequalities among Hispanic groups. Valencia has noted, for example, that there were 381,000 relatively affluent Hispanic households with incomes of more than $50,000 in 1985, and these represented 7.3 percent of all Hispanic households.[41] Thus, although Hispanics as a group have low earnings, some have fared better economically than others. The poverty of Hispanics is not simply a matter of educational deprivation, limited English speaking skills, or assimilation. Long-settled Hispanics of New Mexico, Colorado, and elsewhere are bilingual and culturally adapted to multiethnic settings,[42] yet, they are relatively poor compared to other Hispanics. This issue suggests that effective policies to promote the economic advancement of Hispanics in the United States cannot be designed without some understanding of why some members of the Hispanic population are progressing economically while others are not. We should also be interested in how the characteristics of the communities in which Hispanics live affect their economic progress.

Poverty has been greatest for Hispanics in the Southwest, the major location of Chicanos, which paradoxically is also the region showing the greatest assimilation among Hispanics. But since the area borders Mexico, large-scale immigration of Mexicans and Latinos to the region increases the number of workers with little or no U.S. labor market experience. This increases the competition for jobs and depresses earnings. Tienda and Lii found with census data that Hispanic and nonwhite workers, unlike their white counterparts, lost earnings from residence and work in labor markets with a large share of minority residents.[43] According to them,

> That college-educated whites gained most from minority concentration emphasized how both ascribed (race) and achieved (education) identifiers must coincide to generate white earnings advantages. Considered by themselves, neither racial nor educational divisions explain fully how earnings disparities are accentuated by the ethnic composition of labor markets.[44]

With the recent passage of the Simpson-Rodino Immigration Reform and Control Act of 1986, it was assumed that greater control of the Mexican border and the employment of millions of undocumented aliens would ameliorate the poverty conditions faced by Chicanos. However, much of the immigration policy was based on normative judgments and the conjecture of policy-makers rather than on empirical evidence of net benefits from reform. Given the current trend of increasing poverty levels, it is incumbent upon researchers to study the economic impact of immigration reform in the United States, in the sending nations, and in terms of the structural transformation of industries, occupations, and labor markets. Books edited by Foner, Briggs and Tienda, and research by Bach, and Portes and Bach have provided some empirical data and theoretical groundwork for such inquiry.[45] But the fact that the immigration process is dynamic adds to the complexity of understanding the Hispanic community. Ongoing immigration continuously alters the composition of the Hispanic groups, their geographic locus, and their degrees of assimilation in our society.

Employment, Wages, and Occupations

Among the factors adversely affecting Hispanics are continued high unemployment, especially in the Southwest, and a large number of low-paying jobs that fail to lift families above the poverty line. Even for the Hispanics who worked full-time, year-round in 1985, the census data indicated that one of every fifteen was poor. A big part of the problem is that Hispanics are concentrated in low-earning occupations with little job security.

Since 1973, when annual data on the employment status of Hispanics first became available, Hispanic unemployment rates have been consistently higher than those for non-Hispanics: more than 1.6 times higher than the unemployment rate of whites. In 1987, the Hispanic rate of unemployment reached 8.2 percent compared to 5.1 percent for whites. Although unemployment rates among Hispanics and non-Hispanics sixteen years old and over decreased between March 1982 and March 1987, the current unemployment rate of Hispanics remains high.

Some reports suggest that the unemployment situation for Hispanics reflects the changing economic conditions of the nation, but this does not explain why the level of unemployment for Hispanics is persistently higher. In an attempt to explain the trend, Garcia analyzed unemployment rates during the 1970s, focusing on the times of very high and low national unemployment.[46] His findings indicate that for Mexican Americans, the aggregate rate of joblessness has been both higher and more sensitive to downturns in the economy than it has been for whites. This is true for both women and men. Garcia also discovered that Mexican American women experience longer periods of unemployment after downturns in the economy. The reason for the slower reentrance of Chicanas into the job market has not been studied, but it might be hypothesized that once out of the labor market and at home, it is more difficult for Chicanas to reassert their positions as bread-winners for the family.

In a more recent study with employment data for 1973 through 1984, DeFreitas spotted the same trend in persistent high Hispanic unemployment.[47] He added, however, that "regardless of sex or age, Hispanics are less likely than whites to be unemployed due to quitting their last job and considerably more likely to have been indefinitely laid off or fired."[48] Part of the explanation for the higher unemployment facing Hispanics might be found by examining rates of unemployment by different age groups. Typically persons within the 16-21 age group have the highest rates of unemployment in the labor force. In fact, within this age group, nearly 40 percent of the blacks and 30 percent of the Hispanics are unemployed.[49] As indicated by

Santos, relatively large numbers of young Hispanics are in the labor force, out of school, seeking regular employment at this age when jobs are scarce. Economic necessity forces Chicano youth to look for jobs requiring low wage skills. The combination of high unemployment rates with low school enrollment, whatever the reasons, results in a precarious situation for Hispanic youth, who are discouraged not only from seeking employment, but also from seeking further education and job skills.

This brings us to the issue of whether Hispanics are destined to be relegated to jobs with inherently high employee turnover and unemployment, such as agricultural work. Labor statistics show that about one-fourth of Hispanics are in operative occupations, such as manufacturing machine operators, service station attendants, and truck drivers. This is about twice the proportion for non-Hispanics.[50] Although 9 to 10 percent of Hispanics are employed as professional and technical workers, almost double that proportion of non-Hispanics are employed in these fields. Furthermore, employed Hispanics are less likely to be working as managers and administrators than non-Hispanics. This pattern of employment is expected to continue to the year 2000.[51]

In an earlier study by Kane the occupational patterns of Chicanos were traced between 1969 and 1975, a period which included a major recession.[52] Kane discovered

> . . . that the recession hurt the future income potential of Chicanos as well as their current incomes. In general, the recession has forced Chicanos into occupational groups for which future employment is expected to decline

> relative to total employment, and in which relative wages can be expected to fall as well. . . . By 1975 only 33 percent of Chicanos were located in expanding occupations.[53]

Hispanics are not only concentrated disproportionately in blue-collar jobs, but are also at the low end of the pay scale within many of these job categories.[54] Just to get an idea of the general pattern of earnings, the median income for work performed as an employee during 1985 was $13,587 for whites, $10,883 for blacks, and $10,358 for Hispanics.[55] In addition, a study of earnings between 1979 and 1984 by Mellor and Haugen showed that the Hispanic-to-white earnings ratio, which has hovered around 90 percent, is lower than the ratio of black-to-white earnings, holding gender constant.[56] Moreover, since 1982, the overall Hispanic-to-white ratio has steadily declined, as has the black-to-white earnings ratio. Reimer's 1984 study concluded that the single most important reason for the lower earnings of Hispanics and blacks is lower wages, even after controlling for age, education, and regional distribution. A study of how and why Hispanics are relegated to occupations characterized by low wages and high employee turnover or unemployment needs to be conducted systematically someday. For now, the facts indicate that Hispanics are channeled into low-earning occupations because of limited education and English proficiency.

Hispanics are projected to become an ever-increasing part of the labor force in the coming decades. In 1986, the number of Hispanics in the labor force totaled about 8.1 million. Since 1982, Hispanic employment has risen by 31 percent, the result of sharp increases in both the population level and the percent who are employed. Over the same period, black and white employment levels increased by 21 and 10 percent, respectively. The Bureau of Labor Statistics projects that the Hispanic population will grow by six million workers by the year 2000,[57] which means an increase of 75 percent, or an average of 4.1 percent per year, between 1986 and 2000. However, during the same period, the occupational categories requiring the least educational preparation are expected to grow slowly or to decline, except for the rapidly growing number of service workers. Already, an estimated 1.5 million workers are permanently displaced, their skills obsolete due to a continuing shift from manufacturing to high technology and service industries and to international competition.[58] Figures projected for the rest of the century for the entire economy point to disruptions in the labor market many times more severe than in earlier periods. On the other hand, employment in the broad occupational groups that require the most educational preparation--such as executive, administrative, and managerial workers, professional workers, and technicians and related support workers--will grow faster than average.[59] The nature of the work will also change as technology alters how jobs are performed. Although the number of jobs requiring college degrees is not expected to change significantly, by 1990 an estimated three out of four jobs will require some education or technical training beyond high school. The implications of these future occupational conditions are profound. In contrast to their rising share of new entrants into the labor force, Hispanics will hold a declining fraction of all jobs if they simply retain existing shares of various occupations.[60] Because

Hispanics are currently the least advantaged in terms of their skill levels, English proficiency, and educational backgrounds, the transition for them will be particularly difficult. Unless Hispanics improve their educational accomplishment vis-à-vis future labor market conditions, they may be relegated to declining categories of low wage employment. As Johnston has argued,

> . . . the good fortune to be born in or to immigrate to the United States will make less difference than the luck or initiative to be well-educated and well-trained. For individuals, the good jobs of the future will belong to those who have skills that enable them to be productive in a high-skill, service economy.[61]

Entrepreneurial Activities

In the preceding sections, we have reviewed the current demographic, economic, educational, and occupational status of Hispanics. The overall dismal and depressing state that studies have documented compels us to be extremely concerned with several major problems. Indeed, some scholars have concluded that a time bomb is in the making unless drastic steps are taken to correct complex issues like high fertility, poor education, low English proficiency, low income, and employment disparities.

Although there are tremendous burdens to overcome, as a largely untapped market, Hispanics can contribute directly to a better future. Hispanic populations are growing in key economic regions of the United States: San Antonio, Los Angeles, New York City, Chicago, and Miami. As these groups gain in sheer numbers and overall purchasing power, purveyors of services and products will ultimately have to aim their messages specifically at Hispanics. John J. Wilczak, president of Harvard Consulting, reportedly estimated that Hispanics nationwide have a purchasing power of about $134 billion--$40 billion in California alone.[62] Valencia reported from census data that Hispanics made $84.8 billion in aggregate after-tax income during 1984.[63] In a later article, he added that the after-tax income of Hispanics rose by 10.4 percent to $93.4 billion in 1985.[64] Using the annual growth rate of 12.5 percent in after-tax income from 1980 to 1984, Valencia estimated Hispanic purchasing power at $107.3 billion in 1986 and $172 billion by 1990.[65] He determined that the largest amount of purchasing power is concentrated among Hispanic middle-aged married-couple families in which the head is between 25 and 44 years of age, living in either the Western or Southern regions of the United States. Clearly Hispanics' aggregate purchasing power is growing faster than that of whites or blacks.

It is evident that Hispanics will be in the best position to understand this growing market--in terms of language and its importance, culture and customs, and the strong family orientation that governs household decision-making--which means that Hispanics themselves have tremendous opportunities for investments in Hispanic-oriented business. What, then, have been the entrepreneurial activities of Hispanics?

A look at data from the Economic Census reports, published every five years, reveals 219,335 Hispanic-owned firms in 1977, compared to 117,000 in 1972. In 1977, Hispanic firms accounted for 2.2 percent of the ten million firms in this country and registered sales of $10.4 billion. Hispanics owned 2.4 percent of construction, 2.1 percent of manufacturing, 2.6 percent of transportation and public utilities, 2.4 percent of wholesale and retail trade, 0.9 percent of finance, insurance, and real estate, and 2.4 percent of services. Although for each industry the proportion of Hispanic firms was small, all of them below 3 percent, business ownership was not concentrated in only one or two types of industry.

Census Bureau figures for the period 1977-82 show the number of Hispanic-owned firms increasing by 13.1 percent and total sales by 44.2 percent. In absolute terms, Hispanic companies numbered 248,141 in 1982 with sales of $15 billion. The growth cited may not indicate a proliferation of Hispanic businesses as much as an improvement in the Census Bureau's survey methods. Still, the notable expansion in sales represents a growth of economic power.

Hispanic-owned businesses, as defined by the Census Bureau, include individual proprietorships owned by Hispanics, as well as partnerships and corporations in which at least half the shares are owned by Hispanics. In 1982, the distribution of Hispanic-owned firms by numbers and sales (in thousands of dollars) is shown in Table 2.

According to a report in *Hispanic Business* by Guedella, California had the largest number of Hispanic-owned firms in 1982--74,998--which generated gross receipts of $4.2 billion.[66] Texas was second with 61,540 companies and gross sales of $3.4 billion. Miami alone has 24,898 Hispanic-owned businesses. The New York City-New Jersey SMSA was fourth with 12,292 firms reporting $881.6 million in sales; Hispanic-owned firms with paid employees accounted for 16.1

Table 2

Hispanic-Owned Businesses in the United States, 1982

Firm	Number	Percent	$1,000	Percent
Services	98,279	39.6	3,205,324	21.4
Retail Trade	58,274	23.5	4,850,021	32.4
Construction	26,699	10.8	1,466,338	9.8
Trans. & Pub. Util.	3,155	5.3	656,437	4.4
Fin., Ins., & Real Es.	11,123	4.5	416,632	2.8
Ag., Fish. & Mining	7,640	3.1	239,487	1.6
Manufacturing	4,364	1.8	1,588,714	10.6
Wholesale Trade	3,623	1.5	1,816,631	12.1
Others Not Classified	24,983	10.1	736,751	4.9

percent of the total number of companies, employing 190,000 people. Hispanic retailers topped the list, employing 65,000 workers, followed by service companies with 52,000. Furthermore, 143,177 (about 58 percent) of the 248,141 Hispanic-owned firms were operated by Mexican-Americans. Cubans owned 36,631 firms (15 percent), and Puerto Ricans owned 14,690 (6 percent).

But absolute numbers can be misleading because we would expect more businesses in areas with large Hispanic populations. A better indicator of the strength of Hispanic business is the number of Hispanic-owned businesses per 1,000 Hispanics in the population, or the Hispanic business rate. Nationally the rate is 17 businesses per

1,000. Miami has the highest rate, 42.9 Hispanic-owned businesses per 1,000 Hispanics. The Los Angeles-Long Beach business rate is 14.5/1,000; far lower than Miami's.[67] According to O'Hare, Cuban Americans control most Hispanic businesses in the Florida metropolitan areas. Furthermore, he notes that:

> There is little relationship between the educational level of the local Hispanic population and the rate of Hispanic business participation. But there is a strong positive correlation between the strength of Hispanic business and the level of local Hispanic income relative to white income. In areas where Hispanics earn high incomes relative to whites, there is a higher Hispanic businesses rate.[68]

The link between capital, entrepreneurial activity, and wealth is clear in the Cuban community, showing a workable combination of factors that could spread throughout all Hispanic communities in the United States. Indeed, self-employment is already an important aspect of the Hispanic immigrant experience in the United States. For example, Borjas has shown that: (1) Recent immigration cohorts have higher self-employment rates than earlier cohorts, and (2) immigrants are more likely to be self-employed than similarly skilled native-born workers.[69] A major reason for this pattern, according to Borjas, is that geographic enclaves of immigrants increase self-employment opportunities, particularly for immigrants who share the same national background or language as the residents of the enclave. If these conclusions hold and various segments of the Hispanic population really represent different generations of immigrants, then the continuing immigration should generate further commercial development.

In June 1989, *Hispanic Business* published its annual list of the top 500 companies owned by Hispanics. (To qualify for the list, a company must be 51 percent U. S. Hispanic-owned.) Taken together, they showed aggregate sales of $8.3 billion in 1988. They covered a wide variety of industries: in first place, Bacardi Imports, Inc., with $500.00 million in 1988 sales; second, Goya Foods, $300.00 million; third, Sedano's Supermarkets, $175.76 million; fourth, Van Dyke Dodge, $174.221 million; and fifth, Handy Andy Supermarkets, $166.00 million. The list is impressive, an indication of dynamic business activities and economic success.

There are two further observations that should be made about the business activities of Hispanics in the United States. One is that Hispanic firms tend to hire minorities, but not women. According to the Census report, "Characteristics of Business Owners," based on research partially financed by the Minority Business Development Agency, companies owned by Hispanics and blacks hired fewer women than other businesses, but nearly half had a work force consisting of 75 to 100 percent minorities.[70] The second part of the equation is good, i.e., the hiring of minorities, but the first part about not hiring women is one that should be corrected. The second point is drawn from the same study, which found that two-thirds of minority business owners started their companies without borrowing capital. In some cases start-up capital was not required, while in others, the entrepreneurs used assets from their families' savings. About 64 percent of Hispanic owners began their businesses with less than $5,000 in capital. This level of capital investment can support only small business ventures. The small investments also suggest very limited wealth portfolios in Hispanic families.

Very little research has been carried out on the flow of funds, the institutional sources of credit, and the levels of investments in Hispanic businesses. The book by Dominguez is perhaps the only one of its kind regarding Hispanics.[71] The following findings of his are distressing: (1) minorities, because of their poverty status, seldom get beyond the lowest tier of credit, the stratum that plays host to pawnbrokers, loan sharks, and ghetto merchants; (2) Mexican-Americans have made very limited inroads into the banking industry; and (3) "Due to undercapitalization, many Mexican-American firms are unable to start with a paid staff and as a result of this smallness, they continue to operate with limited help, even though positive incremental revenues may be realized by increasing their work force. Consequently, those that are able to have paid employees manage to enjoy greater per capita revenues."[72] It is highly likely that this same conclusion still applies today.

Conclusions

There is no easy solution to the complex set of issues discussed above. It is apparent, however, that continued efforts are needed to encourage and support higher aspirations for educational attainment among Hispanics. That activity could be promoted by focusing on functional illiterates and programs to increase high school completion rates. The research suggests high economic returns to such investments.

Other activity should be aimed at developing the employability of the growing population of Hispanic workers. The youthfulness of the Hispanic population and its burgeoning size have been identified as major problems for Hispanic communities in the future. Without substantial adjustments in the labor market, Hispanics will have a smaller fraction of the jobs by the year 2000 than they have today, while their share of those seeking work will have risen.

It is apparent that more attention needs to be given to developing Hispanics as a positive resource and not as a burden on society. Each year of delay in seriously and successfully attacking problems of earnings and employment makes it more difficult to turn things around. In the worst case scenario, by the year 2000, Hispanics will be left largely to low-wage, limited-skill jobs that are declining in number, unless new employment programs for Hispanics are supported. Yet, at this time, few policies are being designed and coordinated to handle the up-coming displacement of Hispanic workers. Centers for career planning and placement could be mobilized to support educational goals. Business and government could adopt strategies to help make schooling more effective for Hispanics. One model of business, government, and educational cooperation is the federal Job Training Partnership Act, which requires that potential employers help to oversee training programs for disadvantaged adults so that the training maximizes the probability of getting a job. This model could be studied further with attention to Hispanic rates of participation. Another possibility is the Individual

Retraining Accounts proposed by the Reagan administration and several Democratic candidates for 1988. The idea is to enable workers to deduct contributions into accounts that could be used for retraining when workers' careers are disrupted. Such a system would impose new responsibilities on schools since they would have to develop flexible programs for adult students anxious to reenter the work force. This mobilization would probably require constant checks and monitoring to make sure success is evident.

Traditional job training and employment programs by themselves are unlikely to have any significant impact on the future success of Hispanics. If new efforts to train and employ Hispanics are to succeed where earlier efforts have failed, both individual attitudes and social institutions must change. Radical changes may be required for the public educational system to succeed with Hispanics. If anything, the added Hispanic numbers will require a flexible school system for educating a more diverse student body. In school districts with the most serious problems, experiments with government supported vouchers could be considered, allowing students to shop for the educational programs that suit them best, thereby forcing school districts to improve their offerings. Such schools could also be more directly linked to employers who will hire graduating Hispanics. The reason for establishing a formal linkage between school and work is that, even though unemployment rates fall with age, poor early experiences in the labor market usually lower lifetime earnings.[73]

The complex interconnections among family structure, education, work, income, and living environments make it evident that problems cannot be solved by government fiat or decree. Issues of individual initiative and entrepreneurship must also be considered. However, more research is needed on programs that could promote the entrepreneurial capabilities of Hispanics that develop their capital formation skills and offer business role models for others. Business programs that are usually left to business specialists of the private sector and financial institutions tend to bypass Hispanic communities. Hispanics could be encouraged more strenuously to pursue education with an eye to private business careers; the market for Hispanics is too big and untapped to be left solely to non-Hispanic investors. That impetus could also include efforts to enhance the belief that Hispanics have many positive business attributes which can make whatever they wish to do successful.

Poverty is the result of extenuated circumstances that must be addressed to raise the economic aspirations and opportunities of Hispanics. To date, very little research has been done to enhance our understanding of the correlates, trends, dimensions, and implications of Hispanic poverty. Specific attention must be paid to Hispanic single-headed households, children, and elders. Studies by Angel and Tienda and Frisbie, McCall and Mutchler offer some insights, but the problems require much more research.[74]

In recent times, general attention has strayed from the socioeconomic problems of Hispanics to other issues which the governing society considers more crucial, such as federal indebtedness and international trade. While these are important concerns, they should not consume society's attention at the expense of the interest in people's needs. If progress is to be made in alleviating the plight of Hispanics by the turn of the century, then all segments of American society must make a bona fide effort to meet their social responsibility to a growing minority whose quest is parity citizenship.

Notes

1. Emily Gantz McKay, "The Changing Demographics of the Hispanic Family," *Report of the Policy Analysis Center* (Washington, D.C.: National Council of La Raza: 1987), 4.

2. Ibid.

3. U.S. Bureau of the Census, "The Hispanic Population in the United States: March 1988," *Current Population Reports*, Series P-20, No. 431 (Washington, D.C.: Government Printing Office, 1988).

4. U.S. Bureau of the Census, "Marital Status and Living Arrangements: March 1985," *Current Population Reports*, Series P-20, No. 410 (Washington, D.C.: Government Printing Office, 1986).

5. James V. Koch, "The Incomes of Recent Immigrants: A Look at Ethnic Differences," *Social Science Quarterly* 68 (1987): 294-310.

6. Michael Doyle, "Amnesty Program Rush Hour," *The Sacramento Bee*, 6 May 1988, p. B1.

7. U.S. Bureau of the Census, "Persons of Spanish Origin by State: 1980," *Supplementary Report* PC 80-S1-7 (Washington, D.C.: Government Printing Office, 1982).

8. U.S. Bureau of the Census, Gregory Spenser, "Projections of the Hispanic Population: 1983 to 2080," *Current Population Reports*, Series P-25, No. J995 (Washington, D.C.: Government Printing Office, 1986).

9. U.S. Bureau of the Census, "The Hispanic Population in the United States: March 1986 and 1987," *Current Population Reports*, Series P-20, No. 416 (Washington, D.C.: Government Printing Office, August 1987).

10. Center on Budget and Policy Priorities, "Hispanic Poverty Rises in 1985, Sets Several New Records," (Washington, D.C.: Center on Budget and Policy Priorities, 1986).

11. Ibid., 1.

12. George J. Borjas, "The Self-Employment Experience of Immigrants," *Journal of Human Resources* 21 (1986):485-506; and *idem,* "Immigrants, Minorities, and Labor Market Competition," *Industrial and Labor Relations Review* 40 (1987):382-392.

13. Alejandro Portes and Alex Stepick, "Unwelcome Immigrants: The Labor Market Experiences of 1980 (Mariel) Cuban and Haitian Refugees in South Florida," *American Sociological Review* 50 (1985):493-514.

14. Lisandro Perez, "Immigrant Economic Adjustment and Family Organization: The Cuban Success Story Examined," *International Migration Review* 20 (1986):17.

15. Ibid.

16. Renato Rosaldo, "Chicano Studies, 1970-1984," *American Review of Anthropology* 14 (1985):405-427.

17. Center on Budget and Policy Priorities, "Hispanic Poverty."

18. George J. Borjas, "The Earnings of Male Hispanic Immigrants in the United States," *Industrial and Labor Relations Review* 35 (April 1982); and "Assimilation, Changes in Cohort Quality, and the Earnings of Immigrants," *Journal of Labor Economics* 3 (October 1985):463-489.

19. Cheryl M. Fields, "Closing the Education Gap for Hispanics: State Aims to Forestall a Divided Society," *The Chronicle of Higher Education* (16 September 1987).

20. California Postsecondary Education Commission "From Ninth Grade Through College Graduation: Who Makes It In California," Director's Report No. 85-36 (Sacramento: California Postsecondary Education Commission, 1985).

21. Leon F. Bouvier and Philip Martin, *Population Change and California's Education System* (Washington, D.C.: Population Reference Bureau, Inc., 1987).

22. Franklin J. James and Laura R. Appelbaum, "Education and Labor Market Outcomes of Hispanics: A Survey of the Literature," paper prepared for the Tomas Rivera Center's Seminar on Education and the Economy, Claremont, California, March 1, 1986.

23. Walter S. McManus, "Labor Market Assimilation of Immigrants: The Importance of Language Skills," *Contemporary Policy Issues* 3 (1985):77-89.

24. Koch, "Incomes of Recent Immigrants."

25. Ibid., 297.

26. Ibid., 3.

27. James and Appelbaum, "Education and Labor Market Outcomes"; George J. Borjas and Marta Tienda, eds., *Hispanics in the U.S. Economy* (Orlando, Florida: Academic Press, 1985).

28. Gilles Grenier, "The Effect of Language Characteristics on the Wages of Hispanic-American Males," *Journal of Human Resources* 19 (1984):25-52.

29. Walter McManus, William Gould and Finis Welch, "Earnings of Hispanic Men: The Role of English Language Proficiency," *Journal of Labor Economics* 2 (1983):101-130; C. Reimers, "Sources of Family Income Differentials Among Hispanics, Blacks, and White Non-Hispanics," *American Journal of Sociology* 89 (1984):889-903; and "Labor Market Discrimination Against Hispanics and Black Men,"

Review of Economics and Statistics 65 (1983):570-579; and "The Wage Structure of Hispanic Men: Implications for Policy," *Social Science Quarterly* 65 (1984):401-415.

30. Walter McManus, "Labor Market Costs of Language Disparity: An Interpretation of Hispanic Earnings Differences," *American Economic Review* 75 (1985):818-827.

31. Reimers, "Wage Structure of Hispanic Men."

32. McManus, "Labor Market Costs."

33. McManus, Gould and Welch, "Earnings of Hispanic Men," 101.

34. Borjas, "Assimilation"; George J. Borjas and Marta Tienda, "The Economic Consequences of Immigration," *Science* 235 (1987):645-651.

35. Borjas and Tienda, "Economic Consequences."

36. K. F. McCarthy and R. B. Valdez, *Current and Future Effects of Mexican Immigration in California* (Santa Monica, CA: The Rand Corporation, May 1986).

37. Michael V. Miller and Avelardo Valdez, "Immigration and Perceptions of Economic Deprivation Among Working Class Mexican-American Men," in *The Mexican American Experience*, ed. Rodolfo de la Garza, et al. (Austin: University of Texas Press, 1985), 153-162.

38. Ibid., 116-162.

39. Carlos H. Arce and David L. Torres, "The Effects of Cultural Assimilation and Education on Mexican American Workers' Earnings," *Economic Outlook USA* (Autumn 1983), 87-89.

40. Barry R. Chiswick, "Is the New Immigration Less Skilled Than The Old?" *Journal of Labor Economics* 4 (1986):168-192; Borjas, "Earnings"; "Assimilation"; and "Immigrants."

41. Humberto Valencia, "Disposable Income: A Key Indicator," *Hispanic Business* 8 (1986):28.

42. Annabel Kirschner Cook, "Diversity Among Northwest Hispanics," *The Social Science Journal* 23 (1986):205-216.

43. Marta Tienda and Ding-Tzann Lii, "Minority Concentration and Earnings Inequality: Blacks, Hispanics, and Asians Compared," *American Journal of Sociology* 93 (1987):141-165.

44. Ibid.

45. Robert L. Bach, "Immigration: Issues of Ethnicity, Class, and Public Policy in the United States," *The Annals of the American Academy of Political and Social Sciences* 485 (1986):139-152; Nance Foner, ed., *New Immigrants in New York* (New York: Columbia University Press, 1987); Alejando Portes and Robert L. Bach, *Latin Journey: Cuban and Mexican Immigrants in the United States* (Berkeley and Los Angeles: University of California Press, 1985); Vernon M. Briggs, Jr. and Marta Tienda, eds., *Immigration: Issues and Policies* (Salt Lake City: Olympus Publishing Co., 1984).

46. Philip Garcia, "An Evaluation of Unemployment and Employment Differences Between Mexican Americans and Whites: The Seventies," *The Social Science Journal* 20 (1983):51-62.

47. Gregory DeFreitas, "A Time-Series Analysis of Hispanic Unemployment," *Journal of Human Resources* 21 (1986):24-43.

48. Ibid., 41.

49. Richard Santos, *Hispanic Youth: Emerging Workers* (New York: Praeger and Co., 1985), 55-77.

50. G. T. Silvestri and J. M. Lukasiewicz, "A Look at Occupational Employment Trends to the Year 2000," *Monthly Labor Review* 110 (September 1987):46-63.

51. Ibid.

52. Tim D. Kane, "Chicano Employment Patterns: An Analysis of the Effects of Declining Economic Growth Rates in Contemporary America," *Aztlan: International Journal of Chicano Studies Research* 10 (1979):15-29.

53. Ibid., 28-29.

54. Naomi Turner Verdugo and Richard R. Verdugo, "Earnings Differentials Among Mexican American, Black, and White Male Workers," *Social Science Quarterly* 65 (1984):416-425; David Shapiro, "Wage Differentials Among Black, Hispanic, and White Young Men," *Industrial and Labor Relations Review* 37 (1984):570-581.

55. U.S. Bureau of the Census, "Money Income of Households, Families, and Persons in the United States: 1985," *Current Population Reports*, Series P-60, No. 156 (Washington, D.C.: Government Printing Office, 1987).

56. E. Mellor and S. Haugen, "Hourly Paid Workers: Who They Are and What They Earn," *Monthly Labor Review* 109 (February 1982):20-26.

57. Howard N. Fullerton, Jr., "Labor Force Projections: 1986 to 2000," *Monthly Labor Review* 110 (September 1987):19-29.

58. Ronald E. Kutscher, "Overview and Implications of the Projections to 2000," *Monthly Labor Review* 110 (September 1987): 3-9.

59. Silvestri and Lukasiewicz, "A Look at Occupational Employment."

60. Williams B. Johnston, *Workforce 2000: Work and Workers for the 21st Century* (Indianapolis: Hudson Institute, 1987).

61. Ibid., 103.

62. M. J. Alcott, "Ethnic Consumers Poised to Flex Economic Muscle," *The Sacramento Bee* (27 September 1987).

63. Valencia, "Disposable Income."

64. Humberto Valenica, "Purchasing Power Rises 10 Percent," *Hispanic Business* 9 (1987):15.

65. Ibid.

66. Juan Guedella, "A New Benchmark," *Hispanic Business* (January 1987):12, 16.

67. William O'Hare, "Best Metros for Hispanic Businesses," *American Demographics* 9 (November 1987):30-33.

68. Ibid., 32.

69. Borjas, "Self-Employment."

70. U.S. Bureau of the Census, "Characteristics of Business Owners," *Current Population Reports* (Washington, D.C.: Government Printing Office, 1987).

71. John R. Dominguez, *Capital Flows in Minority Areas* (Lexington, MA: Lexington Books, 1976).

72. Ibid., 140.

73. Bouvier and Martin, *Population Change.*

74. Ronald Angel and Marta Tienda, "Determinants of Extended Household Structure: Cultural Pattern or Economic Need," *American Journal of Sociology* 87 (1982):1360-1383; W. Parker Frisbie, P. L. McCall and J. Mutchler, "The Lonely Crowd?: An Investigation of Hispanic Participation in the Rise of One-Person Households," *Texas Population Research Center Papers* No. 5.006 (Austin: The University of Texas Press, 1983).

Latino Health in the 1980s: Critical Health Policy Issues

Adela de la Torre

Unlike the case in many Western industrialized and socialist countries, health care coverage is not a "right" in the United States. The vast majority of Americans who do not receive Medicaid or Medicare must rely on private insurance coverage contracted through their employers. "Medicaid, long thought to be a source of coverage and recourse for the poor, actually extends eligibility to less than half of those people with incomes below the poverty line." The number of people that fall into the "no care zone" (no health insurance) in the United States is estimated at 35 million. In addition, 7-10 million Americans have only partial insurance coverage during part of the year.[1]

Latinos, as a growing segment of the poor and the working poor, suffer from the same lack of health care access as other low-income Americans.[2] A recent study by the National Center for Health Services Research, using the National Medical Care Expenditure Survey, presented summary statistics illustrating the health care use and insurance state of Hispanics.[3] This study is particularly valuable as it clearly illustrates the striking differences among Latino subgroups with respect to health care access.

Since health care access in the United States is linked to the patient's ability to obtain private insurance or the specifications of Medicaid/Medicare programs, a lack of either type of coverage severely curtails access to medical treatment. Almost 14 percent of Latinos are always uninsured, a higher rate than among the black and white United States populations. Cubans and Mexicans have the largest percentage uninsured, 17.4 percent and 14.7 percent, respectively. Of those with private health insurance, Puerto Rican and Mexican-origin populations have the lowest incidence of private health care insurance coverage. This is somewhat offset by the Puerto Ricans' relatively high rate of Medicaid coverage (almost 50 percent of the Puerto Rican-origin as compared to 27 percent of the Mexican-origin population are covered by Medicaid; see Figure 1).

The limited health care insurance available to Latinos provides a partial explanation for their limited use of health care services. Figure 2 illustrates the pattern of health services used by Latino subgroups. Among the selected Latino subgroups, the Mexican-origin population follows patterns of physician visits and prescribed medicine use similar to those of the black population. Cubans and the Mexican-origin population experience the lowest hospital admissions among these selected ethnic/racial groups. In the case of Cubans, higher per capita income levels and higher rates of private insurance may explain the lower hospital admission rates, as access to private physicians and regular medical care may prevent acute illnesses requiring hospitalization. "A clear pattern of lower use of preventative health services is seen among minority adult populations. . . . A prerequisite

Figure 1

Insurance Coverage of Hispanics, 1977

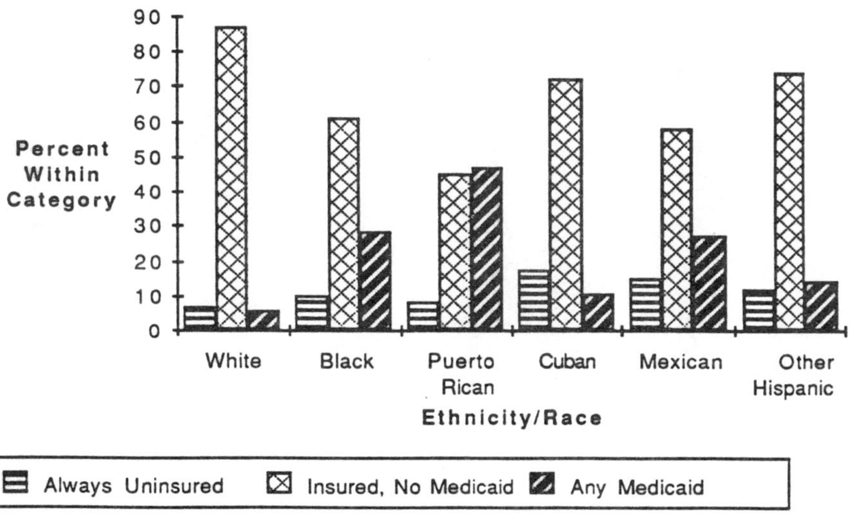

Source: Claudia L. Schur, Amy B. Berstein, and Marc L. Berk, "The Importance of Distinguishing Hispanic Subpopulations in the Use of Medical Care," *Medical Care* 25 (July 1987): 633.

Figure 2

Use of Health Services by Hispanics, 1977

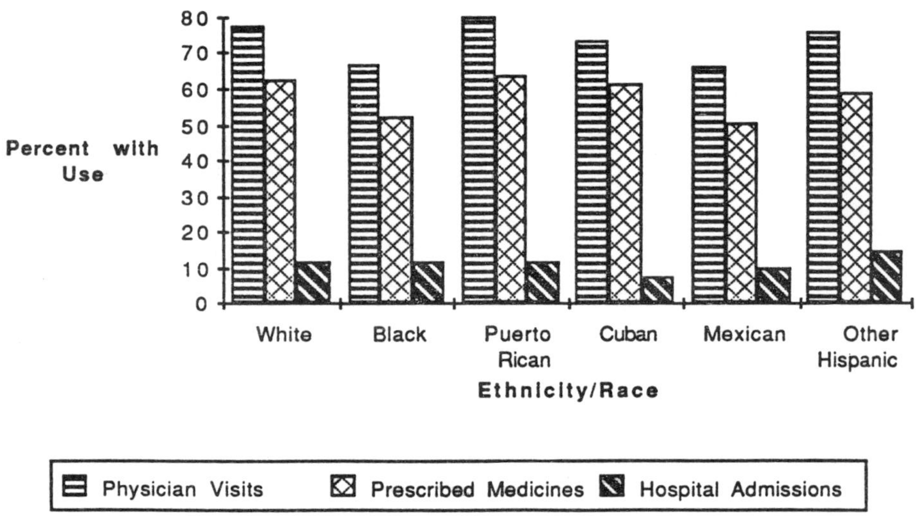

Source: Claudia L. Schur, Amy B. Bernstein, and Marc L. Berk, "The Importance of Distinguishing Hispanic Subpopulations in the Use of Medical Care," *Medical Care* 25 (July 1987): 633.

for access to medical care is the ability to pay for services which in turn largely depends on income and health insurance."[4]

In the Mexican-origin population, which shows a pattern of health service use very similar to the black population, low per capita income combined with limited health insurance coverage may serve as a viable explanation for the pattern of health service use.

In light of the socioeconomic constraints that limit Latinos' access to adequate health care, one can interpret the health status indicators of this growing and diverse minority population. There are an array of indicators one can select in assessing the health status of a population. However, this paper will focus on a few selected indicators that reflect critical health problems facing the Latino community. General mortality rates will first be discussed, followed by a brief assessment of the status of maternal and infant health, including some comments on the impact of the AIDS health crisis on Latinos.

General Mortality Rates

Federal agencies compute national mortality rates for all racial groups from death certificates recorded by the states. However, there is no uniform practice for coding Hispanic ethnicity across states, and for several states ethnicity information on death certificates is optional. Thus, the data are incomplete; due to the lack of precise measures of the total Latino population and exact morbidity and mortality data, only approximate measures of these selected health indicators can be made. In addition to the limitations of traditionally reliable secondary data sets for estimating rates for the Latino community, survey data developed for specific studies of subgroups of the Latino community oftentimes serve as the best detailed health status reports of these communities. Again, bias in these studies limits their generalizability.[5]

Table 1 lists the average annual number of deaths by disease category in the United States between 1979-1981 for Mexican-born and Cuban-born Latinos (Hispanics). Perhaps the most startling fact is the rank of homicide as a major cause of excess deaths among Mexican-born men and women and Cuban-born men. A recent comparative study of immigrants of Cuban, Mexican and Puerto Rican origins also indicates exceptionally high age-adjusted mortality rates due to homicide, "with the Puerto Rican rate equal to that of Blacks."[6] For blacks under age 45, homicide is the largest contributor to excess deaths for males and the second largest for females. Infant mortality is the second cause of excess death for black males and the first cause for black females within this age category.

Infant and Maternal Health and the Impact of AIDS

Fertility and birth rates of the Latino population have been substantially higher than for the non-Latino population.[7] Figures 3 and 4 illustrate the fertility and birth rates between 1983 and 1984, which increased for all Hispanic-origin mothers with the exception of Cuban and "other Hispanic" women. Given the higher levels of childbearing by Latinas, maternal and infant health care issues are of paramount importance.

A major indicator of the success of prenatal care and future

Table 1. HISPANICS (Foreign-Born) Average Annual Number of Deaths by Disease Category, United States, 1979-1981

		CVD*	Cancer	Cirrhosis	Infant Mortality	Diabetes	Unintentional Injuries	Homicide	All Other	Sub-Total***	Total Deaths
Mexican-born Hispanics, Ages 0-64											
Males	Observed	585	334	136	3	32	1,322	848	554	(3,814)	3,814
	Expected**	947	622	106	39	34	769	147	727	(3,391)	3,391
	Excess	−362	−288	30	−36	−2	553	701	−173	(423)	1,284
Percent of Total Excess****		0	0	2	0	0	43	55	0		100
Females	Observed	292	367	39	2	40	184	53	309	(1,286)	1,286
	Expected**	331	512	45	28	28	186	33	357	(1,520)	1,520
	Excess	−39	145	−6	−26	12	−2	20	−48	(−234)	32
Percent of Total Excess****		0	0	0	0	38	0	63	0		100
Cuban-born Hispanics, Ages 0-64											
Males	Observed	351	243	32	0	12	143	179	204	(1,164)	1,164
	Expected**	540	337	53	1	17	172	31	268	(1,419)	1,419
	Excess	−189	−94	−21	−1	−5	−29	148	−64	(−255)	148
Percent of Total Excess****		0	0	0	0	0	0	100	0		100
Females	Observed	114	215	14	0	9	39	25	102	(518)	518
	Expected**	208	307	26	1	16	56	9	158	(781)	781
	Excess	−94	−92	−12	−1	−7	−17	16	−56	(−263)	16
Percent of Total Excess****		0	0	0	0	0	100	0	0		100

*Cardiovascular disease (CVD) combines heart disease and stroke.
**The expected number is calculated from the rate observed in the White population.
***Sub-total is the sum of negative and positive excess deaths. Total deaths sums positive excess deaths only.
****Percentages based on total deaths.
SOURCE: Duke University, analysis commissioned by the Task Force on Black and Minority Health, 1984-1985.

Source: Margaret M. Heckler, *Report of the Secretary's Task Force on Black and Minority Health I: Executive Summary* (August 1985):77.

Figure 3

Fertility Rates by Hispanic Origin of Mother, 1983-84

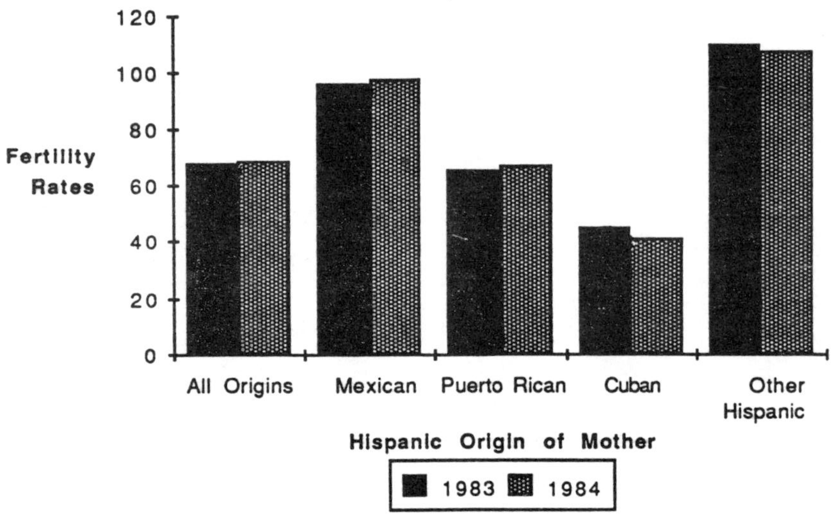

Source: Stephanie J. Ventura, "Births of Hispanic Parentage, 1983 and 1984," *NCHS Monthly Vital Statistic Report* 36, supplement 2 (24 July 1987):10.

Figure 4

Birth Rates by Hispanic Origin of Mother, 1983-84

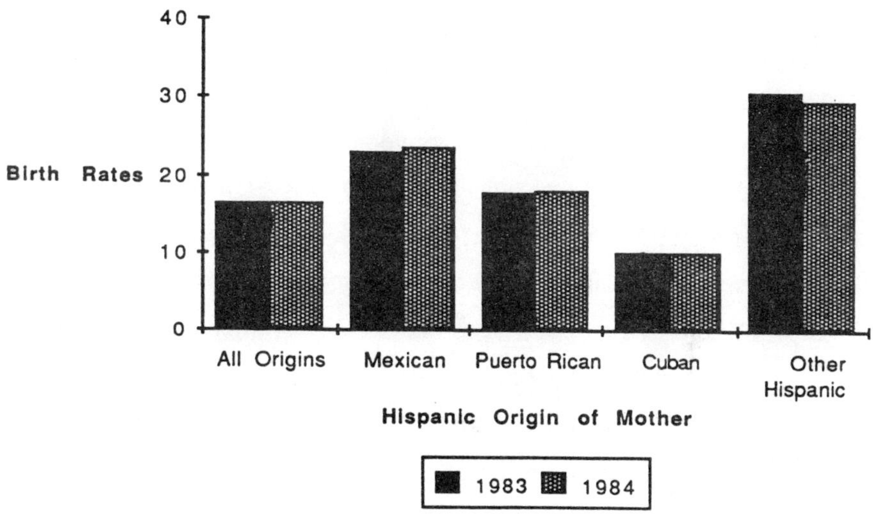

Source: Stephanie J. Ventura, "Births of Hispanic Parentage, 1983 and 1984," *NCHS Monthly Vital Statistics Report* 36, supplement 2 (24 July 1987):10.

health outcomes for infants and children is the infant mortality rate. For the black population, high infant mortality rates are a major cause of death, and some evidence suggests that the white-black infant mortality rate gap is widening.[8] Figure 5 illustrates the black and white neonatal mortality rates (the number of infants dying between 0 and 27 days of life per 1000 live births) and postneonatal mortality rates (the number of infants dying between 28 days and 11 months of life per 1000 live births, i.e., deaths occurring during the remainder of the first year of life).[9] Low-birth-weight infants "account for the majority of deaths in the first year of life and they have a significantly increased risk of permanent disability."[10]

High infant mortality rates have not been a major source of excess deaths for Latinos, nor has a high incidence of low-birth-weight babies been a critical problem. However, low-birth-weight incidence for Latino newborns has been a subject of debate, as problems with the validity and accuracy of the data on Latino infant birth-weight--for example, underreporting of low-birth-weight babies--prevent an adequate assessment of the net impact of low-birth-weight infants on Latino infant mortality rates.[11]

Recent data suggest that Puerto Ricans follow blacks with the highest percent of low-birth-weight infants and infants born prior to thirty-seven weeks of gestation (see Figure 6). Latinos share several risk factors associated with poor birth outcomes with the black childbearing population. First, Latinos experience a high percentage of teenage pregnancies: 18 percent of Mexican-American and 21 percent of Puerto Rican teens, compared to 12 percent of non-Hispanic

Figure 5

Infant Mortality Rates, 1960-1985

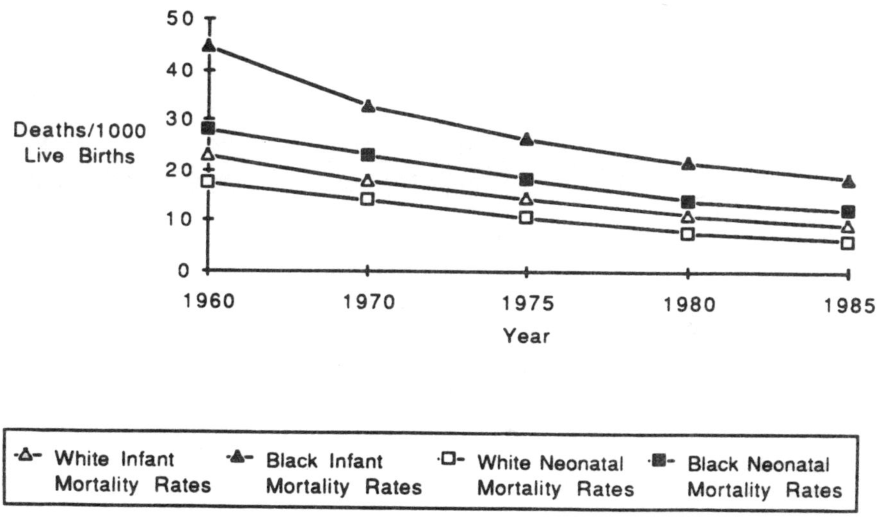

Source: U.S. Bureau of the Census, *Statistical Abstract of the United States, 1988* (Washington, D.C.:Government Printing Office, 1987), based on Table 13, p. 75.

Figure 6

Percent of Births of Low-Birth-Weight Infants and Percent of Births Prior to 37 Weeks

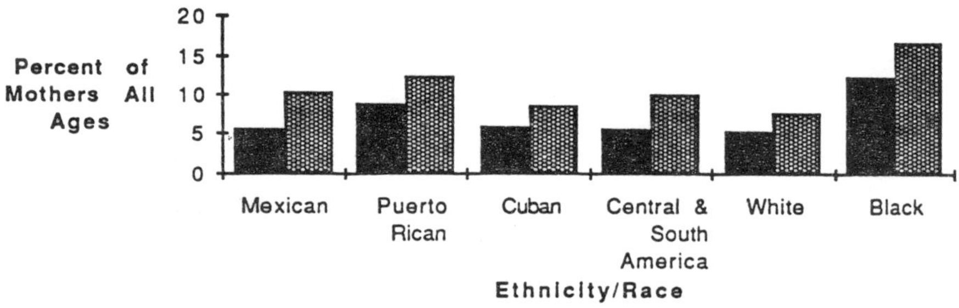

Percent of Births of Low Birth Weight Infants; Percent of Births Born Prior to 37 Weeks of Gestation

Source: Stephanie J. Ventura, "Births of Hispanic Parentage 1983 and 1984," *NCHS Montly Vital Statistics Report* 36, supplement 2 (24 July 1987):10.

teens in 1984. Second, approximately one-half of the births of the Puerto Rican-origin population, one-third of the births of the Central and South American-origin population, and one-quarter of the births of the Mexican-American population were out of wedlock, compared to approximately one-tenth of white non-Hispanic births.[12] In addition, with the exception of Cubans, Latinas show a pattern of first trimester prenatal care similar to that of blacks. On average, approximately 60 percent of Latina mothers begin prenatal care in their first trimester (see Figure 7). Figure 8 highlights this low incidence of prenatal care for Latinas, indicating the percent of mothers who had late or no prenatal care by ethnicity and race. Puerto Rican-, Mexican-, and Central and South American-origin women experienced the highest incidence of late or no prenatal care among the selected groups, higher than that of their black and white counterparts.

The limited use of prenatal care by Latinas may pose even graver birth outcomes for these women with the spread of AIDS as a major health problem. AIDS transmission within the black and Latino communities is not primarily confined to homosexual and bisexual males, as illustrated in Figure 9. Intravenous drug users are almost equally significant in the transmission of AIDS for blacks and Latinos, and heterosexual cases are more common for these groups than for whites. These transmission categories, combined with the lack of prenatal care and screening, particularly during the critical first trimester of pregnancy, may escalate the negative birth outcomes for Latina women. Preliminary evidence of the potential impact of the AIDS epidemic on the health status of Latino infants and children is

Figure 7

Percent of Mothers Who Began Prenatal Care in the First Trimester, by Ethnicity/Race

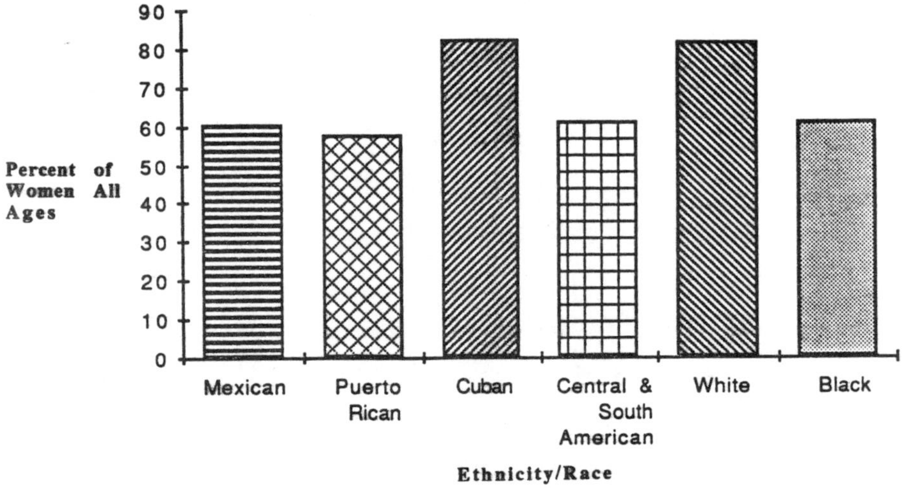

Source: Stephanie J. Ventura, "Births of Hispanic Parentage, 1983 and 1984," *NCHS Monthly Vital Statistics Report* 36 supplement 2 (24 July 1987):16.

Figure 8

Percent of Mothers Who Had Late or No Prenatal Care by Ethnicity/Race

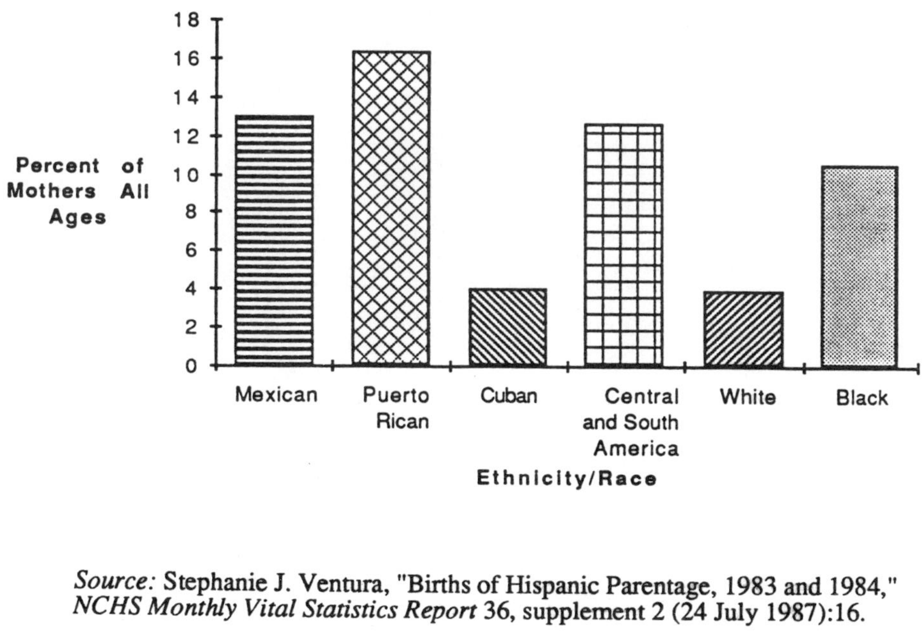

Source: Stephanie J. Ventura, "Births of Hispanic Parentage, 1983 and 1984," *NCHS Monthly Vital Statistics Report* 36, supplement 2 (24 July 1987):16.

Figure 9

AIDS Transmission Categories (Adults/Adolescents)

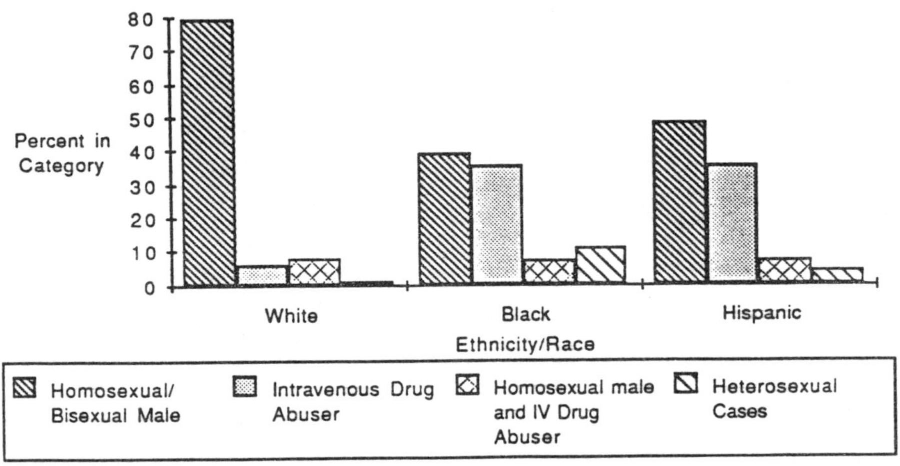

Source: Center for Disease Control, *AIDS Weekly Surveillance Report*, United States AIDS Program, Center for Infectious Diseases (7 December 1987): 1.

apparent in Figure 10. The major AIDS transmission category for both black and Hispanic children is parents with, or at risk for, AIDS. Eighty-one percent of Hispanic children, as compared to only 42 percent of white children, fall within the AIDS transmission category of having a parent with, or at risk for, AIDS. The high transmission category for children among Latinos and blacks is due to the large number of intravenous drug users within these populations. As these individuals become infected with the deadly virus, they place at risk not only their sexual partners but also their unborn children.

Conclusions and Policy Implications

Although the current data on Latinos are sketchy when compared to the data on the black population, health indicators such as mortality rates show similar trends for the two groups. Homicide as a leading killer in both black and Latino communities reflects negative health behaviors of the urban poor which cannot be understood within a narrow medical model. Risk factors associated with negative maternal and infant health outcomes for Latinos are also similar to those in the black community. With the emergence of AIDS as a major public health problem in the 1980s, along with inadequate prenatal care and screening for high-risk mothers, a relatively higher proportion of Latino and black infants and children will suffer the consequences of this dreaded virus.

With the increasing growth and impoverization of the Latino population, the prospects for improved health status and health care access for Latinos, as well as for other minority groups in the United

Figure 10

AIDS Transmission Categories (Children)

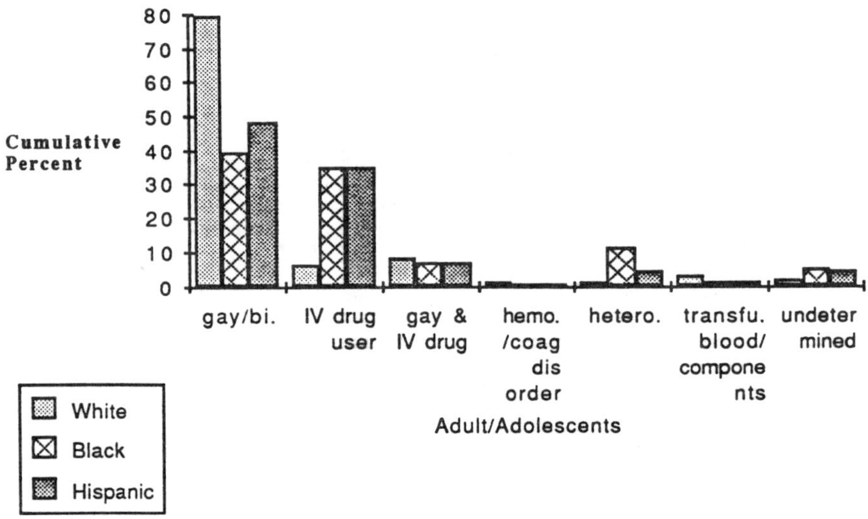

Source: Center for Disease Control, *AIDS Weekly Surveillance Report*, United States AIDS Program, Center for Infectious Diseases (7 December 1987):1.

States, appear bleak. Without the development of a national health insurance program that would give all citizens the "right" to adequate medical care, many of the poor and working poor will be forced to ignore the health needs of themselves and their families, which will result in both economic and social long-term costs to American society.

Notes

1. Donald R. Cohodes, "America: The Home of the Free, the Land of the Uninsured," *Inquiry* 23 (Fall 1986):23.

2. See Refugio I. Rochin, "The Socioeconomic Status of the Hispanic Population," in this volume.

3. Claudia L. Schur, Amy B. Bernstein, and Marc L. Berk, "The Importance of Distinguishing Hispanic Subpopulations in the Use of Medical Care," *Medical Care* 25 (July 1987):627-641.

4. Margaret M. Heckler, *Report of the Secretary's Task Force on Black and Minority Health, U.S. Department of Health and Human Services,* I (1985):188-189.

5. Ibid., 68-70.

6. Ira Rosenwaike, "Mortality Differentials Among Persons Born in Cuba, Mexico, and Puerto Rico Residing in the United States, 1979-81," *American Journal of Public Health* 77 (May 1987):605.

7. Stephanie J. Ventura, "Births of Hispanic Parentage, 1983 and 1984," *NCHS Monthly Vital Statistics Report* 36, supplement 2 (24 July 1987):1-3.

8. Ellice Lieberman, et al., "Risk Factors Accounting for Racial Differences in the Rate of Premature Birth," *The New England Journal of Medicine* 317 (1987):743.

9. Task Force on Infant Mortality, "Statement on Infant Mortality," *Pediatrics* 78 (1986):1155.

10. Richard E. Behrman, "Premature Births among Black Women," *The New England Journal of Medicine* 317 (1987):763.

11. Sylvia Villereal, "Current Issues in Hispanic Health," *Report of the Secretary's Task Force on Black and Minority Health, U.S. Department of Health and Human Services, VIII: Hispanic Health Issues* (1986):24.

12. Ventura, "Births," 2-3.

Income Differentials Between Asian Americans and White Americans in California, 1980

Amado Cabezas, Larry H. Shinagawa, and Gary Kawaguchi

Socioeconomic disadvantage and income inequality are facts of life in America today. The highest one-fifth or quintile of wage and salary workers in the United States earned 49 percent of all income in 1948; 48 percent in 1977, and 50 percent in 1985.[1] By comparison, the lowest quintile earned less than 3 percent of all income in 1985. Even for white males, among whom the income maldistribution is less pronounced, the highest quintile earned 37 percent of all income, the lowest quintile, 8 percent. An arithmetically equal distribution, of course, would have each of the five quintiles accounting for 20 percent of total income. Realistically, however, complete equality may be unattainable, but a distribution pattern that lies somewhere between the actual and the ideal of complete equality would enhance the economic well-being of many groups.

The Myth of the Successful "Model Minority"

This study focuses on income differentials between Asian

Americans and whites. In the 1980s a "media blitz" has portrayed Asian Americans as a model minority.[2] Whether they in fact are has not yet been empirically proven. Eliminating the image of the model minority would help to reduce conflict between Asian Americans and many other Americans, who see Asians as displacing themselves as workers. It would also dismiss the notion that the status of Asian Americans proves that disadvantaged populations can attain success with a minimum number of social programs and that Asian Americans have no need for such programs. Moreover, Asian Americans themselves need to assess more accurately their own economic status.

However, it is not easy to debunk the myth. Part of the problem lies in the use of standard socioeconomic indicators which apply to the majority white population and some minority groups but which are misleading when applied to Asian Americans. Data for these indicators are collected regularly, usually by the government, and are widely disseminated and analyzed. Standard indicators that tend to misrepresent Asian Americans include educational attainment level, labor force participation rate, unemployment, family income, and percentage of families at the poverty level. Fortunately, there also exist other indicators that are more appropriate for Asian Americans: number of workers per family, income per worker by gender, and percentage of unrelated individuals living below the poverty level.

A majority of Asian Americans today are immigrants, most of whom arrived after the 1965 amendments to the Immigration Act were passed. Current United States immigration policy is based on three main criteria: (1) family reunification; (2) preferred immigration status for educated, professional, and skilled workers (when they are needed by the nation's economy); and (3) foreign policy considerations, such as providing asylum for political refugees from designated countries. Asian immigration into the United States since 1965 has occurred mainly on the basis of family reunification and the country's need for educated, skilled workers. These new immigrants, along with the Vietnamese and other Southeast Asian refugees, have accounted for most of the recent growth in the Asian American population in the United States.

Most Americans believe that immigrant Asians, except for Southeast Asian refugees, bring with them social and economic assets. However, though they may be admired for their perceived economic success, Asian Americans are also resented for allegedly displacing U.S.-born whites from jobs. The development of a global economy, which now encompasses all workers here and abroad, including those in Asian countries, has blurred the distinction between Asians in America and Asians in Asia in the minds of many Americans, so that Asian Americans are frequently blamed for the economic difficulties caused by the inability of the U.S. to compete with countries such as Japan in foreign trade.

What in fact is the economic status of Asian Americans today?

Comparing U.S.-born White Males and Foreign-born Asians

First we looked at published 1980 census data for *foreign-born* Asian Americans in the states of California, Illinois, and New York, which, when combined, account for about one-half of the Asian American population in the continental United States. Based on the 1980 census, 63 percent of Chinese Americans, 63 percent of Filipino Americans, and 82 percent of Korean Americans in the U.S. are immigrants. (Japanese Americans are not discussed here because, compared to the other Asian American groups, the percentage of foreign-born among them is much lower.)

According to the 1980 census report series PC-80-1 published for each state, in California 20 percent of the U.S.-born white population had four or more years of college compared to 44 percent for foreign-born Filipinos, 34 percent for foreign-born Koreans, and 26 percent for foreign-born Chinese. It should be noted, however, that the foreign-born Chinese had a bimodal distribution: 15 percent of them, compared with only 2 percent of the U.S.-born white population, 6 percent of the foreign-born Filipinos, and 4 percent of the foreign-born Koreans, had less than a fifth grade education. What these figures document is the high educational attainment level of Asian immigrants who were "pulled" into the United States by an immigration policy designed to attract educated and skilled workers and professionals. This policy was dictated by the needs of the nation in the period following the Soviet launching of Sputnik which started the race for space, the Vietnam war, the full-scale implementation of the Social Security Act of 1966 which spurred national and state health care programs, and the onset of the technological revolution in the early 1960s. Many of the Asian immigrants in the country today were admitted under the third preference (members of the professions, scientists and artists of exceptional ability, and their spouses and children) and the sixth preference (skilled and unskilled workers in occupations for which labor is in short supply in this country and their spouses and children).

In terms of labor force participation among foreign-born Asians, 74 percent of the Filipinos, 64 percent of the Koreans, and 63 percent of the Chinese, compared to 65 percent of U.S.-born whites, were in the labor force in California in 1980. (Labor force participation, a favorite indicator used by labor economists, refers to the proportion of those sixteen years old or over who are currently gainfully employed or are unemployed but seeking work.) The median family income of the U.S.-born white population in California in 1980 was $22,300. By comparison, among Asian immigrants, the median family income was higher for Filipinos at $25,200, comparable for Koreans at $21,700, and lower for Chinese at $19,500. But poverty level indicators, however, show a different picture. Among U.S.-born white families nationwide, 8 percent were living at the poverty level, compared to 6 percent among Filipino, 15 percent among Korean, and 18 percent among Chinese immigrants. Also, among "unrelated individuals," consisting mainly of those in single-person households, 18 percent of the U.S.-born white population were at the poverty level; whereas 26 percent of the Filipino immigrants, 38 percent of the Korean immigrants, and 37 percent of the Chinese immigrants in single-person households were at the poverty level. The latter indicator thus paints quite a different portrait of Asian Americans.

When we turn to per worker or per person income, we get an

even dimmer view of the so-called economic success of Asians. The mean personal income of U.S.-born white men in 1980 in California was $23,400 but was much lower for Asian immigrants: $14,500 for Filipino men, $19,200 for Korean men, and $15,900 for Chinese men. The mean income of U.S.-born white women was only $13,300, or 56 cents to the dollar compared with U.S.-born white men. (The same pattern of income inequality between white men and women has persisted over the last four decades.) The gender inequality between foreign-born Asian women and U.S.-born white men is even more pronounced: the mean income of Filipino immigrant women was only $12,100, Korean immigrant women $11,500, and Chinese immigrant women $10,600.

In considering occupational ranking, whereas only 25 percent of the U.S.-born white population in California are in the blue collar ranks, we find 31 percent of the Filipino immigrants, 36 percent of the Korean immigrants, and 44 percent of the Chinese immigrants in these ranks, figures that are at odds with the high educational attainment of Asians. This poor linkage between education and income suggests extensive underemployment among, as well as employment discrimination against, Asian Americans.

The widely publicized high family income of Asian Americans is merely an arithmetic artifice because there are more workers pooling their incomes per Asian American family. Census data show that the average number of gainfully employed workers is 2.2 in Filipino immigrant families, 1.8 in Korean immigrant families, and 1.9 in Chinese immigrant families, compared to 1.6 in U.S.-born white families.

Thus, the picture that emerges of Asian immigrants in California is that of a highly educated people, many of whom were attracted here by the nation's immigration policy, currently employed but underemployed, with a large percentage of them blue-collar or lower-level white-collar workers, more educated but earning less than their white male counterparts, and pooling their incomes in their larger families. So much for Asian American success in the golden state! The data for Illinois and New York show much the same pattern: high educational attainment level, high family income, more workers per family, and low per capita income.

Income Differentials by Race, Ethnicity, Nativity, and Gender

We shall concentrate on the San Francisco-Oakland-San Jose SCSA (Standard Consolidated Statistical Area) and the Los Angeles-Long Beach SMSA (Standard Metropolitan Statistical Area), the two major labor market areas in California which contain high concentrations of Asians, in comparing income differentials by race, ethnicity, nativity, and gender. The SF-O-SJ SCSA, with a total population of 4,545,700 in 1980, consists of the counties of San Francisco, Alameda, Marin, Contra Costa, San Mateo, and Santa Clara. The LA-LB SMSA consists of Los Angeles County with a total population of 7,477,500 in 1980.

Comparing only employed workers in the civilian labor force--those sixteen years old or older who are not disabled--the mean annual income of U.S.-born white males in 1980 was $19,986 in the San Francisco-Oakland-San Jose SCSA and $19,619 in the Los Angeles-Long Beach SMSA. With U.S.-born white men as the point of reference, the income of others by gender and nativity are as follows:

Table 1

Income Ratios of Various Groups Compared to U.S.-born White Males, 1980

	SF-O-SJ SCSA	LA-LB SMSA
U.S.-born white men	100%	100%
U.S.-born white women	51%	53%
immigrant white men	112%	94%
immigrant white women	50%	49%
U.S.-born black men	70%	68%
U.S.-born black women	49%	50%
immigrant black men	60%	62%
immigrant black women	51%	40%
U.S.-born Filipino American men	64%	72%
U.S.-born Filipino American women	45%	48%
immigrant Filipino American men	64%	70%
immigrant Filipino American women	52%	59%
U.S.-born Mexican American men	72%	68%
U.S.-born Mexican American women	42%	40%
immigrant Mexican American men	61%	50%
immigrant Mexican American women	34%	32%
U.S.-born Chinese American men	86%	87%
U.S.-born Chinese American women	53%	53%

immigrant Chinese American men	71%	59%
immigrant Chinese American women	44%	50%
U.S.-born Japanese American men	94%	90%
U.S.-born Japanese American women	55%	56%
immigrant Japanese American men	102%	102%
immigrant Japanese American women	46%	48%
U.S.-born Korean American men	83%	75%
U.S.-born Korean American women	69%	53%
immigrant Korean American men	78%	69%
immigrant Korean American women	45%	43%
U.S.-born Vietnamese American men	*	*
U.S.-born Vietnamese American women	*	*
immigrant Vietnamese American men	55%	55%
immigrant Vietnamese American women	40%	40%
U.S.-born Asian Indian men	*	*
U.S.-born Asian Indian women	*	*
immigrant Asian Indian men	92%	95%
immigrant Asian Indian women	47%	47%

*sample size too small for computation

The income ratios may be compared with those in 1970.[3]

Table 2

Income Ratios of Various Groups Compared to White Males, 1970

	SF-O SMSA	LA-LB SMSA
white men	100%	100%
white women	52%	51%
Japanese American men	81%	90%
Japanese American women	39%	41%
Chinese American men	55%	67%
Chinese American women	27%	33%
Filipino American men	58%	62%
Filipino American women	38%	47%

Although the 1970 income ratios were not controlled for nativity, we can roughly compare the ratios with those for 1980 as follows. We know that in 1970 most of the Japanese Americans were U.S.-born, the Chinese Americans were about one-half U.S.-born and one-half foreign-born, and the Filipino Americans were mostly foreign-born. The ratios improved significantly for some groups but not much for others. Taking the San Francisco-Oakland SMSA as an example, the ratio rose from 81 percent in 1970 to 94 percent in 1980 for U.S.-born Japanese American men and to 102 percent for foreign-born Japanese American men, but from 39 percent to only 55 percent for U.S.-born Japanese American women and 46 percent for foreign-born Japanese American women. The ratio rose from 55 percent to 71 percent for foreign-born Chinese American men but to 86 percent for U.S.-born

Chinese American men. For Chinese American women, the ratio rose from 27 percent to 44 percent for the foreign-born and to 53 percent for the U.S.-born. For Filipino Americans, the ratio rose from 58 percent to 64 percent for both the foreign-born and U.S.-born men, and from 38 percent to 52 percent for the foreign-born women and 45 percent for the U.S.-born women. However, the improvements are less encouraging in view of the fact that the educational attainment level of the Asian American groups had increased considerably over the same period: from about 20 percent of those twenty-five years old and over having four or more years of college in 1970 to 30-plus percent in 1980.

To understand the causes of income inequality, we shall use the neoclassical human capital model in our analysis. We will explore other models such as institutional and labor market segmentation theories in a forthcoming publication. We have conducted regression analyses of 1980 census microdata for individual respondents. These analyses used personal income as a dependent variable and educational attainment level, work experience, number of weeks worked per year, number of hours worked per week, and marital status as independent variables. In the neoclassical model, these independent variables are considered to be human capital investments which account for income inequality. The model attempts to explain the level of income as the sum of several variables, each representing an investment variable multiplied by a constant, usually called the regression coefficient B, which substantively represents the "returns" of that particular investment to income.

Our regression equation for income as a function of human capital investments is of the following form:

$$\begin{aligned}\text{Income} = {} & A_0 + B_1 \times \text{Education} \\ & + B_2 \times (\#\text{Years Experience}) \\ & + B_3 \times (\#\text{Years Experience})^2 \\ & + B_4 \times (\#\text{ Weeks Worked/Year}) \\ & + B_5 \times (\#\text{ Hours Worked/Week}) \\ & + B_6 \times \text{Marital Status}\end{aligned}$$

where

Income = total wage and salary income received in 1979 for all persons 16 years old and over,

Education = Number of years of schooling,

Years Experience = Age less "Education" less 5

Weeks Worked/Year = number of weeks worked in 1979,

#Hours Worked/Week = Number of hours usually worked per week in 1979,

Marital status = value one for those married or living as if married, and zero if not.

(We have also explored other forms of the regression equation, such as with the logarithm of income as the dependent variable, and will discuss these results in detail in a later publication.)

Our data base is the 5 percent 1980 census public use sample of residents in the San Francisco-Oakland-San Jose SCSA and the Los Angeles-Long Beach SMSA. The sample sizes by race and ethnicity are as follows:

Table 3
Sample Size by Group, 1980

Race/ Ethnicity	San Francisco-Oakland -San Jose SCSA	Los Angeles-Long Beach SMSA
White	10,571	17,730
Black	7,849	17,130
Mexican	6,929	29,574
Japanese	1,633	2,951
Chinese	3,800	1,995
Filipino	3,018	2,460
Korean	347	1,025
Vietnamese	5	284
Asian Indian	367	387
Total	34,519	73,536

Using the above samples, the regression equation was solved for groups stratified by race or ethnicity, nativity, and gender. The statistical procedure used was REGRESSION running in SPSSX, version 10. The procedure calculates means and standard deviations for each of the variables, the regression coefficients and the levels of significance for each, and the percentage of the variance explained by each regression run. The percentage of the variance explained, depending on gender and nativity, ranged from 37 percent to 41 percent for whites; 34 to 38 percent for blacks; 26 to 44 percent for Mexican-Americans; 12 to 46 percent for Japanese Americans; 29 to 50 percent for Chinese Americans; 29 to 49 percent for Filipino Americans and 25 to 39 percent for Korean Americans. These levels are generally regarded as quite acceptable in studies of this type.

Is income inequality between groups due to different investments, to similar investments but different returns, or to a combination of both? Or is the inequality due to incompleteness of the regression equation, or the inadequacy of the human capital model to begin with? The solutions of the equations include calculations of the regression coefficients and mean values of the human capital investments or "productivity" characteristics of each of the study populations. With these solutions, we test the following key hypothesis: the lower income of Asian Americans is not due to less productivity or smaller human capital investment compared to white men; rather, their lower income is due mainly to lower returns from their human capital investment compared to the returns for white men. If the hypothesis proves to be valid, then the problem is structural or societal, rather than one for which individual Asian Americans can be held responsible. We tested this hypothesis by using U.S.-born white male returns with Asian American and black productivity. Our results to date indicate the following:

1. Except for Japanese American men in the Los Angeles metropolitan area, Asian Americans of all ethnicities, both men and women, and both U.S.-born and foreign-born, earn significantly less than U.S.-born white men in both the San Francisco-Oakland-San Jose and the Los Angeles metropolitan areas. This pattern perpetuates the disparity found in the last two decades. This alone is strong empirical evidence refuting the view that Asian Americans are economically successful across the board.

2. In the San Francisco metropolitan area, using the returns for U.S.-born white men with the actual productivity of minorities and women reveals the following pattern: The income gap for both U.S.-born white women and Japanese American women (relative to U.S.-born white men) is due mainly to lower returns rather than to lower (human capital) investments. For both black men and women, however, the income gap is due to both lower returns and lower investments. The gap for U.S.-born Chinese as well as all Filipino Americans, both men and women, is also due to both lower returns and investments, with the lower investments for these groups being traceable to the fact that they are younger populations. White male returns would raise the income of U.S.-born Japanese American men above parity. And finally, lower returns explain most of the gap for

foreign-born Chinese, Filipino, and Korean Americans, all of whom have brought with them high investment characteristics.

3. In the Los Angeles metropolitan area, the pattern is similar. The income gap is due mainly to lower returns for the following U.S.-born populations: white women, black men and women, and Japanese American men and women. As in the San Francisco area, both lower returns and lower investments account for most of the gap for U.S.-born Filipino and Chinese Americans, again because they are younger, second-generation populations. Furthermore, again as in the San Francisco area, lower returns explain most of the gap for foreign-born Chinese, Filipino, and Korean Americans who already have high investment characteristics. Thus income inequality in both the San Francisco and Los Angeles metropolitan areas is explained primarily by lower returns for minorities and women, pointing to continuing race and gender discrimination and structural effects as likely causes of the income disparities. Human capital investments are important, but discrimination and structural effects appear to be even more important at this time.

Comparing our findings with some of the major studies on Asian American economic status which have appeared, we note the following:

1. A study by Harold H. Wong using 1970 census data found that for the most part, structural rather than productivity differences accounted for income differentials among white, Japanese, Chinese, and black men in California. Our results using 1980 census data confirm Wong's findings.[4]

2. We do not agree with Chiswick's results based on a regression analysis of 1970 census data, that U.S.-born Chinese American and Japanese American men in 1970 had already reached parity with white men.[5] Moreover, since we see labor force participation rate as an inadequate measure of Asian American success, we disagree with Chiswick's rationale for using number of weeks worked as a dependent variable with equal standing to personal income, and his use of number of weeks employed as a measurement of economic success for Asian Americans. We believe the number of weeks worked should be an independent rather than a dependent variable in analyses of income inequality.

3. Our results do not agree with Hirschman's and Wong's assessment, based on cross-sectional census data from 1960 to 1976 of educational attainment level,

occupational distribution, and industrial distribution, that U.S.-born Asian Americans had reached parity by 1976 with whites.[6] We do agree, however, that immigrant Asians still lag far behind.

4. We disagree with Nee and Sanders who used occupational attainment as an independent variable in a regression analysis of income. We find it difficult to see occupational attainment as anything other than an outcome or dependent variable.[7]

5. Our results are consistent with the findings of Deborah Woo, also based on 1980 census data, of the continued existence of income disparity between women, both white and Asian American, and white men.[8]

In summary, structural problems confront immigrant Asian American men and women in both major labor market areas of California. Although we have barely scratched the surface in this study, we have shown empirically that Asian Americans, U.S.-born and immigrant, men and women alike, experience significant economic disadvantages. This is the reality that contradicts the myth created by the mass media of their high economic status.

We conclude by listing some of the serious consequences that result from the myth of Asian American economic success. Asian Americans, some of whom themselves misperceive or are silent about their true economic status, unwittingly allow themselves to be scapegoats for some of the economic ills that many Americans face today. Also, sadly, it seems that other minorities have already begun to exclude Asian Americans from the coalitions that deal with issues such as civil rights, equal opportunity, affirmative action, bilingual education, and entitlement in various areas of public life. Asian Americans, instead, are set up (particularly by neoconservatives who aim to reduce the nation's responsibility and commitment to helping the disadvantaged, thus victimizing all minorities) as models for others to follow. Asian Americans, as a result of the misperception of their disadvantaged economic status, thus tend to neglect developing strategies for economic betterment for themselves and other disadvantaged Americans.

Notes

1. Lester C. Thurow, *The Zero-Sum Society: Distribution and the Possibilities for Economic Change* (New York: Basic Books, 1980).

2. Some notable examples are "Asian Americans: The Drive to Excel," *Newsweek* (April 1984); "Asian Americans: Are they Making the Grade?," *U.S. News and World Report* (2 April 1984). In the May 1986 issue of *The Washington Monthly*, a lead article entitled "The Wrong Way to Court Ethnics: Watch Out, Here Comes Another Group to Pander to," by Thomas Massey, a pseudonym for a federal civil rights official, takes as a given the economic success of Asian Americans and bemoans their contributions to some political campaigns:

> The birth of what might be called an Asian American lobby offers an opportunity to raise some important questions about special interest politics in general. When we appeal to groups rather than individuals, do ideals suffer? How can we recognize differences in need among subgroups and among individuals? The rise of Asian-American politics also provides an interesting inverse proportion to the hardships it endures. Asian Americans, like many other groups, had little power in history when they were suffering most from discrimination and poverty. Where were the politicians when the Japanese (sic) were being interned during World War II? Now that Asian Americans are an ethnic success story, presidential candidates cater to them. Is there a better way to approach members of an interest group--one that ensures benefits will go to those who need them most?...

3. Amado Cabezas, *A View of Poor Linkages Between Education, Occupation, and Earnings for Asian Americans* (San Francisco: ASIAN, Inc., 1977).

4. Harold H. Wong, "The Relative Economic Status of Chinese, Japanese, Black, and White Men in California" (Ph.D. diss., University of California, Berkeley, 1974).

5. Barry R. Chiswick, "An Analysis of the Earnings and Employment of Asian American Men," *Journal of Labor Economics* 1, no. 2 (1983).

6. Charles Hirschman and Morrison G. Wong, "Trends in Socioeconomic Achievement among Immigrant and Native-born Asian-Americans, 1960-1976," *The Sociological Quarterly* 22 (Autumn 1981):495-513.

7. Victor Nee and Jimy Sanders, "The Road to Parity: Determinants of the Socioeconomic Achievements of Asian Americans," *Ethnic and Racial Studies* 8, no. 1 (January 1985):75-93.

8. Deborah Woo, "The Socioeconomic Status of Asian American Women in the Labor Force: An Alternative View," *Sociological Perspectives* 28, no. 3 (July 1985):307-338.

The Economic Adaptation of Filipino Americans in California

Edwin B. Almirol

Before coming to the United States, many Filipino immigrants had professional and managerial occupations. The 1970 U.S. Census reported that more than 29 percent of all professional immigrants entering the United States were from the Philippines. In the 1980s, the number of Filipino professionals immigrating into the United States remains high; the only other groups of Asian immigrants with a similarly large proportion of professionals come from Korea and India.[1] In spite of the fact that a majority of the Filipino immigrants are college-educated and professionally-trained, only a minority of them obtain professional jobs after arrival. After finding employment, Filipinos, in their own view, must be "better" and must "work harder" than others in order to retain their jobs, but even those who are employed are not certain that they will advance beyond a certain level.[2] The under-employment of Filipino professionals is a serious, persistent problem because it represents a waste of human resources. Since there is a strong indication that the number of professional and technical workers within the Filipino American population will continue to increase, their rate of socioeconomic mobility is an important issue warranting careful research.

Filipino Americans have made a definite, though moderate, gain in income over the last decade, but their median income level is still lower than that for the United States population as a whole. Filipinos, regardless of their level of education, have lower median incomes compared to Anglos. Close to 10 percent of all Filipinos in California, and nearly 25 percent of the elderly Filipinos, live at the poverty level. Of the latter, most of whom are men, two-thirds live alone.

Despite the fact that Filipinos earn less than their Anglo counterparts, they are satisfied with their jobs, because they feel that their income meets their families' needs. Defining 'family needs' is a critical issue. Many working Filipinos combine their individual incomes, including the salaries of individuals outside the family, in order to augment overall family income. This is at once an economic strategy and a cultural response to being in a comparatively lower-income level.[3] Kin and family interdependence contributes significantly to the feeling of economic satisfaction and successful social adaptation.

Studies of post-war Filipino immigrants in the United States are few and far between. However, although scholarly research on Filipino American topics is limited, there have been some promising recent studies.[4] My study of Filipino American socioeconomic adaptation, based on a questionnaire administered to Filipino Americans in California in 1985, will add to the growing literature.

The questionnaire was part of a larger, ongoing study of social and economic adaptation among Filipinos.[5] This article will describe the background and expectations of the Filipinos before their departure for the United States, document their perceptions of the quality of their lives in California, discuss the extent to which their expectations have been met, and demonstrate their familial ties with relatives in both the United States and the Philippines.

Method

A questionnaire was sent out to 1,500 Filipino respondents who were chosen at random from the membership lists of approximately 680 Filipino voluntary associations in four California counties--Los Angeles, Monterey, San Joaquin, and San Francisco. Additional names were randomly chosen from the *Telephone Directory of Filipino Business in California, 1984*.

The questionnaire was divided into three parts: (1) questions on the respondents' sociological background, including age, gender, marital status, family size, level of education, living arrangement, occupation, and income; (2) questions on immigration patterns, including reasons for leaving the Philippines, occupation prior to departure, expectations of American life, and reasons for choosing California as a destination; and (3) questions on their life in the United States, including current status as well as changes in income levels and occupations, job satisfaction and preference, social adjustment, definitions of success, and contacts with the homeland communities.

Qualitative data were collected through formal and informal interviews and participant observation. The forty people interviewed in-depth were selected primarily on the basis of their availability and willingness to be interviewed. Rapport between interviewer and interviewee helped to determine the choice of respondents, who were interviewed in a language they preferred. Twenty-eight percent of the respondents were interviewed in Tagalog and thirty percent in Ilocano; the rest were interviewed in English. All interviews took place in the homes of the respondents. Five men and five women were chosen from each of the four counties. In addition, participant observation provided considerable versatility and exploratory advantage in the gathering of information. Since my contact with members of the Filipino community was not segmented and rigidly formal, I believe that the responses were spontaneous and honest.

About 42 percent of the respondents to the questionnaire live in San Francisco, 35 percent in San Joaquin and Monterey, and 23 percent in Los Angeles. Excluding those who were born in the United States, the respondents have spent an average of 12.3 years in the United States. Their ages range from 21 to 75 years and the mean age is 39.3.

Historical Background

Filipinos comprise one of the fastest growing ethnic groups in the United States today. They number close to 1.5 million, with the largest concentrations in California, Hawaii, Chicago, New York, Seattle, and New Jersey. In California, where more than half of the Filipinos in the United States reside, the Filipino American population increased almost two-fold during the last decade, making it the state's largest Asian American population today. They rank below only the white, Latino, and black populations in size. According to the 1980 census, 357,514 Filipinos lived in California as compared to 327,348 Chinese Americans and 261,817 Japanese Americans. More than two-thirds of the Filipinos in California reside in six counties, namely, San Francisco, Santa Clara, Alameda, San Mateo (all in the San Francisco Bay Area), and San Diego and Los Angeles in southern California. A decade ago, of the 336,731 Filipinos in the United States, 46.8 percent were American-born. Today two-thirds of them are United States citizens: one-third are U.S.-born and another third are naturalized Americans.

It was not until the 1920s that large numbers of Filipinos started coming to California. Most of those who arrived in the continental United States before the 1920s were students from prominent, wealthy families who came on government scholarships to be trained for government service. In 1920 there were only 5,603 Filipinos in the continental United States, with 3,360 of them in California.[6] Between 1920 and 1929, 31,092 Filipinos, mostly farm laborers, were admitted into the United States through California.[7] By 1930, some 45,000 Filipinos lived in the United States mainland. In 1934, the Filipino immigration quota fell to 50 persons per year, as stipulated in a clause of the Tydings-McDuffie Act, which promised the Philippines eventual independence; in 1945, the immigration quota for Filipinos increased to 100 per year. As a result of these restrictions, the 1950 census counted only 45,563 Filipinos in the United States. Between 1960 and 1970, however, there was a 95 percent increase, partly as a result of the repeal of the "national origins" provision of U.S. immigration laws.

From the 1920s until after World War II, Filipinos, like Chinese and Japanese immigrants, were considered at best a "problem" and at worst a "menace." Political and labor leaders condemned Filipinos as "cheap labor," but at the same time, American-owned steamship company agents and farm labor contractors actively recruited Filipino laborers with guarantees of work and good pay. The departure of the Chinese and Japanese for small-scale truck farming and urban occupations had left a vacuum in the supply of laborers in West Coast agribusiness, and Filipinos were specifically recruited to fill it. According to Carey McWilliams, "there is scarcely a Filipino who did not leave the Philippines at the invitation, expressed or implied, of some employer."[8]

Most early Filipino arrivals were young single males: 93 percent of them were male and 84 percent were under 30 years of age, with almost 5 percent under age 16.[9] The majority were single, but even the few who were married invariably came alone, leaving their families behind. These early Filipino immigrants generally worked in either farm labor or domestic service. Domestic work included jobs such as houseboy, waiter, busboy, cook, elevator operator, and dishwasher. The domestic workers usually lived in Los Angeles, Seattle, or San Francisco. Since farm labor was seasonal, the Filipinos employed in it followed the crops up and down the West Coast. In the summer and fall they worked in the Salinas and San Joaquin valleys in California or in the Yakima Valley in Washington; in the winter, they worked in San Diego and the Imperial Valley in southern California;

in the spring and summer, they worked in the salmon canneries in Alaska. Because of this mobility, stable Filipino communities comparable to the European immigrant communities were never established until after World War II.

Occupational Background

Filipino Americans no longer become farm workers in large numbers. Among my respondents, 54 percent were in professional and managerial occupations prior to coming to the United States, 12 percent were in clerical jobs, 10 percent were in service-related jobs, 2 percent were operatives, 2 percent were farm laborers, and 20 percent were in "other" occupations, which include students, housewives, and other uncodable categories. These recent immigrants are most likely to have fathers in professional and managerial occupations (31 percent), followed by fathers in farm work (18 percent), and service (11 percent), which includes the military. The remaining occupations for fathers are, in rank order, craft and kindred workers (10 percent), operatives and nonfarm laborers (5 percent each), sales (4 percent), and clerical (1 percent). All other occupations of the fathers comprise 6 percent, while 8 percent did not respond. Most respondents' mothers are housewives (43 percent), followed by professional occupations: teaching (28 percent), nonfarm labor (10 percent), clerical (5 percent), service (4 percent), sales, crafts and operatives (1 percent each). Six percent of the respondents did not answer the question on their mothers' occupation.

Using the respondents' fathers' occupation as a reference point, the data suggest that there has been a modest degree of intergenerational upward mobility into professional and managerial jobs. Only 31 percent of the respondents' fathers have professional occupations, but 47 percent of the respondents themselves are professionals or managers--a 16 percent increase. The occupational distributions of Filipinos and Filipinas differ greatly; however, about the same percentage of each is employed in professional and managerial occupations.

Motives for Emigration

Why did the respondents leave the Philippines? The most frequently cited reason is to be with family and friends (27 percent), followed by an expectation of better opportunity (25 percent). Another 24 percent thought the United States would provide them and their children with improved standards of living. Another 15 percent, all females, came because of their husbands. (The item they chose on the questionnaire was, "I had no choice; my husband wanted to come.") Six percent listed "adventure" and "self-improvement" as motives for leaving the Philippines and another 3 percent came to attend school in the United States.

Who held what expectations of the United States before leaving the Philippines? The more highly educated immigrants expected to find higher standards of living in the United States. Those who have larger families, those who live in San Francisco, and those who are currently holding professional jobs also expected a higher standard of living. Respondents who had "other expectations" and "no expectations" tended to have held service, clerical, or other occupations in the Philippines, and to have fathers employed in sales. These respondents tended to be more satisfied with their jobs than those who had expectations of higher living standards, and were more likely to send money to relatives in the homeland.

Settlement Pattern

Where have they settled after they arrived in America? An impressive majority (60 percent) of the respondents have relatives who had come ahead of them and who were already living in California. More than half (57 percent) of the Filipinos in the study chose California because of the presence of family and friends. More than 28 percent had a spouse already settled here. California's climate and geography drew 7 percent of the respondents, while 8 percent were attracted by job possibilities. (The data on where to settle exclude the American-born and those who did not respond.)

Clearly, Filipino immigration and settlement patterns follow closely the phenomenon called "chain migration"[10] and are strikingly similar to Mexican migration patterns.[11] Mexican immigrants to the United States, however, differ from Filipino immigrants in that the proportion of professionally-trained Mexican immigrants is insignificant.

Household Composition

The respondents have a mean family size of 4.9 persons. This measure probably includes unrelated individuals since it is impossible from the questionnaire data to differentiate unrelated household members from related ones.

Ninety-four percent of the respondents report that at least one person in the household works. In 60 percent of the households, two or more people work. Overall, an average of 1.62 people are dependent or unemployed in the California Filipino household. (It is not possible to separate out the aged, children, disabled, or employable-but-unemployed in the questionnaire data.) Fairly good data on the relationship of the respondent to the other household workers are available, however. Of the 790 working household members, 20 percent are siblings of the respondents, 18 percent are husbands, 18 percent are parents, 19 percent are sons or daughters, 15 percent are wives, 5 percent are friends, and 5 percent are in-laws. These statistics suggest a considerable degree of economic familism within Filipino households.

Income

Of the 520 respondents who reported income and were Philippine-born, the average income is $14,671 per year. Females average $564 more than males, but the difference does not approach statistical significance. This study attempts to "explain" the income levels of the respondents and to determine how their incomes are affected by education, the number of years spent in the United States, age, job-hunting skills, and residential location. Table 1 shows these variables correlated with income. The two variables most closely associated with high income are high level of education and professional or managerial occupation. Although a positive correlation is found for length of stay in the United States, the data suggest that to feel it is sufficient.

Those whose relatives had come to the United States ahead of them are also more likely to feel their income is sufficient. Those who feel that their income is sufficient would like their children to have jobs like theirs; they also feel that their expectations of the United States have been met.

About 17 percent of the respondents report extra sources of income. Almost 38 percent among them hold jobs other than their primary occupation, 36 percent are engaged in small-scale business in addition to wage work, 15 percent receive retirement pensions, 6 percent social security, and 4 percent government aid. Individuals who have other sources of income are likely to be more educated, older, from the San Francisco Bay Area, and they regularly send money to their relatives in the Philippines.

Job Satisfaction and Preference

A majority (60 percent) of the respondents report that they are satisfied with their jobs, although 22 percent are dissatisfied and 14 percent have mixed opinions. Four percent did not respond. Those satisfied with their jobs feel their incomes are sufficient to meet their needs; they do not desire different jobs, would not mind their children having jobs similar to theirs, do not feel life in the United States is as hard as it was in the Philippines, and do not feel that their standards of living and quality of life are worse than they had expected before immigrating. Overall, job satisfaction is significantly correlated with the feeling that one's income is sufficient to meet one's needs.

Individuals who find life harder in the United States are not in professional jobs but desire to be. Males and females do not differ on this point. Individuals who are professionals in the United States as well as those who had been professionals in the Philippines are more likely to prefer professional jobs in America. Filipino Americans who currently work as operatives are more likely to desire other non-professional jobs. People in sales, followed by service workers, are least likely to desire professional jobs.

Generally, people who came to the United States recently and have closer attachments to their Philippine relatives want their children to have jobs similar to their own, but respondents' feelings on this issue are not closely tied to their present occupations. Many respondents whose fathers are professionals, and who are themselves trained as professionals but do not hold such jobs in the United States, wish their children to have jobs different from their own current occupations.

Definitions of Success

About 25 percent of the respondents define success in terms of career goals or pecuniary accumulation, 11 percent mention "happiness" or good health, and 16 percent mention both. There is no gender difference among those who state that success means pecuniary accumulation. The modal response to this item, however, is a more abstract goal of "life fulfillment" or some other general statement (47 percent). Only one respondent admits not knowing how to define success.

The correlates of these different responses provide an insight into the perceptions of Filipino Americans. Those stressing pecuniary goals had worked as operatives or in farm labor in the Philippines. They indicate that a desire to improve their standard of living was the main reason they left the Philippines. They also feel that their standard of living and quality of life in the United States are worse than they had expected them to be.

The number of years spent in the United States is not strongly correlated with different definitions of success, but those who have spent more time in the United States are least likely to express an abstract success goal. Those who left the Philippines for schooling or self-improvement tend to stress an abstract goal. The respondents whose fathers are occupied in craft or kindred work are also more likely to desire an abstract or health/happiness goal, and to have mixed feelings about whether or not they are satisfied with their jobs. These findings paint a picture of frustration among those most interested in the American ideal of material accumulation.

Is Life Harder in the United States?

Respondents who find life in the United States harder than they had expected are those who send money home regularly, who write to relatives in the Philippines moderately frequently, who would like to have a job different from their current employment, and professionals. Gender and occupational status are significant factors in the perception of whether life is harder in America. Filipino women, especially those who had held professional occupations in the Philippines, find life in the United States harder than they had expected. A significant percentage of Filipino men who had professional and technical occupations in the Philippines also find that life in America is harder than they had expected. Filipino professionals are highly motivated and extremely ambitious, but due to economic and social barriers, many fail to get professional jobs here, hence their perception of hardship. There is also a positive, though not strong, correlation between age and the feeling that life is harder in the United States: older Filipinos (55 years and older), regardless of sex, are somewhat more likely to feel that life is harder in America.

Expectations Met

In response to the question "How would you compare your standard of living and quality of life in America to your expectations before you arrived?" almost half of the respondents (49.1 percent) report that their standard of living and quality of life in the United States are better than they had expected. In general, those who had service, clerical, or "other" jobs in the Philippines reported that their standard of living in California is better than they had expected. But 14.8 percent of the respondents find life in America worse than they had expected, and they are more likely to have low incomes, or incomes insufficient for their needs, to live alone or not have close family members, to be dissatisfied with their present job, and to have had craft/kindred occupations in the Philippines. Respondents who find their standard of living and quality of life to be the same as they had expected amount to 36.1 percent.

Have the respondents' expectations of the United States been met? More than half of the respondents (55 percent) report that their expectations of the United States have been met. Those whose expectations have been met feel that their standard of living and quality of life have improved. Respondents who expected to find greater opportunity are far more likely to feel that their expectations have been met. A correlation exists among age, income, and the feeling that expectations have been met. Younger respondents (those under 35 years old) are more likely to report that their expectations have been met. These younger respondents frequently are more successful in getting professional jobs; they also tend to land jobs which are higher-paying. In general, younger Filipino Americans, regardless of gender, tend to have more skills and advantages when looking for jobs: they have greater proficiency in English, more education and professional training, and more appropriate marketable skills such as computer literacy.

Links with the "Old Country"

More than 95 percent of the respondents still have relatives living in the Philippines. About 45 percent write to their relatives one or more times a month; 19 percent once every 3 to 6 months, 4 percent only once every 10 to 12 months. Another 19 percent indicate they write but do not specify how often. Twelve percent did not respond.

To understand who writes and with what frequency, the responses to this item were grouped into three categories: (1) little or not at all (not at all or once every 10 to 12 months), (2) moderately (once every 3 to 6 months), and (3) frequently (once or more often per month). These three categories were then correlated with selected items in the questionnaire.

The frequency of letter writing to relatives in the Philippines is closely related to the respondent's occupation and his or her parents' occupations in the Philippines: former operatives and nonfarm laborers write little or not at all; those who fathers' occupation is in craft or kindred work also write little or not at all. People who had expected a higher standard of living in the United States also write little or not at all. People with higher incomes write little, as do those who find life harder in the United States, and those who had moved to the United States because of marriage.

The moderate writers had some apparently contradictory characteristics: they left the Philippines to seek better opportunities and they feel that life is better in the United States than in the Philippines, but they also report that their expectations of the United States have not been met in terms of their standard of living and quality of life. These people are more likely to have moved to California because of a job offer, the climate, or school and career plans.

Frequent writers are people who prefer a different job from what they currently have; they left the Philippines to seek economic opportunities. It is somewhat surprising that the correlation between letter-writing and having relatives is not high. Interesting, but not strong, correlations exist between the frequency of letter-writing and some other variables. For instance, those who have lived in the United States for a shorter time period write more frequently, and those who write frequently are more likely to send money to the Philippines. Thus, letter-writing and money-giving go hand-in-hand, to reinforce family support, commitment, and loyalty.

Many of the respondents (about 88 percent) send money to relatives in the Philippines. Those who send money are more likely to have been professionals in the Philippines but to no longer have professional jobs in California. People who find life hard in the United States also send significantly more money more frequently than other groups. Those less likely to send money had held clerical, service, or "other" occupations in the Philippines. Individuals who have lived in the United States for a relatively short period, come from larger families, have other sources of income, and do not want their children to have jobs similar to theirs, are also less likely to send money to relatives in the Philippines.

Summary

In summary, a large proportion of post-war Filipino immigrants to the United States had professional and managerial occupations prior to leaving the Philippines. Recent Filipino immigration patterns underscore the "brain drain" nature of this influx. "Brain drain," a serious problem in the Philippines, as in other Third World countries, "refers to those persons whose education and professional training have been possible through the efforts and resources of one country, but whose services are being utilized by another."[12] Filipino "brain drain" to the United States is partly a symptom of the depressed Philippine labor market which is unable to absorb a significant portion of its trained professionals. Filipino professionals who wish to make full use of their skills and training have to emigrate. Beginning in the 1960s, about 25 percent of all Filipino physicians and surgeons, more than 40 percent of all pharmacists and dentists, and 58 percent of dieticians, emigrated to the United States.[13]

Although they have experienced slight upward mobility in the United States, there is still an alarming number of college-educated and professionally-trained Filipinos who have not found appropriate jobs. The under-utilization of Filipino professionals is increasingly becoming a serious problem, both within and without the ethnic community.

The number of professional and technical workers within the Filipino American population will probably continue to increase. Many people left the Philippines in search of stable and well-paying jobs, but the most frequent reason for leaving was to be with family and relatives, a phenomenon called "chain migration." The very choice of where they would settle and establish themselves is also dependent on "chain migration." A majority of Filipino immigrants stay in California because they have family members who have already settled in California.

Unlike the early Filipino arrivals in the 1920s who came to find work, make money, and return home, present-day Filipino immigrants come to stay. A majority have permanent jobs, some even have second jobs. Although there have been definite, albeit moderate, income gains over the last decade, the Filipino American median income level is still lower than the median for the United States population as a whole. Filipinos, regardless of their level of education or length of stay in the United States, have lower median incomes compared to the American mainstream population. The experiences of Filipino immigrants, especially professionals, contradict assimilation theories that maintain that the length of stay in the United States plays a critical role in economic integration. As this study has shown, length of stay in the United States does not significantly affect income levels or feelings of economic satisfaction.

In spite of the fact that Filipinos earn less than their Anglo counterparts and their incomes are not commensurate with their level of education, many are satisfied with their jobs. This job satisfaction results from the feeling that their income is sufficient to meet their needs, which in turn is correlated with the presence of supportive family members and kin groups in the United States. Family needs are frequently met by combining individual incomes to augment the overall family income.

The feeling of economic satisfaction also emerges from the respondents' definition of success. To them, success is fulfillment of one's life goals. For many Filipinos who come to the United States, finding work and being with family and kin here represent the fulfillment of their life goals. Those who seem most satisfied with their lives here are those who have their families here. Kin support and family interdependence, then, are essential to the Filipino American's feeling of successful social and economic adaptation.

Notes

1. Bok-Lim C. Kim, *The Asian Americans: Changing Patterns, Changing Needs* (Mountclair, N.J.: Association of Korean Christian Scholars in North America, 1978).

2. A recent study of Chinese Americans in the San Francisco Bay Area found that they had a similar perception of their lot (Yuan-Li Wu, "Income, Employment, and Occupational Patterns: Three Decades of Change," *The Economic Condition of Chinese Americans*, ed. Yuan-Li Wu [Chicago: Pacific/Asian American Mental Health Research Center, 1980]).

3. Evidently, this practice of income collectivization within the extended kin group is also widespread among Chinese Americans (Wu, *Economic Condition*). Ricardo Abad, "Social Links, Perception of Opportunities, and the Propensity of Migrants to Return Home: The Case of Filipino Medical Graduates in New York City" (Ph.D. diss., Fordham University, 1975).

4. Abad, "Social Links"; Ruben Alcantra, *Sakada: Filipino Adaptation in Hawaii* (Washington, D.C.: University Press of America, 1981); James Allen, "Recent Immigration from the Philippines and Filipino Communities in the United States," *Geographical Review* 67, no. 2 (1977):195-208; Edwin B. Almirol, *Ethnic Identity and Social Negotiation: A Study of a Filipino Community in California* (New York: AMS Press, 1985); Purita Asperilla, "The Mobility of Filipino Nurses" (Ph.D. diss., Columbia University, 1971); Erlinda Clark, "Filipino Labor Experiences in the United States" (Ph.D. diss., Texas Technical University, 1971); Stephen Griffiths, "Emigrants and Entrepreneurs: Social and Economic Strategies in a Philippine Peasant Community" (Ph.D. diss., University of Hawaii, 1978); Josefine Jayme, "Demographic and Socio-Psychological Determinants of the Migration of Highly Trained Filipinos to the United States" (Ph.D. diss., University of Hawaii,

1971); Charles Keely, "Philippine Immigration: Internal Movements and Emigration to the United States," *International Migration Review* 7, no. 2 (1972):177-187; Barbara Posadas, "Crossed Boundaries in Interracial Chicago: Pilipino American Families since 1925," *Amerasia Journal* 8, no. 2 (1981):31-52; Sonja Solland, "A Study of Conflict in a Multi-Ethnic Community" (Ph.D. diss., University of Washington, Seattle, 1974).

5. Edwin Almirol, "Filipino Americans: Cultural Continuity and Change," Unpublished ms., 1986.

6. Louis Block, *Facts About Filipino Immigration into California* (San Francisco: California Department of Industrial Relations, 1930).

7. Ibid.

8. Carey McWilliams, *Brothers Under the Skin* (Boston: Little, Brown, and Co., 1964), 236.

9. Louis Block, *Facts About Filipino Immigration into California* (San Francisco: California Department of Industrial Relations, 1930).

10. J. MacDonald, "Urbanization, Ethnic Groups, and Social Segmentation," *Social Research* 25 (1962):433-448; Juan Gomez-Quinones, *Mexican Immigration to the United States and the Internationalization of Labor, 1848-1980: An Overview of Mexican Immigrant Workers in the United States,* ed. Antonio Rios-Bustamante (University of California, Los Angeles: Chicano Studies Research Center, 1981).

11. Antonio Pido, "Brain-Drain Filipinos," *Society* (Sept.-Oct. 1977):50-58.

12. James Allen, "Recent Immigration."

Marriage Patterns of Asian Americans in California, 1980

Larry Hajime Shinagawa and Gin Yong Pang

Introduction

The sociological literature on marriage patterns of racial and ethnic minorities has focused almost exclusively upon studies of intermarriage.[1] Two schools of thought have emerged to account for intermarriages.[2] The first, assimilation theory, provides the major explanation for the intermarriage patterns of white ethnic and religious minorities.[3] Since the Second World War, it has also been applied to the study of the intermarriage patterns of nonwhite racial minorities.[4] Asian Americans,[5] in particular, have come to be viewed as a group whose intermarriage demonstrates that race no longer remains a barrier to the full acceptance of minority groups by the majority. A second alternative view, hypergamy theory, emphasizes that intermarriage is a function of the inequality within a class and racially stratified society. Scholars have yet to explore the use of hypergamy theory to explain the intermarriage patterns of Asian Americans. In this paper, by using the hypergamy model, we will offer a structural socioeconomic analysis of the marriage patterns of Asian Americans.

Assimilation theory postulates that intermarriage is a sign of the growing acceptance of a minority group by the majority group.[6]

Thus, interracial marriages involving Asian Americans and whites are a sign of white acceptance of people of Asian ancestry in the United States.[7] In particular, John Tinker's study of Japanese American intermarriage stresses that past racial antagonism can ultimately be overcome so that a racially distinct minority can be accepted and can consequently assimilate into the dominant society.[8] Tinker suggests that the high rate of intermarriage between Japanese Americans and whites demonstrates that race is no longer a boundary between the two groups.[9] Not all of the recent scholarship shares this opinion about the declining significance of race in the everyday experience of racial minorities, but most studies based on assimilation theory do view Asian Americans as embarking on the assimilation path blazed by white ethnics and argue that the intermarriage of Asian Americans should be seen as an important indicator of the assimilation of Asian Americans into American society.[10]

The alternative theory of hypergamy suggests that intermarriage performs a specific function for the upper castes or classes. First used as a concept in anthropological studies of marriage patterns in India, hypergamy describes the intermarriage between higher caste males and lower caste females. Kingsley Davis argues that in societies such as India a higher caste male may exchange his social position for the extraordinary achievement, beauty, intelligence, youth, or wealth brought to the marriage by the female partner of a lower caste.[11] In contrast to India, according to Kingsley Davis, intermarriage in the United States--a society which is racially stratified--allows racial minority males with higher socioeconomic status but lower racial status and females with higher racial status but lower socioeconomic status to mutually benefit each other. Davis stresses that such marriages between racial minority males and majority females tend to occur especially in highly industrialized, democratic societies.[12] In an important development of the original concept, Pierre Van Den Berghe underscores the fact that hypergamy principally involves the "maximization of status" for each marital partner.[13] Hypergamous intermarriage occurs when the female can obtain a status gain for herself or her children while the male suffers no substantial loss of status for himself. For racial minority males married to higher racial status females, the marriage is both hypergamous and hypogamous: hypergamous because his *socioeconomic status* is higher than that of his wife, but also hypogamous because his *racial status* is lower than that of his wife. Emphasizing the structural and "functional necessity" of stratification,[14] the motor of hypergamy is the existence of caste and class inequalities between the genders.

The hypergamy model has become increasingly unpopular in the analysis of intermarriage since the early 1970s. Non-assimilationist-oriented scholars of race relations from the cultural nationalist and Marxist traditions, responding to the racial and ethnic awareness movements of the 1960s and 1970s, tended to react negatively to the structuralist-functionalist foundations of the hypergamy theory propounded by Davis and Moore.[15] In particular, the tendency of functionalist theory to justify the unequal distribution of goods and services among individuals and groups appeared to them as rather "morally-toned," validating an oppressive but "moral" social order that neglects the role of racial and class conflict in American society.[16] Nevertheless, they failed to provide alternative theoretically-oriented explanations for the intermarriage patterns of racial minorities. Consequently, few articles appeared challenging the predominant assimilation theory of intermarriage.

Unlike past research on Asian American intermarriages, this essay assesses the marriage patterns of Asian Americans by drawing upon hypergamy theory. Assimilation theory tends to be blind to the internal stratifications within populations, viewing American society as one without rigid barriers that might hinder the socioeconomic progress of minority groups. Hypergamy theory, however, allows us to look at the internal and external stratification within and between racial/ethnic populations through an analysis of the marital partners' nativity, gender, age, education, and socioeconomic characteristics. In this study, we analyze the intraethnic, interethnic, and interracial marriage patterns among Asian Americans and their spouses. A person of Asian ancestry who is married to someone from his or her own ethnic group is defined as intramarried, regardless of whether the spouse is U.S.-born or foreign-born. An Asian American who is married to a member of an Asian American group other than his or her own is defined as interethnically married. An Asian American married to a person of non-Asian American background is considered to be interracially married. Both interethnic and interracial marriage are subsumed under intermarriage.[17] We hypothesize that assimilation theory has overlooked systematic hierarchical relations of inequality in the marriage patterns of Asian Americans. We argue that the marriage patterns of Asian Americans can be better understood by the application of a hypergamous model of intermarriage.

Data Design

Unlike recent studies of intermarriage patterns among Asian Americans which have relied on marriage license applications as their data base,[18] we will use the 1980 U.S. Census of Population which provides specific information on nativity, veteran status, age, education, income, and labor force characteristics of both the husband and wife of married individuals living together. In the past, the computational complexity of gathering this information from the census has probably deterred usage of this data base.[19]

We include all of the married husbands and wives of the major Asian American groups and their spouses from the 5-percent Public User Microdata Sample (PUMS) for the state of California.[20] The result is a data base of 231,394 individuals living together in married households, of whom 12,010 are Asian American husbands and 13,656 are Asian American wives.

We have restricted the major part of our study to U.S.-born whites and the following Asian American groups:

1. U.S.-born Chinese
2. Foreign-born Chinese
3. U.S.-born Japanese
4. Foreign-born Japanese
5. U.S.-born Filipino
6. Foreign-born Filipino
7 Foreign-born Korean
8. Foreign-born Asian Indian
9. Foreign-born Vietnamese

Blacks, Hispanics, and foreign-born whites are excluded from this study because of the small number of such individuals having spouses of Asian American descent. U.S.-born Korean, U.S.-born Asian Indian, and U.S.-born Vietnamese, and other unreported Asian American groups are also not included due to their small numbers. Unless otherwise stated, the chi-square statistics for the marriage patterns are statistically significant for all bivariate comparisons of the remaining groups.

Sometimes, the exclusion of these other groups from the study complicates the interpretation of the data. For example, most U.S.-born white females, when they marry out of their own race/ethnicity/nativity group, marry into the foreign-born white population. Similarly, Asian Americans who marry into the "other" race/ethnicity category marry mainly foreign-born whites. Generally, however, the exclusion of certain racial/ethnicity/nativity groups does not present a problem.[21] The majority of the marriage patterns of Asian Americans are presented by race/ethnicity/nativity groupings in the following tables.

Methodology

Paul Besanceney, in a widely influential research note, has suggested that all future research on intermarriage should (1) make a distinction between rates and prevalences based on marriages rather than on individuals, (2) acknowledge group size as operating through mathematical necessity when it is found to be inversely related to intermarriage rates, and (3) when possible, report the ratio of a group's actual rate or prevalence of intermarriage to its expected intermarriage rate or prevalence.[22] Rates determine the amount of change from one point in time to another, while prevalence shows the extent to which various characteristics of a given population exist at a specific moment in time. We decided not to use marriages as the unit of analysis because reports based upon marriages count intramarriages once and intermarriages twice. Double counting the latter inflates the number of intermarriages. On the other hand, when the unit of analysis is the individual, we count each marriage twice, since each individual marriage partner is counted. Thus, the extent of intermarriage appears smaller. In our opinion, using the individual as the unit of analysis is more accurate in describing the nature of marital relationships, since we are able to describe the contributions and characteristics of both spouses involved in the marriage. For these reasons, we have elected to conduct our research and present our findings using the individual as the unit of analysis.

The analysis utilizes a flat rectangular file structure of household members and their characteristics from the original hierarchical format of the census data. The statistical program used for our analysis is the Statistical Package for the Social Sciences, Version X 3.0 (SPSSX). Distributions of the population by marriage pattern are presented in the initial cross-classification tables, followed by detailed socioeconomic characteristics of the individuals by marriage pattern for whites and selected Asian American groups. [23]

Findings

In California in 1980, the majority of Asian Americans are married within their own ethnic groups. However, Asian Americans are more likely to be intermarried than other racial/ethnic groups. Population distributions derived from the 1980 U.S. Census for California show that 12.6 percent of all husbands are interethnically or interracially married, compared to 4.9 percent for all wives. The overall percentage of all spouses who are interethnically or interracially married is 8.2 percent. On the other hand, 14.4 percent of Asian American husbands and 25.0 percent of Asian American wives are interethnically or interracially married. The overall percentage of Asian American spouses--male and female combined--who are intermarried is 19.9 percent. These statistics indicate that Asian American women are much more likely to intermarry than Asian American men.

Table 1 shows the marriage prevalence of whites and Asian Americans in California, 1980. It shows that the majority of intermarriages involving Asian Americans are with whites. Among Asian Americans, Japanese Americans are the most likely group to marry whites (31.6 percent), followed by Filipino Americans (23.9 percent), and then Asian Indians (23.0 percent).

A significant proportion of intermarriages among Asian Americans are to other Asian Americans. Japanese Americans and Chinese Americans, when they interethnically marry, are likely to marry each other. Of those Korean Americans who interethnically marry, a sizable proportion marry Japanese Americans (3.4 percent), even though historical animosity between Koreans and Japanese have existed for a long time. Perhaps because many Vietnamese Americans are overseas Chinese, more Vietnamese Americans are married to Chinese Americans (1.9 percent) than to any other Asian American ethnic group.

Does this mean then that intermarried Asian Americans are most likely to marry whites? The answer to this question is both yes

TABLE 1

Marriage Prevalence of Whites and Asian Americans, California, 1980

	Race/Ethnicity*						
Race/Ethnicity	White **	Chinese	Japanese	Filipino	Korean	Asian Indian	Vietnamese
White**	**89.7**	13.7	31.6	23.9	18.8	23.0	14.6
Chinese	0.3	**77.8**	3.3	1.2	1.8	0.0	1.9
Japanese	0.7	3.5	**56.6**	1.0	3.4	0.5	0.4
Filipino	0.5	1.3	1.1	**61.6**	1.2	0.8	0.6
Korean	0.1	0.6	1.2	0.4	**69.4**	0.1	0.6
Asian Indian	0.1	0.0	0.1	0.1	0.1	**69.9**	0.0
Vietnamese	0.1	0.3	0.1	0.1	0.3	0.0	**78.8**
Other Race/Ethnicity	8.5	2.8	6.0	11.7	5.0	5.7	0.0
Total	100%	100%	100%	100%	100%	100%	100%
N	187,048	3,758	3,993	4,220	1,338	773	669

Sources: 1980 U.S. Census Bureau 5-percent Public User Microdata Sample (PUMS) and special unpublished tabulations of the Asian American population.

*Vertical Percentages **U.S.-born Non-Hispanic White

and no. In absolute numbers, unquestionably, the largest proportion of Asian Americans, when they marry outside of their ethnic group, marry whites. As noted by Besanceney and Blau, however, the mathematical probability of a smaller group marrying out into the larger population is very high.[24] Correspondingly, the probability of a large group, such as whites, marrying out is very low. By controlling for the size of the population, we get a truer representation of the statistical likelihood of marriages between and among Asian Americans and others. We find that once these controls are made, the likelihood of an Asian American marrying another Asian American is higher than an Asian American marrying a white.

Although there are many ways to control for the size of the population, we use the technique prescribed by Besanceney, Glick, and Barnett.[25] It is based upon a cross tabulation table presenting the actual (Fe) and expected (Fo) frequencies between husband's race/ethnicity and wife's race/ethnicity. The statistic, called R, has the formula:

$$R = Fe/Fo$$

The procedure has the added convenience of making it possible to calculate the C^2 statistic. Since the expected frequencies show what would result in the cell frequency if only the marginals of the tables were taken into account, we can easily interpret the expected frequency as the number of individuals who should have been married in a particular cell if there were no racial and socioeconomic characteristics that distinguish the populations. The ratio R is equal to one when the observed and expected frequencies are the same, i.e., hypothetically, when there is true racial equality in our society. Unlike the "intermarriage distance scale" devised by Parkman and Sawyer,[26] it is not affected by differences in composition created by a marriage relationship between a large population with a low percentage of individuals intermarried and a small population with a high percentage of individuals intermarried.[27]

Table 2 shows the ratio of actual versus expected marriages by husband's background/wife's background. Unlike the Parkman and Sawyer statistic, it is assymetrical: the results for the marital position of a husband of the same race/ethnicity are different from the results for a wife. Using the R statistic, which controls for group size, we discover that regardless of whether it is a husband or wife, the probability of an Asian American marrying another Asian American is higher than that of an Asian American marrying a white. For example, a marriage involving a Japanese American man and a white woman has a ratio of .14, as opposed to 1.27 if his wife were Chinese American, and 1.68 if his wife were Korean American. Similarly, a marriage involving a Japanese American woman and a white man results in a ratio of .37, as opposed to 1.98 if her husband were Chinese American, and .46 if her husband were Korean American.

Thus, for a Japanese American man, the probability that he would marry a Chinese American woman rather than a white woman is approximately nine times greater. The probability of a Japanese American man marrying a Korean American woman is twelve times that of marrying a white woman. For a Japanese American woman, the probability that she would marry a Chinese American man is five and a quarter times greater than her marrying a white man. Similarly,

TABLE 2

Ratio of Actual to Expected Marriages Calculated from Husband's Race/Ethnicity by Wife's Race/Ethnicity Whites and Asian Americans, California, 1980

	Husband's Race/Ethnicity						
Wife's Race/Ethnicity	White *	Chinese	Japanese	Filipino	Korean	Asian Indian	Vietnamese
White*	**1.29**	.07	.14	.14	.03	.18	.02
Chinese	.13	**63.09**	1.27	.38	.36	.66	.53
Japanese	.37	1.98	**76.46**	.65	.46	.31	.13
Filipino	.25	.64	.28	**53.61**	.34	.63	.00
Korean	.24	1.05	1.68	.58	**172.83**	.29	.34
Asian Indian	.17	.00	.14	.00	.00	**310.00**	.00
Vietnamese	.19	.92	.28	.46	1.11	.00	**365.00**

Sources: 1980 U.S. Census Bureau 5-percent Public User Microdata Sample (PUMS) and special unpublished tabulations of the Asian American population.
*U.S.-born Non-Hispanic White

a marriage involving a Japanese American woman and a Korean American man is one and a quarter times that of one involving a white man. The aggregate findings support Parkman and Sawyer's observation that whom Asian Americans choose as spouses are (1) first, members of their own ethnic groups, (2) second, other Asian Americans, (3) third, whites, and (4) Hispanics and blacks.

Marriage Prevalence by Race/Ethnicity

Table 3 shows the percentage of husband's race/ethnicity by wife's race/ethnicity in California in 1980. Correspondingly, Table 4 shows the percentage of wife's race/ethnicity by husband's race/ethnicity in California in 1980. The data presented in Tables 3 and 4 demonstrate that the majority of intermarried Asian American individuals are interracially married, specifically, mostly to whites. Among intermarried Asian American men, 54 percent have white wives, while among intermarried Asian American women, 73 percent have white husbands. Of the intermarried individuals, 20.8 percent of the Asian American men are married interethnically to Asian American wives, while 10.4 percent of the Asian American women are married interethnically to Asian American husbands.

Marriage Prevalence by Race/Ethnicity and Nativity

In Tables 5 and 6, we disaggregated the populations further by specifying both race/ethnicity and nativity in order to see if there are differences between U.S.- and foreign-born. These tables demonstrate that taking into account the nativity of married individuals for both men and women is very important. For example, if we look at Table 4, we find that 27.5 percent of all Japanese American women are

TABLE 3

**Husband's Race/Ethnicity by Wife's Race/Ethnicity in Percentages
Whites and Asian Americans, California, 1980**

	Husband's Race/Ethnicity						
Wife's Race/Ethnicity	White *	Chinese	Japanese	Filipino	Korean	Asian Indian	Vietnamese
White*	**94.2**	4.9	9.9	10.6	2.0	13.0	1.7
Chinese	0.2	**89.5**	1.8	0.5	0.6	0.0	0.8
Japanese	0.6	2.5	**83.8**	1.0	2.2	0.5	0.2
Filipino	0.4	0.9	0.4	**79.7**	0.5	0.9	0.0
Korean	0.1	0.6	0.9	0.3	**93.6**	0.2	0.2
Asian Indian	0.0	0.0	0.0	0.0	0.0	**82.6**	0.0
Vietnamese	0.1	0.3	0.1	0.1	0.3	0.0	**96.4**
Other Race/Ethnicity	4.4	1.3	3.1	7.8	0.8	2.8	0.0
Total	100%	100%	100%	100%	100%	100%	100%
N	170,562	3,173	2,654	3,168	979	638	530

Sources: 1980 U.S. Census Bureau 5-percent Public User Microdata Sample (PUMS) and special unpublished tabulations of the Asian American population.

*U.S.-born Non-Hispanic White

TABLE 4

Wife's Race/Ethnicity by Husband's Race/Ethnicity in Percentages
Whites and Asian Americans, California, 1980

	Wife's Race/Ethnicity						
Husband's Race/Ethnicity	White *	Chinese	Japanese	Filipino	Korean	Asian Indian	Vietnamese
White*	**95.0**	9.6	27.5	18.3	17.9	12.7	14.1
Chinese	0.1	**86.4**	2.3	0.9	1.4	0.0	1.3
Japanese	0.2	1.5	**64.2**	0.3	1.9	0.2	0.3
Filipino	0.2	0.5	0.9	**73.4**	0.8	0.0	0.6
Korean	0.0	0.2	0.6	0.1	**73.5**	0.0	0.5
Asian Indian	0.0	0.0	0.1	0.2	0.1	**83.8**	0.0
Vietnamese	0.0	0.1	0.0	0.0	0.1	0.0	**80.9**
Other Race/Ethnicity	4.5	1.7	4.4	6.8	4.3	3.3	0.0
Total	100%	100%	100%	100%	100%	100%	100%
N	169,129	3,285	3,466	3,439	1,247	629	632

Sources: 1980 U.S. Census Bureau 5-percent Public User Microdata Sample (PUMS) and special unpublished tabulations of the Asian American population.

*U.S.-born Non-Hispanic White

married to white husbands. By controlling for nativity, Table 6 shows that only 14.4 percent of U.S.-born Japanese American women are married to U.S.-born white husbands, compared to 42.1 percent of foreign-born Japanese American women who are married to U.S.-born white husbands. (The latter group of women are mainly G.I. war brides.) The opposite is true for Filipino Americans. The general figures by race alone in Tables 3 and 4 indicate that 10.6 percent of Filipino American men are married to white wives, compared to 18.3 percent of Filipino American women who are married to white husbands. Controlling for nativity, however, Tables 5 and 6 show that U.S.-born Filipino American men are significantly more likely to marry white women than foreign-born Filipino American men (33.2 percent for U.S.-born Filipino American men compared to 6.0 percent for foreign-born). Likewise, U.S.-born Filipino American women are also more likely to marry whites than the foreign-born (33.3 percent versus 15.0 percent).

For those populations where we have both U.S.-born and foreign-born categories, in all instances, U.S.-born Asian American men intermarry more than the foreign-born. The same pattern holds for U.S.-born Asian American women, except for Japanese Americans. We hypothesize that for the Japanese Americans, the difference is due to the large number of military wives who have come to the United States. Between 1947 and 1977, a total of 69,699 Japanese wives of U.S. servicemen entered the United States.[28] With over 36 percent of Asian Americans living in California in 1980, it means that there are a significant proportion of G.I. wives in

TABLE 5

**Husband's Race/Ethnicity and Nativity by Wife's Race/Ethnicity and Nativity in Percentages
Whites and Asian Americans, California, 1980**

Wife's Race/Ethnicity And Nativity	Husband's Race/Ethnicity and Nativity: U.S.-born White*	U.S.-born Chinese	Foreign-born Chinese	U.S.-born Japanese	Foreign-born Japanese	U.S.-born Filipino	Foreign-born Filipino	Foreign-born Korean	Foreign-born Asian Indian	Foreign-born Vietnamese
U.S.-born White*	**90.0**	11.3	2.3	9.9	6.0	33.2	6.0	1.4	6.6	1.1
U.S.-born Chinese	0.1	**48.8**	6.3	1.5	0.2	0.5	0.2	0.1	0.0	0.0
Foreign-born Chinese	0.1	26.9	**87.6**	0.8	0.2	0.0	0.3	0.2	0.0	0.8
U.S.-born Japanese	0.2	5.2	0.8	**69.1**	23.8	1.9	0.2	0.3	0.2	0.0
Foreign-born Japanese	0.4	0.9	0.5	12.9	**65.5**	0.9	0.5	0.1	0.2	0.2
U.S.-born Filipino	0.1	0.9	0.0	0.3	0.0	**21.5**	3.7	0.0	0.2	0.0
Foreign-born Filipino	0.3	0.9	0.6	0.2	0.3	18.5	**82.2**	0.5	0.8	0.0
Foreign-born Korean	0.1	0.4	0.4	0.7	0.6	0.5	0.3	**95.9**	0.2	0.2
Foreign-born Asian Indian	0.0	0.0	0.0	0.1	0.0	0.0	0.0	0.0	**84.2**	0.0
Foreign-born Vietnamese	0.1	0.1	0.3	0.1	0.0	0.2	0.1	0.3	0.0	**96.0**
Other Race/Ethnicity	8.6	4.6	1.2	4.4	3.4	22.8	6.5	1.2	7.6	1.7
Total	100%	100%	100%	100%	100%	100%	100%	100%	100%	100%
N	156,597	763	2,410	1,990	664	428	2,740	930	603	528

Sources: 1980 U.S. Census Bureau 5-percent Public User Microdata Sample (PUMS) and special unpublished tabulations of the Asian American population.
*Non-Hispanic White

TABLE 6

Wife's Race/Ethnicity and Nativity by Husband's Race/Ethnicity and Nativity in Percentages Whites and Asian Americans, California, 1980

Husband's Race/Ethnicity And Nativity	Wife's Race/Ethnicity and Nativity: U.S.-born White*	U.S.-born Chinese	Foreign-born Chinese	U.S.-born Japanese	Foreign-born Japanese	U.S.-born Filipino	Foreign-born Filipino	Foreign-born Korean	Foreign-born Asian Indian	Foreign-born Vietnamese
U.S.-born White*	**91.3**	17.1	6.6	14.4	42.1	33.3	15.0	15.9	2.6	13.2
U.S.-born Chinese	0.1	**51.3**	8.0	2.0	0.5	1.5	0.2	0.3	0.0	0.2
Foreign-born Chinese	0.0	21.0	**82.4**	1.0	0.8	0.2	0.5	0.8	0.0	1.1
U.S.-born Japanese	0.1	4.1	0.6	**69.2**	17.4	1.1	0.1	1.2	0.2	0.3
Foreign-born Japanese	0.0	0.1	0.0	8.0	**29.4**	0.0	0.1	0.3	0.0	0.0
U.S.-born Filipino	0.1	0.3	0.0	0.4	0.3	**19.9**	2.7	0.2	0.0	0.2
Foreign-born Filipino	0.1	0.8	0.4	0.3	0.9	22.0	**75.7**	0.7	0.0	0.5
Foreign-born Korean	0.0	0.1	0.1	0.2	0.1	0.0	0.2	**74.8**	0.0	0.5
Foreign-born Asian Indian	0.0	0.0	0.0	0.1	0.1	0.2	0.2	0.1	**93.0**	0.0
Foreign-born Vietnamese	0.0	0.0	0.2	0.0	0.1	0.0	0.0	0.1	0.0	**80.7**
Other Race/Ethnicity	8.3	5.2	1.7	4.4	8.3	21.8	5.3	5.6	4.2	3.3
Total	100%	100%	100%	100%	100%	100%	100%	100%	100%	100%
N	154,440	725	2,560	1,987	1,479	463	2,976	1,193	546	628

Sources: 1980 U.S. Census Bureau 5-percent Public User Microdata Sample (PUMS) and special unpublished tabulations of the Asian American population.
*Non-Hispanic White

California. To see whether our hypothesis is valid, we next analyze the veteran status of the husbands of Asian American women.

The Effects of Husband's Veteran Status

Comparing the breakdowns by nativity status in Tables 7 and 8, we observe that the probability of foreign-born Asian American women being intermarried is greater if their husbands are in the military or are veterans. Note that 67.9 percent of the foreign-born Japanese American women are married to veterans who are U.S.-born whites, compared to 10.9 percent of foreign-born Japanese American women who are married to non-veterans who are white. The same pattern appears among Korean American women: 44.8 percent of foreign-born Korean American women are married to veterans who are U.S.-born whites, compared to 4.1 percent of foreign-born Korean American women who are married to non-veterans who are white. However, we did not discern this fact before Tables 7 and 8 because of the significantly smaller number of Korean American women who are intermarried compared to those who are intramarried. Given the continuing immigration of Koreans to the United States, the 37,063 Korean American women who married U.S. servicemen between 1947 and 1977 are dwarfed by the large number of Korean American women who have Korean American husbands.[29]

Among the Asian American women married to veterans, the proportion of foreign-born women who are intermarried is greater than that of the U.S.-born. The exception to this pattern is among Filipino American women, of whom a larger proportion of U.S.-born than the foreign-born are married to white veterans. For Asian American women married to non-veterans, the opposite pattern holds:

TABLE 7

White and Asian American Wives of Veterans in California, 1980
Wife's Race/Ethnicity and Nativity by Husband's Race/Ethnicity and Nativity

Husband's Race/Ethnicity And Nativity	Wife's Race/Ethnicity and Nativity: U.S.-born White*	U.S.-born Chinese	Foreign-born Chinese	U.S.-born Japanese	Foreign-born Japanese	U.S.-born Filipino	Foreign-born Filipino	Foreign-born Korean	Foreign-born Asian-Indian	Foreign-born Vietnamese
U.S.-born White*	**93.4**	18.1	27.4	15.4	67.9	41.1	27.0	44.8	25.0	35.8
U.S.-born Chinese	0.0	**57.5**	20.0	1.6	0.7	1.0	0.2	0.6	0.0	0.6
Foreign-born Chinese	0.1	14.4	**45.7**	0.4	0.4	0.0	0.1	0.9	0.0	1.1
U.S.-born Japanese	0.0	3.6	1.9	**76.1**	15.6	1.6	0.1	3.2	0.0	0.6
Foreign-born Japanese	0.0	0.3	0.0	2.3	**2.8**	0.0	0.1	0.9	0.0	0.0
U.S.-born Filipino	0.1	0.3	0.0	0.4	0.5	**19.3**	2.6	0.6	0.0	0.0
Foreign-born Filipino	0.0	0.3	1.0	0.3	1.0	19.8	**63.0**	2.0	0.0	0.6
Foreign-born Korean	0.0	0.0	0.0	0.0	0.0	0.0	0.0	**30.6**	0.0	0.0
Foreign-born Asian Indian	0.0	0.0	0.0	0.0	0.0	0.0	0.0	0.0	**50.0**	0.0
Foreign-born Vietnamese	0.0	0.0	0.2	0.0	0.0	0.0	0.0	0.0	0.0	**53.1**
Other Race/Ethnicity	6.4	5.5	3.8	3.5	11.1	17.2	6.9	16.4	25.0	8.2
Total	100%	100%	100%	100%	100%	100%	100%	100%	100%	100%
N	81,128	332	420	938	810	192	1,346	346	36	179

Source: 1980 U.S. Census Bureau 5-percent Public User Microdata Sample (PUMS) and special unpublished tabulations of the Asian American population.
*Non-Hispanic White

TABLE 8

White and Asian American Wives of Non-Veterans in California, 1980
Wife's Race/Ethnicity and Nativity by Husband's Race/Ethnicity and Nativity

Husband's Race/Ethnicity And Nativity	Wife's Race/Ethnicity and Nativity: U.S.-born White*	U.S.-born Chinese	Foreign-born Chinese	U.S.-born Japanese	Foreign-born Japanese	U.S.-born Filipino	Foreign-born Filipino	Foreign-born Korean	Foreign-born Asian-Indian	Foreign-born Vietnamese
U.S.-born White*	**88.9**	16.3	2.6	13.5	10.9	27.7	5.2	4.1	1.0	4.2
U.S.-born Chinese	0.1	**46.1**	5.7	2.4	0.1	1.8	0.2	0.1	0.0	0.0
Foreign-born Chinese	0.1	26.5	**89.6**	1.5	1.3	0.4	0.9	0.8	0.0	1.1
U.S.-born Japanese	0.2	4.6	0.4	**63.0**	19.6	0.7	0.2	0.4	0.2	0.2
Foreign-born Japanese	0.0	0.0	0.0	13.0	**61.6**	0.0	0.1	0.1	0.0	0.0
U.S.-born Filipino	0.1	0.3	0.0	0.4	0.0	**20.3**	2.7	0.0	0.0	0.2
Foreign-born Filipino	0.1	1.3	0.2	0.3	0.7	23.6	**86.1**	0.1	0.0	0.4
Foreign-born Korean	0.0	0.3	0.1	0.3	0.1	0.0	0.3	**92.8**	0.0	0.7
Foreign-born Asian Indian	0.1	0.0	0.0	0.0	0.1	0.4	0.3	0.1	**96.1**	0.0
Foreign-born Vietnamese	0.0	0.0	0.1	0.0	0.1	0.0	0.0	0.0	0.0	**91.8**
Other Race/Ethnicity	10.4	4.6	1.3	5.6	5.5	25.1	4.0	1.5	2.7	1.4
Total	100%	100%	100%	100%	100%	100%	100%	100%	100%	100%
N	73,312	393	2,140	1,049	669	271	1,630	847	510	449

Source: 1980 U.S. Census Bureau 5-percent Public User Microdata Sample (PUMS) and special unpublished tabulations of the Asian American population.
*Non-Hispanic White

it is more likely that a U.S.-born Asian American wife, than a foreign-born Asian American wife, is intermarried. Thus the veteran status of the husband of an Asian American woman does indeed make a difference.

We now turn our attention to selected socioeconomic characteristics of individuals and their marriage patterns as shown in Tables 9 through 12. Table 9 highlights the characteristics of U.S.-born white and Asian American husbands; Table 10 depicts the characteristics of U.S.-born white and Asian American wives; Table 11 shows those of foreign-born Asian American husbands; while Table 12 presents those of foreign-born Asian American wives. Hereafter, these aggregate summary characteristics tables will be referred to as the "summary tables."

Age as a Proxy for Generation

One of the major tenets of the assimilationist model is that each successive generation in the United States is more likely to intermarry into the general population than the previous generation. Since nativity is not equivalent to generational cohorts, it is somewhat difficult to discern whether this is true or not. The census does not contain data on immigrant generation, so we will use age as a proxy for generation. Because nativity can only differentiate between U.S.-born and foreign-born, it has limited utility in helping us understand generational marriage patterns. Given what we know about a particular population's immigration history, we can use age ranges to study the effects of generation on the marriage patterns of that specific population.

We analyze only the data for Japanese Americans because the composition of this ethnic group has not been complicated by recent immigration, with the exception of G.I. war brides. Japanese Americans have traditionally been differentiated into four generations: *Issei*, *Nisei*, *Sansei*, and*Yonsei*. Thus, it is fairly accurate to use age ranges as proxies for generation.[30]

The summary tables show the husband's race/ethnicity by age range (in percentages). Let us assume that in California in 1980 that the *Yonsei* generation of Japanese Americans is between the ages of 0-25, *Sansei* 25-45, *Nisei* 45-65, and *Issei* 65+. The tables confirm that each successive generation in the United States is indeed more likely to intermarry than the preceding generation.

Among U.S.-born Japanese American men, intermarriages of the *Nisei* and *Sansei* are primarily to whites. Our data, which support the findings of Montero, Gurak and Fitzpatrick, and Kitano et. al., show that interethnic and interracial marriages tend to increase with the amount of time a population has resided in the United States.[31]

By comparing the *Nisei* age category with the *Sansei*, the age distributions at the top of Tables 9 and 10 shows that the proportion of interethnically married *Sansei* increases at a faster rate than interracially married *Sansei*, though more *Sansei* are interracially married in absolute numbers than are interethnically married *Sansei*. Among Japanese American women, each successive generation exhibits a greater proportion of interracial marriages than found among Japanese American men. Among Japanese American men, each successive generation shows a greater proportion of interethnic marriages than among Japanese American women. Interethnic

TABLE 9

Selected Characteristics of U.S.-born White* and U.S.-born Asian American Husbands In Percentages California, 1980

Characteristic	White IT	White IR	Chinese IT	Chinese IE	Chinese IR	Japanese IT	Japanese IE	Japanese IR	Filipino IT	Filipino IE	Filipino IR
	Race/Ethnicity and Marriage Pattern**										
Marriage Pattern											
Percentage	94.1	5.9	75.6	9.6	14.8	82.0	4.6	13.4	40.0	6.1	54.0
Count	147431	9166	577	73	113	1632	92	266	171	26	231
Age											
00-18	.1	.1	0	0	0	0	0	0	0	0	0
18-25	6.0	10.5	2.6	5.5	7.1	1.2	5.4	11.3	10.5	3.8	17.7
25-30	10.1	16.0	11.1	19.2	15.9	3.5	12.0	21.4	15.2	19.2	25.1
30-35	11.8	17.4	11.3	28.8	20.4	7.2	25.0	13.9	19.9	19.2	21.6
35-40	10.4	14.2	10.4	4.1	15.0	7.4	12.0	16.2	11.7	23.1	13.9
40-45	8.9	10.5	9.9	11.0	13.3	9.8	14.1	9.0	11.7	11.5	10.8
45-50	8.9	9.8	13.7	16.4	6.2	14.2	12.0	10.2	8.8	11.5	6.5
50-55	9.8	8.0	16.5	9.5	11.5	17.0	10.9	8.6	12.3	7.7	2.2
55-60	10.6	5.5	11.1	1.4	7.1	20.2	5.4	5.3	5.8	3.8	1.8
60-65	8.8	4.0	6.8	1.4	.9	12.4	2.2	3.4	1.8	0	0
65+	14.6	4.0	6.6	2.6	2.6	7.1	1.0	.7	2.3	.2	.4
Mean Age	47.7	40.1	46.3	38.8	40.0	51.0	40.2	38.3	39.4	38.0	33.7
Spouse's Mean Age	45.0	37.4	42.7	36.3	36.0	47.6	36.6	35.4	36.7	35.6	30.8
Educational Level											
High School or Less	46.3	45.3	28.2	19.2	19.5	44.6	29.3	27.1	45.0	50.0	46.3
Some College	25.5	30.6	23.9	27.4	27.4	23.7	31.5	32.7	33.3	30.8	41.6
4-5 Years College	17.3	15.3	30.2	31.5	31.9	21.7	23.9	26.7	17.0	3.8	8.7
Graduate/Professional	11.0	8.8	17.7	21.9	21.2	10.0	15.2	13.5	4.7	15.4	3.5
Mean Educational Level											
# Years of Education	14.9	14.9	16.6	17.3	17.3	15.7	16.7	16.6	15.2	15.8	15.0
Spouse's Educational Level											
High School or Less	55.5	60.0	38.6	26.0	35.4	53.4	40.2	44.0	50.3	57.7	63.6
Some College	27.6	27.3	27.0	32.9	36.3	26.7	25.0	33.5	29.2	26.9	30.7
4-5 Years College	13.1	8.3	26.0	27.4	18.6	16.3	28.3	18.4	18.1	7.7	5.2
Graduate/Professional	3.8	3.4	8.3	13.7	9.7	3.6	6.5	4.1	2.3	7.7	0.4
Spouse's Mean Educational Level											
# Years of Education	14.9	14.4	15.3	16.6	16.0	15.2	15.5	15.2	14.8	14.9	14.3
Location in Labor Force											
Employed Civilian	75.2	81.6	87.7	94.5	88.5	91.7	92.4	92.5	83.6	80.8	87.9
Unemployed Civilian	2.4	3.4	.9	0	2.7	.7	1.1	1.9	4.1	3.8	3.0
Employed Military	2.0	5.3	.3	2.7	.9	.4	2.2	.8	6.4	15.4	4.3
Not in Labor Force	20.4	9.7	11.1	2.7	8.0	7.2	4.3	4.9	5.8	0	4.8
Spouse's Location In Labor Force											
Employed Civilian	45.4	53.3	64.3	52.1	62.8	65.5	58.7	64.3	67.8	57.7	61.0
Unemployed Civilian	2.1	3.4	2.3	4.1	1.8	1.3	3.3	2.6	6.4	7.7	5.2
Employed Military	.1	.1	0	0	0	.1	0	0	.6	3.8	.4
Not in Labor Force	52.5	43.1	33.4	43.8	35.4	33.0	38.0	33.1	25.1	30.0	33.3

Sources: 1980 U.S. Census Bureau 5% Public User Microdata Sample (PUMS) for California and unpublished tabulations of the Asian American population.

*Non-Hispanic White **IT = Intramarriage IE = Interethnic Marriage IR = Interracial Marriage

[a]U.S.-born Non-Hispanic White Household Income [b]U.S.-born Non-Hispanic White Male Income

TABLE 9

Selected Characteristics of U.S.-born White* and U.S.-born Asian American Husbands In Percentages California, 1980 (Continued)

	Race/Ethnicity and Marriage Pattern**										
	White		Chinese			Japanese			Filipino		
Characteristic	IT	IR	IT	IE	IR	IT	IE	IR	IT	IE	IR
Occupational Position											
Managerial	19.7	15.1	19.4	23.2	20.0	14.3	12.9	12.6	10.5	4.8	10.3
Professional	16.2	13.8	27.5	27.5	28.0	20.3	18.8	25.2	10.5	19.0	4.7
Technical/Sales/Clerical	21.6	22.6	28.7	20.3	23.0	22.6	25.5	22.0	29.4	9.5	22.2
Blue Collar	42.5	48.5	24.5	29.0	29.0	43.0	42.4	40.2	49.7	66.7	62.6
Spouse's Occupational Position											
Managerial	11.7	9.2	12.3	15.8	14.9	7.2	11.1	11.8	6.5	0	6.6
Professional	16.9	12.0	18.7	28.9	23.9	13.8	18.5	19.5	10.3	14.3	6.6
Technical/Sales/Clerical	51.4	48.3	50.1	44.7	38.8	53.3	50.0	50.3	43.0	64.3	55.1
Blue Collar	20.1	30.4	18.9	10.5	22.4	25.7	20.4	18.3	40.2	21.4	31.6
Mean Household Income in 1979											
Dollars	28587	26779	34798	33770	30145	33940	31195	30234	26565	28513	25110
Ratio to White HH Income[a]	1.00	.94	1.22	1.18	1.05	1.19	1.09	1.06	.93	1.00	.88
Distribution of Household Income In Quintiles ($1000)											
Bottom Fifth	9.65	10.01	14.89	22.16	14.01	15.61	11.49	13.52	11.41	15.15	9.57
Second Fifth	18.32	18.36	24.77	26.71	22.87	25.18	21.22	20.86	19.01	21.01	17.31
Third Fifth (Median Income)	25.60	24.62	32.21	32.00	29.01	32.22	29.79	27.79	24.01	24.36	22.81
Fourth Fifth	34.06	32.01	40.73	36.57	33.83	40.02	39.41	34.51	32.33	33.16	30.01
Top Fifth	51.68	45.60	59.52	50.10	48.61	54.43	50.37	49.57	44.55	43.32	41.52
Number of Spouses Working	1.23	1.40	1.52	1.49	1.52	1.58	1.53	1.58	1.58	1.58	1.54
Mean Individual Earnings in 1979											
Dollars	18652	18089	21223	22716	22013	20569	22998	20775	15509	17093	17100
Ratio to White Male Income[b]	1.00	.97	1.14	1.22	1.18	1.0	1.23	1.11	.83	.92	.92
Spouse's Individual Earnings in 1979											
Dollars	4556	5309	7862	7729	5844	7117	7135	7284	6474	8204	5444
Ratio to White Male Income[b]	.24	.28	.42	.41	.31	.38	.38	.39	.35	.44	.29
Family Structure											
Nuclear Family without Children	44.7	39.1	30.7	28.8	35.4	32.0	29.3	33.5	18.1	15.4	19.9
Nuclear Family with Children	48.8	59.3	63.3	60.3	55.8	60.6	65.2	54.4	64.9	76.9	71.0
Extended Family	6.5	9.1	6.1	11.0	8.8	7.4	5.4	7.1	17.0	7.7	9.1
Mean Total Number Of Workers in Household	1.62	1.78	2.13	1.90	1.89	2.13	1.87	1.84	2.23	2.00	1.96
Work Status											
Full Time	80.0	81.2	85.5	88.9	84.0	85.8	90.1	85.3	80.9	73.1	80.2
Part Time	20.0	18.8	14.5	11.1	16.0	14.2	9.9	14.7	19.1	26.9	19.8
Spouse's Work Status											
Full TIme	43.2	46.9	54.1	58.0	44.9	53.0	50.8	52.4	52.7	57.1	45.6
Part Time	56.8	53.1	45.9	42.0	55.1	47.0	49.2	47.6	47.3	42.9	54.4

Sources: 1980 U.S. Census Bureau 5% Public User Microdata Sample (PUMS) for California and unpublished tabulations of the Asian American population.

*Non-Hispanic White **IT = Intramarriage IE = Interethnic Marriage IR = Interracial Marriage

[a]U.S.-born Non-Hispanic White Household Income [b]U.S.-born Non-Hispanic White Male Income

TABLE 10

Selected Characteristics of U.S.-born White* and U.S.-born Asian American Wives In Percentages California, 1980

	Race/Ethnicity and Marriage Pattern**										
	White		Chinese			Japanese			Filipino		
Characteristic	IT	IR	IT	IE	IR	IT	IE	IR	IT	IE	IR
Marriage Pattern											
Percentage	95.0	5.0	72.3	6.5	21.2	77.2	5.1	17.8	41.9	5.0	53.1
Count	146699	7741	524	47	154	1533	101	353	194	23	246
Age											
00-18	.4	1.2	0	0	0	.1	0	0	0	0	.8
18-25	9.8	21.9	5.0	2.1	9.1	2.7	8.9	20.4	13.4	21.7	24.4
25-30	11.6	20.1	15.6	25.5	28.6	5.9	23.8	22.9	15.5	26.1	23.2
30-35	12.4	17.1	21.2	27.7	32.5	9.3	20.8	19.0	17.5	17.4	28.9
35-40	10.2	12.2	10.5	10.6	7.1	9.9	17.8	11.0	7.7	4.3	9.8
40-45	8.7	7.7	11.3	10.6	5.8	10.8	8.9	7.1	10.8	13.0	4.9
45-50	8.6	6.1	13.5	8.6	8.4	15.5	8.9	6.5	11.9	8.7	3.7
50-55	9.8	4.6	12.6	8.6	1.9	16.8	5.9	8.2	11.9	8.7	3.3
55-60	9.8	4.0	10.9	6.4	4.5	17.0	2.0	4.0	6.2	0	.4
60-65	7.8	2.6	5.3	0	.6	9.2	2.0	.3	3.6	0	.4
65+	11.0	2.6	3.1	0	1.3	4.4	1.0	.6	1.5	0	.4
Mean Age	45.0	35.4	43.5	37.5	35.0	48.3	36.5	35.0	40.0	33.9	31.7
Spouse's Mean Age	47.8	38.7	46.6	40.0	37.6	51.7	39.1	37.5	44.4	36.0	33.9
Educational Level											
High School or Less	54.4	58.3	35.3	31.9	25.3	52.9	33.7	30.0	52.6	47.8	58.9
Some College	27.5	28.0	29.6	34.0	25.3	27.3	25.7	33.1	32.0	43.5	30.9
4-5 Years College	13.2	10.3	26.1	31.9	30.5	16.2	29.7	27.2	13.9	8.7	8.5
Graduate/Professional	3.9	3.4	9.0	2.1	18.8	3.6	10.9	9.6	1.5	0	1.6
Mean Educational Level											
# Years of Education	14.9	14.8	15.8	16.2	16.9	15.1	16.4	16.4	14.7	14.7	14.7
Spouse's Educational Level											
High School or Less	46.6	48.7	28.6	21.3	18.8	46.2	23.8	26.1	42.3	39.1	48.0
Some College	25.3	29.9	22.7	29.8	27.3	21.5	24.8	31.2	33.5	34.8	32.9
4-5 Years College	17.2	13.0	29.6	29.8	27.3	21.9	28.7	25.2	19.1	17.4	13.4
Graduate/Professional	10.9	8.3	19.1	19.1	26.6	10.5	22.8	17.6	5.2	8.7	5.7
Spouse's Mean Educational Level											
# Years of Education	15.4	15.1	16.6	17.3	17.4	15.7	16.9	16.9	15.0	15.3	15.2
Location in Labor Force											
Employed Civilian	45.3	54.6	66.0	66.0	72.1	66.5	61.4	72.0	66.0	60.9	67.5
Unemployed Civilian	2.1	3.6	1.1	2.1	.6	1.2	2.0	1.1	6.7	4.3	4.5
Employed Military	.1	.2	0	2.1	0	.1	0	0	.5	0	.4
Not in Labor Force	52.6	41.6	32.8	29.8	27.3	32.1	36.6	26.9	26.8	34.8	27.6
Spouse's Location In Labor Force											
Employed Civilian	74.9	83.6	86.5	93.6	92.9	90.0	94.1	88.7	88.4	91.3	84.1
Unemployed Civilian	2.4	4.6	.8	0	1.3	.6	2.0	3.1	3.1	4.3	4.1
Employed Military	1.9	2.1	.2	4.3	.6	.1	2.0	2.8	3.6	0	4.9
Not in Labor Force	20.8	9.7	12.6	2.1	5.2	9.3	2.0	5.4	12.9	4.3	6.9

Sources: 1980 U.S. Census Bureau 5% Public User Microdata Sample (PUMS) for California and unpublished tabulations of the Asian American population.

*Non-Hispanic White **IT = Intramarriage IE = Interethnic Marriage IR = Interracial Marriage

[a]U.S.-born Non-Hispanic White Household Income [b]U.S.-born Non-Hispanic White Male Income

TABLE 10

Selected Characteristics of U.S.-born White* and U.S.-born Asian American Wives in Percentages California, 1980 (Continued)

	Race/Ethnicity and Marriage Pattern**										
	White		Chinese			Japanese			Filipino		
Characteristic	IT	IR	IT	IE	IR	IT	IE	IR	IT	IE	IR
Occupational Position											
Managerial	10.3	8.6	11.7	5.6	11.2	7.6	9.3	13.2	8.5	13.3	10.4
Professional	16.1	12.0	18.9	25.0	32.0	14.4	21.3	24.2	7.8	6.7	6.9
Technical/Sales/Clerical	51.8	52.8	55.7	52.8	42.2	53.9	56.0	48.0	54.3	66.7	58.4
Blue Collar	21.9	26.6	13.7	16.7	8.6	24.1	13.3	14.7	29.5	13.3	24.3
Spouse's Occupational Position											
Managerial	19.1	13.6	21.6	23.3	17.8	13.2	24.6	17.7	11.9	35.7	11.4
Professional	16.2	13.0	24.9	26.7	30.8	20.6	24.6	23.0	10.9	7.1	10.8
Technical/Sales/Clerical	22.4	19.6	26.7	26.7	20.6	23.1	18.0	23.4	22.0	28.6	24.1
Blue Collar	42.3	53.8	26.7	23.3	30.8	43.2	32.8	35.9	55.9	28.6	53.8
Mean Household Income in 1979											
Dollars	28517	24891	35193	32341	33509	34121	32190	33132	26137	25791	25021
Ratio of White HH Income[a]	1.00	.87	1.23	1.13	1.17	1.19	1.13	1.15	.91	.90	.88
Distribution of Household Income In Quintiles ($1000)											
Bottom Fifth	9.58	8.91	16.36	16.64	15.50	15.01	15.42	15.01	9.40	7.71	11.62
Second Fifth	18.21	16.76	25.42	22.05	25.11	25.34	25.36	22.53	17.69	20.01	18.21
Third Fifth (Median HH Income)	25.51	23.01	33.01	26.27	31.33	32.69	32.00	30.01	24.02	24.01	23.01
Fourth Fifth	34.02	29.84	41.02	37.10	39.16	40.51	37.56	38.63	31.01	30.73	30.01
Top Fifth	51.62	42.54	59.21	55.69	56.59	54.57	50.28	56.52	46.43	47.89	40.12
Number of Spouses Working	1.22	1.41	1.53	1.66	1.66	1.57	1.57	1.63	1.51	1.52	1.67
Mean Individual Earnings in 1979											
Dollars	4546	5301	8015	8649	9799	7340	7083	9276	6445	6291	7124
Ratio of White Male Income[b]	.24	.28	.43	.46	.53	.39	.38	.50	.35	.34	.38
Spouse's Individual Earnings in 1979											
Dollars	18558	16704	21475	21806	21542	20091	21890	21730	13036	16160	14525
Ratio of White Male Income[b]	1.00	.90	1.15	1.17	1.16	1.08	1.17	1.17	.70	.87	.78
Family Structure											
Nuclear Family without Children	44.8	29.3	30.7	27.7	42.2	34.3	23.8	43.1	13.0	13.0	22.8
Nuclear Family with Children	48.7	62.4	64.1	68.1	51.9	57.9	71.3	49.9	52.9	78.3	65.0
Extended Family	6.5	8.3	5.2	4.3	5.8	7.8	5.0	7.1	34.1	8.7	12.2
Mean Total Number Of Workers in Household	1.61	1.79	2.10	1.94	1.90	2.13	1.85	1.91	2.21	2.04	1.89
Work Status											
Full Time	43.1	45.8	56.2	50.0	58.1	53.4	50.7	56.8	57.4	60.0	59.7
Part Time	56.9	54.2	53.8	50.0	41.9	46.6	49.3	43.2	42.6	401.0	40.3
Spouse's Work Status											
Full Time	77.7	79.5	85.4	91.3	78.2	84.5	79.8	85.5	74.9	86.4	80.6
Part Time	22.3	20.5	14.6	8.7	21.8	15.5	20.2	14.5	25.1	13.6	19.4

Sources: 1980 U.S. Census Bureau 5% Public User Microdata Sample (PUMS) for California and unpublished tabulations of the Asian American population.

*Non-Hispanic White **IT = Intramarriage IE = Interethnic Marriage IR = Interracial Marriage

[a]U.S.-born Non-Hispanic White Household Income [b]U.S.-born Non-Hispanic White Male Income

TABLE 11
Selected Characteristics of Foreign-born Asian American Husbands in Percentages
California, 1980

Characteristic	Chinese IT	Chinese IE	Chinese IR	Japanese IT	Japanese IE**	Japanese IR	Filipino IT	Filipino IE	Filipino IR	Korean IT	Korean IE**	Korean IR**	Asian Indian IT	Asian Indian IE**	Asian Indian IR	Vietnamese IT	Vietnamese IE**	Vietnamese IR**
Marriage Pattern																		
Percentage	93.9	2.9	3.2	89.3	1.2	9.5	85.9	2.0	12.1	96.6	1.6	1.8	85.6	1.8	12.6	96.6	1.1	23
Count	2262	70	78	593	8	63	2354	54	332	898	15	17	516	11	76	510	6	12
Age																		
00-18	0	0	0	0	0	0	0	0	0	0	0	0	0	0	0	0	0	0
18-25	1.3	2.6	3.8	2.0	25.0	11.1	2.6	1.9	7.8	1.8	0	0	2.7	9.1	3.9	6.9	0	50.0
25-30	10.6	15.7	21.8	10.0	37.5	30.2	21.1	9.3	10.5	9.5	0	35.3	11.0	9.1	23.7	17.5	66.6	25.0
30-35	14.4	28.6	15.4	19.7	25.0	23.8	18.9	16.7	11.1	19.3	26.7	17.6	25.8	18.2	17.1	16.5	16.7	8.0
35-40	12.6	10.0	17.9	16.9	0	12.7	16.1	11.1	8.7	21.5	26.7	17.6	24.2	45.4	19.7	15.9	16.7	17.0
40-45	14.5	7.1	17.9	11.5	12.5	15.9	13.1	13.0	6.0	22.5	26.7	23.6	12.2	18.2	14.4	14.9	0	0
45-50	12.4	15.7	9.0	7.9	0	1.6	8.0	13.0	6.6	9.8	6.7	0	12.0	0	3.9	12.0	0	0
50-55	8.4	8.6	6.4	5.9	0	1.6	8.2	18.3	6.6	6.0	6.7	0	5.4	0	9.2	8.0	0	0
55-60	9.2	7.1	2.6	4.4	0	0	4.9	0	1.5	4.0	6.5	0	3.1	0	5.3	4.7	0	0
60-65	5.7	0	2.6	3.3	0	1.6	3.9	3.7	2.0	2.4	0	0	1.5	0	0	2.0	0	0
65+	10.9	4.3	2.6	18.4	0	1.5	12.2	13.0	39.2	3.2	0	5.9	2.1	0	2.7	1.4	0	0
Mean Age	46.4	40.5	39.4	46.6	30.1	36.1	44.2	46.0	51.6	41.5	41.1	36.2	39.6	35.5	39.0	40.0	30.7	27.6
Spouse's Mean Age	41.9	36.7	35.1	42.3	30.0	31.0	40.0	39.6	44.0	37.5	36.6	30.9	34.7	33.1	36.2	35.2	30.8	25.4
Educational Level																		
High School or Less	45.5	30.0	17.9	38.8	25.0	30.2	33.4	38.9	60.5	25.9	13.3	5.9	36.2	9.1	7.9	40.2	33.3	16.7
Some College	12.7	30.0	21.8	13.7	50.0	34.9	24.8	33.3	20.5	13.7	13.3	23.5	10.1	9.1	13.2	34.3	33.3	50.0
4-5 Years College	19.6	24.3	24.4	35.1	12.5	22.2	33.4	16.7	11.1	42.8	53.3	52.9	19.4	27.3	25.0	13.7	0	25.0
Graduate/Professional	22.2	15.7	35.9	12.5	12.5	12.7	8.4	11.1	7.8	17.6	30.0	17.6	44.4	54.5	53.9	11.8	33.3	8.3

(Column groups: Race/Ethnicity and Marriage Pattern*)

TABLE 11
Selected Characteristics of Foreign-born Asian American Husbands in Percentages
California, 1980 (Continued)

	Race/Ethnicity and Marriage Pattern*																	
	Chinese			Japanese			Filipino			Korean			Asian Indian			Vietnamese		
Characteristic	IT	IE	IR	IT	IE**	IR	IT	IE	IR	IT	IE**	IR**	IT	IE**	IR	IT	IE**	IR**
Mean Educational Level																		
# Years of Education	13.0	16.1	15.6	15.0	13.9	13.9	16.0	16.7	14.2	15.2	14.0	13.1	15.0	19.0	15.2	12.6	11.9	13.0
Spouse's Educational Level																		
High School or Less	56.4	35.7	35.9	50.6	87.5	41.3	29.1	66.7	73.5	45.9	40.0	23.5	41.3	18.2	27.6	63.9	33.3	58.3
Some College	15.8	28.6	28.2	30.4	0	41.3	19.3	16.7	19.3	18.3	26.7	47.1	20.3	9.1	38.2	27.1	16.7	25.0
4-5 Years College	19.0	31.4	24.4	17.4	12.5	11.1	44.0	13.0	6.0	32.3	32.3	17.1	22.5	45.5	13.2	6.3	16.7	16.7
Graduate/Professional	8.8	4.3	11.5	1.7	0	16.3	7.7	3.7	1.2	3.6	0	11.8	15.9	27.3	21.1	2.7	33.3	0
Spouse's Mean Educational level																		
# Years of Education	13.1	15.1	16.1	15.2	15.5	15.2	16.0	13.8	12.7	15.2	15.3	16.1	15.0	18.2	16.4	12.6	14.7	14.6
Location in Labor Force																		
Employed Civilian	80.0	87.1	92.3	82.5	75.0	90.5	74.6	79.6	59.6	87.2	86.7	82.4	89.3	90.9	94.7	66.3	83.3	83.3
Unemployed Civilian	1.7	0	1.3	.2	0	3.2	2.3	0	4.2	2.8	6.7	0	4.1	9.1	1.3	5.3	0	16.7
Employed Military	.1	1.4	1.3	.3	25.0	3.2	11.0	7.4	4.8	.6	0	11.8	.4	0	0	.4	0	0
Not in Labor Force	18.2	11.4	5.1	17.0	0	3.2	12.0	13.0	31.3	9.5	6.7	5.9	6.2	0	3.9	28.0	16.7	0
Spouse's Location In Labor Force																		
Employed Civilian	56.8	60.0	48.7	34.2	62.5	42.5	77.5	70.4	42.8	62.1	53.3	35.3	45.9	72.7	66.6	46.9	50.0	50.0
Unemployed Civilian	3.6	4.3	2.6	1.0	0	6.3	3.2	0	4.2	1.7	0	0	7.9	9.1	5.3	3.7	0	0
Employed Military	0	0	0	0	0	0	.2	0	0	0	0	0	0	0	0	0	0	0
Not in Labor Force	37.7	35.7	48.7	64.8	37.5	50.8	19.1	29.6	53.0	36.2	46.7	64.7	46.1	18.2	38.2	49.4	50.0	50.0

TABLE 11
Selected Characteristics of Foreign-born Asian American Husbands in Percentages
California, 1980 (Continued)

Characteristic	Chinese IT	Chinese IE	Chinese IR	Japanese IT	Japanese IE**	Japanese IR	Filipino IT	Filipino IE	Filipino IR	Korean IT	Korean IE**	Korean IR**	Asian Indian IT	Asian Indian IE**	Asian Indian IR	Vietnamese IT	Vietnamese IE**	Vietnamese IR**
	Race / Ethnicity and Marriage Pattern*																	
Occupational Position																		
Managerial	17.3	18.0	22.2	35.5	0	14.0	11.4	11.6	10.1	19.0	53.8	21.4	7.1	30.0	22.2	8.6	0	0
Professional	22.7	18.0	31.9	15.7	33.3	12.3	11.4	9.3	11.1	11.4	7.7	21.4	38.2	30.0	40.3	15.4	20.0	0
Technical / Sales / Clerical	20.1	29.5	20.8	18.0	0	17.5	31.9	25.6	21.2	26.9	30.8	35.7	18.2	30.0	29.2	28.7	20.0	10.0
Blue Collar	39.9	34.4	25.0	35.8	66.7	56.1	44.1	53.9	57.6	42.7	7.7	21.4	26.5	10.0	8.3	47.3	60.0	90.0
Spouse's Occupational Position																		
Managerial	12.0	16.7	13.2	6.6	0	7.7	8.0	3.1	8.1	7.3	0	30.0	11.0	12.5	11.6	7.3	0	0
Professional	8.9	11.9	28.9	8.2	0	11.5	19.2	0	13.7	9.3	28.6	0	14.4	25.0	27.9	3.0	0	0
Technical / Sales / Clerical	37.0	45.2	42.1	37.7	60.0	65.4	45.1	43.8	43.5	32.0	42.9	60.0	41.9	50.0	41.9	36.1	33.3	66.7
Blue Collar	42.0	26.2	15.8	47.5	40.0	15.4	27.7	53.1	34.7	51.4	28.6	20.0	32.6	12.5	18.6	53.6	66.7	33.3
Mean Household Income in 1979																		
In Dollars	26048	27241	30335	26289	19931	21939	27919	27499	21056	24023	33977	25703	27695	32942	29885	16852	16068	19983
Ratio of White HH Income[a]	.91	.95	1.06	.92	.59	.77	.98	.96	.74	.84	1.18	.90	.97	1.15	1.05	.59	.56	.70
Distribution of Household Income In Quintiles ($1000)																		
Bottom Fifth	6.01	7.36	12.06	7.01	1.21	10.91	11.01	14.34	6.91	6.51	11.01	8.92	6.93	20.21	11.24	1.25	5.21	5.01
Second Fifth	15.37	16.59	20.64	15.61	12.01	17.01	19.49	21.30	12.01	13.61	23.01	18.01	17.47	21.11	21.91	8.28	6.06	8.32
Third Fifth (Median Income)	24.00	23.16	28.51	23.09	17.61	20.56	26.01	25.89	17.75	21.26	30.77	21.99	25.78	26.35	28.52	14.75	13.45	18.26
Fourth Fifth	32.03	33.00	35.60	31.64	23.01	25.80	33.53	31.52	25.78	29.01	34.51	28.51	34.01	37.72	34.01	22.05	21.51	24.62
Top Fifth	49.54	53.34	55.02	50.01	39.82	34.21	46.53	41.64	39.01	48.01	72.02	48.44	50.01	52.05	52.01	34.39	36.73	32.02
Number of Spouses Working	1.37	1.49	1.42	1.17	1.63	1.37	1.63	1.57	1.07	1.50	1.40	1.29	1.36	1.64	1.51	1.14	1.33	1.33
Mean Individual Earnings in 1979																		
In Dollars	14587	16593	21790	18713	15248	15295	12887	14581	10828	15657	24679	21954	20381	23942	21447	7898	10928	12904
Ratio of White Male Income[b]	.78	.89	1.17	1.00	.81	.82	.69	.78	.58	.84	1.32	1.17	1.09	1.28	1.14	.42	.59	.69

TABLE 11
Selected Characteristics of Foreign-born Asian American Husbands in Percentages
California, 1980 (Continued)

Characteristic	Race/Ethnicity and Marriage Pattern*																	
	Chinese			Japanese			Filipino			Korean			Asian Indian			Vietnamese		
	IT	IE	IR	IT	IE**	IR	IT	IE	IR	IT	IE**	IR**	IT	IE**	IR	IT	IE**	IR**
Spouse's Individual Earnings In 1979																		
In Dollars	5783	7011	5493	3349	4232	5304	8954	6278	4190	5757	7005	2854	4849	7144	5925	3710	4622	3943
Ratio of White Male Income[b]	.31	.38	.29	.30	.23	.28	.48	.34	.22	.31	.38	.15	.26	.38	.31	.20	.25	.21
Family Structure																		
Nuclear Family w/o Children	20.2	34.3	32.1	34.6	50.0	38.1	12.9	29.6	30.4	13.9	6.7	29.4	16.3	100.0	36.8	8.6	33.3	5.4
Nuclear Family with Children	58.5	62.9	56.4	59.2	50.0	52.4	52.6	50.0	50.9	67.9	66.7	70.6	64.7	0	56.6	52.7	66.7	58.3
Extended Family	21.1	12.9	11.5	6.2	0	9.5	34.5	20.4	18.7	18.2	26.7	0	19.0	0	6.6	38.6	0	38.3
Mean Total Number Of Workers In Household	1.95	1.87	1.69	1.41	1.50	1.65	1.80	2.19	1.58	1.80	1.93	1.59	1.79	1.82	1.75	1.60	1.33	1.83
Work Status																		
Full Time	78.6	68.8	75.7	81.2	100.0	84.7	77.7	74.5	63.9	70.2	71.4	100.0	78.5	90.9	83.8	65.5	60.0	66.7
Part Time	21.3	31.3	24.3	18.8	0	15.3	22.3	25.5	35.1	29.8	28.6	0	21.5	9.1	16.2	34.5	40.0	33.3
Spouse's Work Status																		
Full Time	54.7	53.1	56.1	49.6	75.0	63.2	65.3	65.9	45.6	55.3	60.0	36.4	43.6	57.1	40.0	58.8	50.0	28.6
Part Time	45.3	46.9	43.9	50.4	25.0	36.8	34.7	34.1	53.4	44.7	40.0	63.6	56.4	42.9	60.0	41.3	50.0	71.4

Sources: 1980 U.S. Census Bureau 5% Public User Microdata Sample (PUMS) for California and special unpublished tabulations of the Asian American population.

*IT = Intramarriage IE = Interethnic Marriage IR = Interracial Marriage **Cases are too few to interpret reliably

[a]U.S.-born Non-Hispanic White Household [b]U.S.-born Non-Hispanic White Male

TABLE 12
Selected Characteristics of Foreign-born Asian American Wives in Percentages
California, 1980

Characteristic	Chinese IT	Chinese IE	Chinese IR	Japanese IT	Japanese IE**	Japanese IR	Filipino IT	Filipino IE	Filipino IR	Korean IT	Korean IE**	Korean IR**	Asian Indian IT	Asian Indian IE**	Asian Indian IR	Vietnamese IT	Vietnamese IE**	Vietnamese IR**
	Race/Ethnicity and Marriage Pattern*																	
Marriage Pattern																		
Percentage	90.4	1.4	8.2	46.8	3.2	50.0	78.3	1.9	19.7	75.2	4.0	20.8	93.6	.4	6.0	80.9	2.9	16.2
Count	2315	35	210	692	47	740	2331	58	587	897	48	248	511	2	33	508	18	102
Age																		
00-18	0	0	0	0	2.1	.1	0	0	.2	.1	0	0	.2	50.0	0	.4	0	0
18-25	4.3	2.9	4.4	4.3	2.1	3.2	6.0	20.7	15.2	8.1	14.6	16.5	13.1	0	15.2	16.1	16.7	12.7
25-30	17.1	34.3	22.9	15.2	10.6	8.0	15.0	24.1	21.8	15.7	13.8	18.5	24.7	15.0	18.2	21.5	16.7	32.4
30-35	18.3	20.0	32.9	21.2	8.5	8.5	21.3	24.1	19.8	22.7	22.9	25.0	25.6	0	24.2	18.3	22.2	24.5
35-40	12.6	14.3	15.7	14.7	14.9	10.3	17.5	12.5	17.9	22.2	12.5	17.5	14.9	0	9.1	15.6	16.7	20.6
40-45	12.2	14.3	9.0	10.0	12.8	19.7	13.2	12.1	11.6	14.5	12.5	11.3	9.8	0	3.0	11.4	16.7	7.8
45-50	11.1	11.4	2.4	12.6	31.9	28.9	9.1	0	6.5	7.4	12.5	7.3	5.3	0	9.1	7.1	5.6	0
50-55	9.0	0	1.9	9.8	12.8	15.1	6.9	5.2	2.9	1.4	2.1	2.4	3.9	0	6.1	5.5	5.6	1.0
55-60	6.0	2.9	1.0	4.5	0	4.3	5.1	0	2.7	1.4	2.1	1.2	.8	0	6.1	3.3	0	1.0
60-65	4.2	0	.5	1.3	4.3	.8	2.8	0	.5	1.6	0	0	.6	0	0	.4	0	0
65+	5.2	0	1.4	6.4	0	.9	3.0	1.7	1.0	2.1	0	0	1.2	0	9.1	.4	0	0
Mean Age	41.8	35.3	33.9	41.5	42.3	43.8	39.8	33.6	35.1	37.5	34.9	34.3	34.4	27.0	39.2	35.2	34.9	32.2
Spouse's Mean Age	46.3	40.5	37.6	45.6	47.1	45.6	43.9	36.3	37.5	41.1	40.3	37.3	39.3	25.0	42.8	39.6	38.8	40.0
Educational Level																		
High School or Less	56.8	31.4	36.7	52.0	55.3	71.2	28.7	27.6	54.3	46.0	70.8	77.4	41.7	0	39.4	63.8	83.3	72.5
Some College	15.5	22.9	32.9	28.6	31.9	20.9	19.0	17.2	21.8	18.2	12.5	16.1	19.8	50.0	27.3	27.2	5.6	20.6
4-5 Years College	19.1	28.6	19.5	17.3	8.5	6.4	44.6	44.8	17.7	32.3	12.5	5.2	22.5	0	18.2	6.3	5.6	4.9
Graduate/Professional	8.7	17.1	11.0	2.0	4.3	1.5	7.8	10.3	6.1	3.5	4.2	1.2	6.0	50.0	15.2	2.8	5.6	2.0

TABLE 12
Selected Characteristics of Foreign-born Asian American Wives in Percentages
California, 1980 (Continued)

Characteristic	Chinese IT	Chinese IE	Chinese IR	Japanese IT	Japanese IE**	Japanese IR	Filipino IT	Filipino IE	Filipino IR	Korean IT	Korean IE**	Korean IR**	Asian Indian IT	Asian Indian IE**	Asian Indian IR	Vietnamese IT	Vietnamese IE**	Vietnamese IR**
	Race/Ethnicity and Marriage Pattern*																	
Mean Educational Level																		
# Years of Education	18.0	16.1	15.6	15.0	13.9	13.9	16.0	16.7	14.2	15.2	14.0	13.1	15.0	19.0	15.2	12.6	11.9	13.0
Spouse's Educational Level																		
High School or Less	45.0	20.0	16.7	36.1	44.7	40.0	33.5	29.3	52.1	26.0	37.5	48.8	26.6	0	30.3	40.0	44.4	25.5
Some College	13.2	28.6	32.4	20.1	19.1	36.9	24.7	31.0	28.3	13.8	31.3	31.9	10.2	50.0	24.2	34.4	22.2	35.3
4-5 Years College	20.0	25.7	28.1	32.8	27.7	14.9	33.3	22.4	12.4	42.8	16.7	10.9	19.2	0	15.2	13.8	22.2	24.5
Graduate/Professional	21.8	25.7	22.9	11.0	8.5	8.2	8.4	17.2	7.2	17.4	14.6	8.5	44.0	50.0	30.3	11.8	11.1	14.7
Spouse's Mean Educational Level																		
# Years of Education	14.7	17.0	17.5	16.0	15.1	15.6	15.7	16.4	15.3	16.8	16.0	15.5	17.5	19.5	17.2	14.7	15.5	16.6
Location in Labor Force																		
Employed Civilian	56.5	62.9	60.0	36.4	59.6	43.2	77.8	70.7	63.0	61.9	50.0	43.5	45.8	50.0	51.5	46.7	61.1	52.0
Unemployed Civilian	3.8	0	2.4	1.3	0	1.9	3.2	1.7	3.6	1.8	10.4	4.4	8.0	50.0	12.1	3.5	0	7.8
Employed Military	0	0	0	0	0	0	.2	0	0	0	0	0	0	0	0	0	0	0
Not in Labor Force	39.7	37.1	37.6	62.3	40.4	54.9	18.9	27.6	33.4	36.3	39.6	52.0	46.2	0	36.4	49.8	38.9	40.2
Spouse's Location In Labor Force																		
Employed Civilian	80.5	91.4	78.6	87.7	63.8	74.3	74.8	87.9	60.1	87.2	75.0	67.3	89.6	50.0	78.8	66.1	77.8	81.4
Unemployed Civilian	1.7	0	2.4	.6	2.1	3.2	2.4	3.4	2.6	2.7	0	2.4	3.9	0	0	5.3	0	2.0
Employed Military	.1	0	13.3	.9	12.8	10.0	11.3	5.2	28.1	.7	18.8	25.8	.4	0	6.1	.4	0	10.8
Not in Labor Force	17.7	8.6	5.7	10.8	21.3	12.4	11.5	3.4	9.2	9.5	6.3	4.4	6.1	50.0	15.2	28.1	22.2	5.9

TABLE 12
Selected Characteristics of Foreign-born Asian American Wives in Percentages
California, 1980 (Continued)

Characteristic	Chinese			Japanese			Filipino			Korean			Asian Indian			Vietnamese		
	Race/Ethnicity and Marriage Pattern*																	
	IT	IE	IR	IT	IE**	IR	IT	IE	IR	IT	IE**	IR**	IT	IE**	IR	IT	IE**	IR**
Occupational Position																		
Managerial	11.8	15.4	11.4	5.8	14.3	7.4	7.8	10.6	9.7	7.3	8.3	3.4	9.5	0	10.0	7.6	0	5.2
Professional	9.5	15.4	18.7	8.8	9.5	6.2	19.0	21.3	10.7	9.5	8.0	2.6	15.8	0	35.0	3.6	0	10.3
Technical/Sales/Clerical	35.6	46.2	51.8	36.3	38.1	30.6	43.9	53.2	38.6	32.2	28.0	37.1	38.2	0	30.0	36.7	18.2	27.6
Blue Collar	43.1	23.1	18.0	49.1	38.1	55.8	29.4	14.6	41.0	50.9	56.0	56.9	36.5	100.0	25.0	52.2	81.8	56.9
Spouse's Occupational Position																		
Managerial	17.8	13.6	13.9	14.5	33.3	18.7	11.4	22.5	14.6	17.8	15.0	20.0	17.6	100.0	6.7	9.9	0	11.9
Professional	20.9	18.2	25.9	12.0	4.8	9.5	11.3	7.5	13.4	8.3	30.0	16.5	32.6	0	33.3	15.5	9.1	21.4
Technical/Sales/Clerical	21.1	40.9	31.5	22.4	4.8	33.9	33.1	32.5	27.2	25.7	25.0	20.0	22.7	0	46.7	29.7	18.2	31.0
Blue Collar	40.3	27.3	28.7	51.0	57.1	37.8	44.2	37.5	44.8	48.2	40.0	43.5	27.0	0	13.3	44.8	72.7	35.7
Mean Household Income in 1979																		
In Dollars	26159	30249	29498	26982	27556	27167	27968	27993	23696	23913	26206	22543	27705	18360	30090	16870	19588	25356
Ratio to White HH Income[a]	.92	1.06	1.03	.94	.97	.95	.98	.98	.83	.84	.92	.79	.97	.64	1.05	.59	.69	.89
Distribution of Household Income In Quintiles ($1000)																		
Bottom Fifth	6.04	8.01	12.25	8.64	9.34	11.01	11.01	12.70	9.30	6.40	10.86	8.04	6.82	3.71	12.01	1.25	6.01	12.51
Second Fifth	15.51	23.51	19.83	17.70	21.21	19.81	19.57	22.51	15.53	13.61	15.49	14.81	17.47	3.71	20.22	8.29	11.07	18.01
Third Fifth (Median Income)	34.01	31.08	26.21	24.01	26.07	25.81	26.02	24.49	21.58	21.07	23.26	20.01	25.79	18.36	27.01	14.75	16.59	22.57
Fourth Fifth	32.22	36.73	32.07	31.76	30.28	32.19	33.82	32.01	28.01	28.61	34.17	28.03	34.09	33.01	33.63	22.07	24.71	28.01
Top Fifth	49.62	44.32	56.86	50.01	48.03	43.96	46.49	47.94	41.49	47.80	43.02	40.15	50.01	33.01	54.52	34.52	41.50	42.92
Number of Spouses Working	1.37	1.54	1.52	1.25	1.36	1.28	1.64	1.64	1.51	1.50	1.44	1.37	1.36	1.00	1.36	1.13	1.39	1.44
Mean Individual Earnings in 1979																		
In Dollars	5796	7270	7078	3394	5503	4110	8981	9054	6103	5717	4940	3523	4890	2355	8137	3708	4775	3680
Ratio to White Male Income[b]	.31	.39	.38	.18	.30	.22	.48	.49	.33	.31	.26	.19	.26	.13	.44	.20	.26	.20

TABLE 12
Selected Characteristics of Foreign-born Asian American Wives in Percentages
California, 1980 (Continued)

Characteristic	Chinese IT	Chinese IE	Chinese IR	Japanese IT	Japanese IE**	Japanese IR	Filipino IT	Filipino IE	Filipino IR	Korean IT	Korean IE**	Korean IR**	Asian Indian IT	Asian Indian IE**	Asian Indian IR	Vietnamese IT	Vietnamese IE**	Vietnamese IR**
	Race/Ethnicity and Marriage Pattern*																	
Spouse's Mean Earnings In 1979																		
In Dollars	14682	21574	19711	30039	16907	17076	13035	16160	14534	15607	17969	16035	20430	16005	22671	7911	12969	18157
Ratio to White Male Income[b]	.79	1.16	1.06	1.07	.91	.92	.70	.87	.78	.84	.96	.86	1.10	.86	1.22	.42	.70	.97
Family Structure																		
Nuclear Family w/o Children	20.4	31.4	36.2	29.0	38.3	36.2	13.0	31.0	30.8	14.2	33.3	32.7	16.0	100.0	45.5	8.5	22.2	12.7
Nuclear Family with Children	58.7	54.3	51.4	65.3	53.2	58.4	52.9	50.0	56.7	67.8	56.3	56.9	65.4	0	42.4	52.8	55.6	71.6
Extended Family	21.0	14.3	12.4	5.6	8.5	5.4	34.1	19.0	12.4	18.1	10.4	10.5	18.6	0	12.1	38.8	22.2	15.7
Mean Total Number Of Workers in Household	1.96	2.03	1.78	1.52	1.94	1.73	2.30	1.98	1.81	1.80	1.71	1.67	1.79	2.00	1.64	1.60	1.67	1.68
Work Status																		
Full Time	54.2	54.2	54.9	48.4	66.7	50.5	65.0	55.3	49.1	54.9	40.7	38.7	43.5	0	42.1	58.8	61.5	35.5
Part Time	45.8	45.8	45.1	51.6	33.3	49.5	35.0	44.7	50.9	45.1	59.3	61.3	56.5	100.0	57.9	41.2	38.5	64.5
Spouse's Work Status																		
Full Time	78.9	73.5	82.3	85.2	69.2	81.5	78.2	87.0	82.8	70.1	80.4	78.0	78.3	50.0	79.3	65.4	56.3	76.0
Part Time	21.1	26.5	17.7	14.8	30.8	18.5	21.8	13.0	17.2	29.9	19.6	13.0	21.7	50.0	[illegible]	34.6	43.8	24.0

Sources: 1980 U.S. Census Bureau 5% Public User Microdata Sample (PUMS) for California and special unpublished tabulations of the Asian American population.
*IT = Intramarriage IE = Interethnic Marriage IR = Interracial Marriage **Cases are too few to interpret reliably
[a]U.S.-born Non-Hispanic White Household [b]U.S.-born Non-Hispanic White Male

marriages for each generation is smaller numerically than interracial marriages, yet the rate of growth from one generation to the next increases. For both *Sansei* men and women, the growth rate of interethnic marriages has picked up considerably, although interracial marriages were predominant among intermarried *Sansei*. We believe this is a product of the increasing ethnic awareness brought on by the Asian American movement.[32] Since the *Yonsei* generation is not yet at the peak years of marriage age, it is too early to discern their marriage patterns.

Using age as a generational proxy for Japanese Americans shows that successive generations increasingly intermarry, both interethnically and interracially. For all Asian American populations, the younger the individuals, the more likely they will intermarry. Whether intermarriage rates will continue to increase in the direction toward interethnic or interracial marriages cannot be predicted, however.

Educational Attainment

Many studies have shown that the Asian American population has a high educational attainment.[33] Our data support these findings. According to the educational characteristics shown below the age distributions in the summary tables, Asian Americans have on average a higher educational attainment than other racial groups in California. Over and above this high attainment, we are interested in investigating how educational achievement relates to the marriage patterns of Asian Americans. Hypergamy theory predicts that highly educated racial minority men and women may opt to exchange their higher socioeconomic and educational status with the higher racial status of their spouses.

The marriage patterns and characteristics of Asian American women validate hypergamy theory more than those shown for Asian American men.[34] For both the U.S.-born and foreign-born, Asian American women are likely to have a higher educational level when they are intermarried than when they are intramarried. The exception to this rule appears in populations with a high proportion of marriages involving U.S. servicemen: foreign-born Chinese American, foreign-born Japanese American, U.S.- and foreign-born Filipino American, foreign-born Korean American, and foreign-born Vietnamese American women. We believe that these G.I. marriages account for the lower educational levels of those subpopulations.

White husbands, in general, of interracially married U.S.-born Chinese American, U.S.-born Japanese American, and U.S.-born Filipino American women have a higher mean educational level than Asian American husbands of the same categories of women. On the other hand, white husbands who are interracially married to foreign-born Japanese American, foreign-born Filipino American, foreign-born Korean American, and foreign-born Vietnamese American women have lower levels of education than Asian American men intramarried to those groups of women.[35]

To test the exchange hypothesis of hypergamy theory, we take as an example the experiences of U.S.-born Chinese American and U.S.-born Japanese American women. Summary Table 10 shows that U.S.-born Chinese American and U.S.-born Japanese American women who are interracially married have considerably higher educational attainment than their counterparts who are intramarried: interracially married Chinese American women have 16.9 mean years of education compared to 15.8 for those who are intramarried; among Japanese American women, it is 16.4 compared to 15.1. White women who are interracially married, on the other hand, have only 14.8 years of education, compared to 14.9 years for those who are intramarried. White husbands of the U.S.-born Chinese American and U.S.-born Japanese American women are also better educated than Asian American husbands of such women. White husbands of U.S.-born Chinese American women have 17.4 mean years of education, compared to 16.6 years among the Chinese American husbands of U.S.-born Chinese American women; white husbands of U.S.-born Japanese American women have 16.9 mean years of education, compared to 15.7 years for Japanese American husbands of U.S.-born Japanese American women.

These data support the exchange hypothesis of hypergamy theory and indicate that U.S.-born Asian American women who intermarry have higher educational attainment than U.S.-born Asian American women who intramarry. These women also have higher levels of education than white women in general. When intermarried, the largest percentage of U.S.-born Asian American women are married to white men who are themselves better educated than their wives. Additionally, these white men are better educated than both intramarried white men and intramarried Asian American men.[36] Interracially married Asian American men also have higher levels of educational attainment than intramarried Asian American men.

Class Effects

Members of the same class usually have similar occupational positions and incomes. The sociological literature is replete with concepts of class that are based upon the individual's and family members' labor force status, occupational position, and income.

Hypergamy theory predicts that intermarriage will occur when the class indicators (labor force status, occupational position in the labor market, and the household and individual income characteristics) of a racial minority individual are higher than those of his spouse, if male, and lower than those of her spouse, if female. It also predicts that these class factors will be higher for the intermarried individual than for the intramarried individual.[37] Hence, according to hypergamy theory, only the most socioeconomically advantaged class segment of the Asian American population is likely to intermarry with the white population.

On the other hand, if marital assimilation, as Milton Gordon points out, is "an inevitable by-product of structural assimilation," then Asian Americans, as a whole, must have the same locations in the societal structure and have very similar socioeconomic characteristics as the dominant majority.[38] It follows, therefore, from assimilation theory, that each and every class segment of the Asian American population will have a proportionate number of individuals who intermarry with whites. Unfortunately, much of the assimilationist literature on Asian American intermarriage has reversed the causal relationship between marital assimilation and structural assimilation.[39] Although structural assimilation might occur without marital assimilation, marital assimilation does not happen until the structural underpinnings of social and economic equality between the two groups are evident, and when they interact with each other and partake of the rewards of American society in proportion to their numbers within the U.S. population. Few studies on Asian American intermarriage are explicit in delineating this difference between marital assimilation and intermarriage. The terms are not analogous. One can have intermarriage, as shown by Davis and Merton's studies of marriages between blacks and whites, without the social and economic equality (structural assimilation) that Gordon postulated as a necessary precondition for marital assimilation.[40] Thus, intermarriage, by itself, is not equivalent to marital assimilation, nor does the existence of marital assimilation imply structural assimilation has taken place.

In the following subsections, shown in the summary tables below the educational characteristics of the spouses, we present various indicators of structural assimilation--those class characteristics that are necessary to discern which of the two theories is most accurate in describing the nature of marriage patterns among Asian Americans. (These figures are given in the bottom parts of the summary tables.) If assimilation theory is valid, then intermarried Asian Americans and whites must show little or no difference in their class characteristics vis-à-vis those who are intramarried. Differences in the class characteristics between intermarried and intramarried would demonstrate that the alternative--hypergamy theory--is more accurate. We now turn to what are generally considered structural assimilation variables involving class--labor force status, occupational position, and household and individual income--to see if they are related to race/ethnicity, nativity, gender, and marriage pattern.

Labor Force Status.[41] A greater percentage of the interracially married U.S.-born Asian American men are employed in the labor force than intramarried U.S.-born Asian American men. In Table 9, among the interracially married, 88.5 percent of Chinese American men, 92.5 percent of Japanese American men, and 87.9 percent of Filipino American men are employed in the labor force compared to 87.7 percent for Chinese American men, 91.7 percent for Japanese American men, and 83.6 percent for Filipino American men among the intramarried. U.S.-born Asian American women, regardless of who they are married to, are considerably more likely to be in the labor force than white women. U.S.-born Asian American women with white husbands across the board are more likely to be in the labor force than intramarried or interethnically married Asian American women. Table 10 shows that among the U.S.-born Asian American women who are interracially married, 72.1 percent of the Chinese American women, 72.0 percent of the Japanese American women, and 67.5 percent of the Filipino American women are in the labor force. The comparable figures for intramarried women are 66.0 percent for Chinese American women, 66.5 for Japanese American women, and 66.0 percent for Filipino American women. Among interethnically married women, the proportions are 66.0 percent for Chinese American women, 61.4 percent for Japanese American women, and 60.9 percent for Filipino American women. Comparing white spouses of U.S.-born Asian American men to Asian American spouses of U.S.-born Asian American men, a smaller percentage of the former than the latter are in the labor force. These findings indicate that while U.S.-born Asian American women, in general, have higher labor force participation than white women, U.S.-born Asian American women in interracial marriages have a higher labor force participation than U.S.-born Asian American women in intramarriages.

Occupational Position in the Labor Market. In general, interracially married individuals occupy higher positions in the labor market than those who are intramarried. Chinese American and Japanese American men, both U.S.-born and foreign-born, who are married to white women are more likely than Asian American men married to Asian American women to be in managerial/professional occupations. White husbands of Asian American women, both U.S.- and foreign-born, also generally have a higher position in the occupational labor market than Asian American husbands of U.S.-born Asian American women.

Intramarried U.S.-born Asian American women generally have lower occupational positions in the labor market than interethnically and interracially married U.S.-born Asian American women. Because of the large influx of already married professional Asian women in the 1970s, foreign-born intramarried Asian American women, however, are more likely to be in the professional ranks than foreign-born interracially married Asian American women (G.I. wives). Intramarried foreign-born Asian American women in populations without large numbers of military marriages (i.e., Chinese and Asian Indian) and interracially married Asian American women who are married to U.S. servicemen (Japanese, Filipino, Korean, and Vietnamese) are more likely to be in the clerical/blue collar occupations.

Family and Individual Income. Family income consists of the sum total of interest earnings, subsidies given by outside agencies, and the combined wages of individual members of the family. In the typical nuclear family with no children, the major income sources are the husband and wife. In extended families or in families with working children, a significant proportion of the family income may come from the wages of individuals other than the husband and wife. The children, brothers, sisters, nieces, nephews, aunts, uncles, parents, grandparents of the heads of the families, as well as unrelated individuals, can all contribute to the family income of an extended family.

The summary tables show that intramarried Asian American families are more likely to contain wage-earning children. They are also more likely to have other members of the family contributing to the income pool. Interethnically and interracially married Asian American families are more likely to be nuclear, without the presence of children, and with fewer additional workers in the family.

The summary tables show that the family income hides some of the disparities in the income of individuals within intramarried versus interracially married Asian American populations. At first glance, the family mean and median incomes of intramarried Asian American families seem the same as, or higher than, those of intramarried white families. This is due to the fact that intramarried Asian American families compensate for the lack of opportunities and the low earning returns of the husbands by having more workers contributing to the family income, as well as by having a higher labor force participation of the wife in order to enjoy a lifestyle similar to that of white families.

The pattern of individual contributions to the family income is statistically significant. With the exception of foreign-born Filipino Americans (a high percentage of whom are older former farmworkers and stewards who call themselves *Pinoys*) and foreign-born Japanese Americans (many of whom are businessmen working for Japan-based corporations), both U.S.-born and foreign-born Asian American men who are interracially married have higher *individual* incomes than intramarried Asian American men even though their *family* incomes may be lower. For example, in Table 9 the individual income of interracially married U.S.-born Chinese American, Japanese American, and Filipino American men are respectively $22,013, $20,755, and $17,100, compared to $21,223, $20,569, and $15,509 for the intramarried men.

Interracially married Asian American women, except for those who have very recently arrived or who are members of groups with a large proportion of military wives, also tend to have higher incomes than those who are intramarried. According to Table 10, the mean individual income of interracially married U.S.-born Chinese American, Japanese American, and Filipino American women are $9,799, $9,276, and $7,124, compared to $8,015, $7,340, and $6,445 for those who are intramarried.

The individual characteristics thus support hypergamy theory, especially among the U.S.-born Asian American population: interracially married Asian Americans have higher class characteristics than intraethnically married Asian Americans.

Conclusion

The majority of Asian Americans in California in 1980 are married within their own ethnic groups, although a substantial proportion (19.9 percent) are intermarried. Japanese Americans have the largest proportion of intermarried individuals, followed by Filipino Americans and Asian Indians. Asian American women intermarry more than Asian American men (25 percent vs. 14.4 percent). For both intermarried Asian American men and women, the intermarriages are primarily to non-Hispanic whites. When population size and composition are controlled, Asian Americans marry in the following order: first, members of their own ethnic groups; second, other Asian Americans; third, whites; and lastly, Hispanics and blacks.

Intermarriage among certain groups of Asian Americans is associated with participation of the husband in the military. For the Asian American population as a whole, it is related to the increasing number of generations in the United States, higher educational attainment, higher socioeconomic status, and the relative youthfulness of the married Asian American individual. U.S.-born Asian Americans intermarry more than foreign-born ones. The exceptions to this pattern are in populations with a sizable proportion of G.I. wives. Younger individuals show a marked tendency to marry spouses who are white or of another Asian American ethnic group.

Neither Asian American men nor women follow the patterns of intermarrriage hypothesized by proponents of assimilation theory. Instead of finding the number of interracially married individuals from each socioeconomic class being proportionate to the size of that class vis-à-vis the total Asian American population, we find that, on the average, the most advantaged members of the Asian American population enter into marriages with similarly advantaged members of the white population. The exception to this pattern is among foreign-born wives from Asia married to white U.S. servicemen, who tend to be lower in socioeconomic standing.

Hypergamy theory is based upon the concept that individuals tend to maximize their status through marriage in a racially stratified society. The intermarriage patterns among Asian Americans show that highly accomplished Asian American women can maximize their status by intermarrying with the most advantaged individuals with the highest racial position. Asian American men also have higher status and class characteristics in interracial marriages, but their spouses tend to have lower educational and socioeconomic status although they are higher in racial position. Thus, our findings show a distinct gender difference, supporting both the Indian caste hypergamy model emphasizing the marriage of lower caste status women with higher caste status men; and the hypergamy-hypogamy model applied to the study of the marriage between lower racial status minority men and higher racial status women. The overall findings suggest that the hypergamous nature of the marriage patterns of Asian Americans systematically reflect the significance of nativity and generation, as well as the functional nature of racial, gender, educational, and socioeconomic class inequalities in American society.

Notes

1. We define racial minorities as the four major nonwhite "racial" groups in the United States: Asian Americans, blacks, Hispanics, and Native Americans. Within these racial groups are ethnic subpopulations defined by their national ancestry or by cultural distinctions.

2. A third major conceptual framework, not discussed in this article, is the theorem that heterogeneity is positively correlated with increasing intermarriage. Blau et. al. advance this theory to show that while ingroup marriages prevail in the United States, greater cultural and ethnic diversity, concomitant with the associated higher probabilities of social contact between different groups, will lead to increases in the rate of intermarriage. In a future article, we shall offer an empirical test of this theorem. On the heterogeneity school, see Peter M. Blau, *Inequality and Heterogeneity* (New York: Free Press, 1977) and Peter M. Blau, Terry Blum, and Joseph Schwartz, "Heterogeneity and Intermarriage," *American Sociological Review* 47 (1982): 45-62.

3. In the past, the intermarriage literature has focused upon the marriages between members of various white ethnic and religious groups, partly as a result of the concern of American sociologists regarding the assimilability of Southern and Eastern Europeans who were entering into the metropolitan areas of the United States during the early twentieth century. See Julian Drachsler, *Intermarriage in New York City* (New York: Columbia University Press, 1921); Bessie

B. Wessel, "Comparative Rates of Intermarriage among Different Nationalities in the United States," *Eugenical News* 15 (1930): 105-107; Reuben B. Resnik, "Some Sociological Aspects of Intermarriage of Jew and Non-Jew," *Social Forces* 11 (1933): 94-102; James H. S. Bossard, "Nationality and Nativity as Factors in Marriage," *American Sociological Review* 4 (1939): 792-798; Maurice R. Davie and Ruby Jo Reeves, "Propinquity of Residence before Marriage," *American Journal of Sociology* 44 (1939): 510-517; Ruby Jo Reeves Kennedy, "Premarital Residential Propinquity and Ethnic Endogamy," *American Journal of Sociology* 48 (1943): 580-584; Ruby Kennedy, "Single or Triple Melting Pot? Intermarriage Trends in New Haven, 1870-1940," *American Journal of Sociology* 49 (1944): 331-339; Milton L. Barron, *People Who Intermarry: Intermarriage in a New England Industrial Community* (Syracuse, New York: Syracuse University Press, 1946); August Hollingshead, "Cultural Factors in the Selection of Marriage Mates," *American Sociological Review* 15 (1950): 619-627; John L. Thomas, "The Factor of Religion in the Selection of Marriage Mates," *American Sociological Review* 16 (1951): 489-496; Alfred C. Clarke, "Residential Propinquity as a Factor in Mate Selection," *American Sociological Review* 17 (1952): 17-22; Loren E. Chancellor and Thomas P. Monahan, "Religious Preference and Interreligious Mixture in Marriages and Divorce in Iowa," *American Journal of Sociology* 61 (1955): 233-239; Harvey Locke, Georges Sabagh, and Mary Margaret Thomas, "Interfaith Marriages," *Social Problems* 4 (1957): 329-333; Paul C. Glick, "Intermarriage and Fertility Patterns among Persons in Major Religious Groups," *Eugenics Quarterly* 7 (1960): 31-38; Jerold S. Heiss, "Premarital Characteristics of the Religiously Intermarried in an Urban Area," *American Sociological Review* 25 (1960): 47-55; and David Heer, "Marital Status of Second Generation Americans," *American Sociological Review* 26 (1961): 233-241.

4. As stated above, we define four U.S. racial minorities: Asian Americans, blacks, Hispanics, and Native Americans. Within these racial populations, there are subpopulations of ethnic groups. For example, Mexicans, Puerto Ricans, Cubans, and El Salvadoreans

within the Hispanic population, and Chinese, Japanese, Filipinos, and Koreans within the Asian American population, are racial minority ethnic groups. They, too, have been the subjects of sociological inquiry in the intermarriage literature.

5. In this article, "Asian American" refers to people of Asian or Pacific Islander descent living in the United States. Both U.S.- and foreign-born Chinese, Japanese, Filipinos, Koreans, Asian Indians, and Vietnamese are considered Asian Americans.

6. Milton Gordon, *Assimilation in American Life* (New York: Oxford University Press, 1964) is a classic work that sees intermarriage as "an inevitable by-product of structural assimilation," (p. 80) one of the seven types of assimilation necessary for total assimilation into the dominant society. Other works sharing the assimilation perspective include Emory S. Bogardus, "Filipino Americans," in *Our Racial and National Minorities*, ed. F. S. Brown and J. S. Roucek (New York: Prentice-Hall, Inc., 1937), 510-525; James H. S. Bossard, "Nationality and Nativity as Factors in Marriage," *American Sociological Review* 4 (1939): 792-798; William Smith, *Americans in the Making* (New York: D. Appleton-Century, 1939); Milton L. Barron, *People Who Intermarry* (Syracuse, New York: Syracuse University Press, 1946); Ruby Jo Reeves Kennedy, "Single or Triple Melting Pot? Intermarriage Trends in New Haven, 1870-1940," *American Journal of Sociology* 29 (1944): 67-81; and Robert E. Park, *Race and Culture: Essays in the Sociology of Contemporary Man* (New York: Free Press, 1950). More recently, such studies as John H. Tinker, "Intermarriage and Assimilation in a Plural Society: Japanese-Americans in the United States," *Marriage and Family Review* 5 (1982): 61-74; Edward Murguia, *Chicano Intermarriage: A Theoretical and Empirical Study* (San Antonio: Trinity University Press, 1982); Ernest Porterfield, "Black American Intermarriage in the United States," *Marriage and Family Review* 5 (1982): 17-34; Harry Kitano, Wai-tsang Yeung, Lynn Chai, and Herbert Hatanaka, "Asian-American Interracial

Marriage," *Journal of Marriage and the Family* 46 (1984): 179-90; and Betty Lee Sung, "Intermarriage Among the Chinese in New York City," in *Chinese America: History and Perspectives* (San Francisco: Chinese Historical Society of America, 1987), 101-118, extend the assimilation model to include the intermarriage patterns of racial minorities.

7. Milton Gordon has termed this stage of assimilation "marital assimilation," occuring only after the structural assimilation of a minority group into the larger dominant group has taken place. See Gordon, *Assimilation in American Life*, 61-83.

8. John N. Tinker, "Intermarriage and Assimilation," 72-73. John Tinker's scholarship epitomizes how the dominant assimilation theory has been applied to studies of the intermarriage between Asian Americans and whites.

9. John N. Tinker, "Intermarriage and Ethnic Boundaries: The Japanese American Case," *Journal of Social Issues* 29 (1973): 64-65.

10. The assimilationist perspective is evident in numerous other studies discussing Asian American and white intermarriage: Emory S. Bogardus, "Filipino Americans"; Andrew W. Lind, "Assimilation in Rural Hawaii," *American Journal of Sociology* 45 (1939):200-214; Clarence C. Glick, "The Relation between Position and Status in the Assimilation of Chinese in Hawaii," *American Journal of Sociology* 47 (1942):667-679; Gerald J. Schnepp and Agnes Masako Yui, "Cultural and Marital Adjustment of Japanese War Brides," *American Journal of Sociology* 61 (1955):48-50; C.K. Cheng and Douglas S. Yamamura, "Interracial Marriage and Divorce in Hawaii," *Social Forces* 36 (1957):77-84; Margaret Parkman and Jack Sawyer, "Dimensions of Ethnic Intermarriage in Hawaii," *American Sociological Review* 32 (1967):593-607; Akemi Kikumura and Harry H. L. Kitano,

"Interracial Marriage: A Picture of the Japanese Americans," *Journal of Social Issues* 29 (1973):67-81; Tinker, "Intermarriage and Ethnic Boundaries"; Harry H. L. Kitano and Lynn K. Chai, "Korean Interracial Marriage," *Marriage and Family Review* 5 (Spring 1982): 75-89; Harry H. L. Kitano and Wai-tsang Yeung, "Chinese Interracial Marriage," *Marriage and Family Review* 5 (1982):35-48; John N. Tinker, "Intermarriage and Assimilation in a Plural Society: Japanese-Americans in the United States," *Marriage and Family Review* 5 (1982):61-74; Charles Hirschman, "America's Melting Pot Reconsidered," *Annual Review of Sociology* 9 (1983):397-423; Kitano et. al., "Asian-American Interracial Marriage" Sharon Lee and Keiko Yamanaka, "Intermarriage in the Asian American Population," unpublished paper presented at the annual meeting of the American Sociological Association, New York, 1987; and Sung, "Intermarriage among the Chinese."

11. Kingsley Davis, "Intermarriage in Caste Societies," *American Anthropologist* 43 (1941):386.

12. Davis, "Intermarriage," 389 and 393. Robert K. Merton, "Intermarriage and Social Structure: Face and Theory," *Psychiatry* 4 (1941):364-374. This is not to say that sexual relations between racial majority men and racial minority women do not occur in democratic societies. Both Kingsley Davis and Robert K. Merton are clear in demonstrating that white men have access to racial minority women, but do not necessarily need to consummate this relationship by marriage. According to Davis, on page 389, ". . . caste inequality makes it easy for the white man to take sexual advantage of Negro women without marrying them." Robert K. Merton similarly states on page 374, "the sex morality supports sex advances by the male; the caste morality more easily enables the dominant upper-caste member to initiate cross-caste sexual overtures. . . . Given the dominance of the white male with his relative immunity from active retaliation by the

lower-caste male, there is no pressure to legitimize his liaison by marriage."

13. Pierre Van Den Berghe, "Hypergamy, Hypergenation, and Miscegenation," *Human Relations* 13 (1960): 84.

14. Kingsley Davis and Wilbert E. Moore, "Some Principles of Stratification," in *Class, Status and Power: Social Stratification in Comparative Perspective*, 2d ed., ed. Reinhard Bendix and Seymour Martin Lipset (New York: The Free Press, 1966), 47-48.

15. Banton, Michael, *Racial and Ethnic Competition* (New York: Cambridge University Press, 1983), 84-85, and 91-94.

16. Melvin M. Tumin, "Some Principles of Stratification: A Critical Analysis," in *Class, Status and Power*, 53-58.

17. Intermarriage is analogous to outmarriage, while intraethnic marriage is synonymous with intramarriage and inmarriage.

18. The inherent strengths of using marriage licenses are their immediacy and the ease of calculating an intermarriage rate. Their weaknesses are that first, they give us no information regarding the prevalence of the number of individuals who are intra- or intermarried, i.e., the distribution of who people are married to at a given time. Second, the researchers must make a best guess estimate of the race of the individuals involved. Third, due to the nature of the marriage license applications, there is little specific information regarding the socioeconomic characteristics of the individuals. Intermarriage rates for individuals are determined by dividing the total number of individuals in a particular group intermarrying by the

total number of individuals in that group marrying at that particular time period and place, and multiplying that figure by 100. See Akemi Kikumura and Harry H. Kitano, "Interracial Marriage: A Picture of the Japanese Americans," *Journal of Social Issues* 29 (1973):67-81; Tinker, "Intermarriage and Ethnic Boundaries," 49-66; Kitano and Chai, "Korean Interracial Marriage"; Kitano, et. al., "Asian American Interracial Marriage"; Harry Kitano and Wai-tsang Yeung, "Chinese Interracial Marriage," *Marriage and Family Review* 5 (1982):35-48; and Russell Endo and Dale Hirokawa, "Japanese American Intermarriage," *Free Inquiry in Creative Sociology* 11 (1983):159-166.

19. In the 1980 U.S. Census, there is specific information on the socioeconomic, racial/ethnic, and nativity characteristics of both the husband and wife of married individuals living together. A great advantage of this census data base is that it has information regarding each individual's marriage pattern and socioeconomic characteristics. To our knowledge, the only studies of intermarriage of Asian Americans using this alternative data base are by Betty Lee Sung and the research team of Sharon Lee and Keiko Yamanaka. The first to appear was Betty Lee Sung's article based upon data from the 1980 U.S. Census for the City of New York and summarizing the characteristics of both those Chinese Americans who were intramarried and those who were outmarried. It was subsequently followed by Lee and Yamanaka's paper presented at the 1987 American Sociological Association meeting, which analyzes the characteristics of Asian Americans nationwide who are outmarried from their ethnic group, using a social distance scale for intermarried. See Sung, "Intermarriage among the Chinese," 101-118; and Lee and Yamanaka, "Intermarriage in the Asian American Population."

20. Bureau of the Census, *Census of Population and Housing, 1980: Public Use Microdata Sample Technical Documentation* (Washington, D.C.: U.S. Government Printing Office, 1983).

21. For the summary tables only, we report the marriage patterns without breakdowns by nativity. For example, interracial marriages of Asian Americans may be with U.S.- or foreign-born whites.

22. Paul Besanceney, "On Reporting Rates of Intermarriage," *American Journal of Sociology* 70 (1965):717.

23. The chi-square statistics for the tables are available upon request from the authors.

24. Besanceney, "On Reporting Rates," 718-719; and Blau, "Heterogeneity and Intermarriage," 45-48.

25. Besanceney, "On Reporting Rates," 720-721; Paul C. Glick, "Intermarriage among Ethnic Groups in the United States," *Social Biology* 17 (1970):292-298; and Larry D. Barnett, "Interracial Marriage in California," *Marriage and Family Living* 25 (1963):424-427.

26. Margaret A. Parkman and Jack Sawyer, 593-607.

27. The indexing technique used by Parkman and Sawyer is very similar to that of the Index of Dissimilarity (used in segregation research) and its related measures. For a critique of the Index of Dissimilarity, see Stanley Lieberson, "Measuring Population Diversity," *American Sociological Review* 34 (1969): 850-862; and *idem*, "An Assymetrical Approach to Segregation," in *Ethnic Segregation in Cities*, ed. Ceri Peach et. al. (London: Croom-Helm, 1981), 51-82.

28. Bok Lim Kim, *Women in Shadows* (La Jolla, California: National Committee Concerned with Asian Wives of U.S. Servicemen, 1981), 12.

29. Ibid., 11.

30. Japanese Americans have not had large-scale immigration to the United States since the Gentleman's Agreement of 1908, with the exception of the Japanese G.I. war brides who arrived in the United States between 1946 and 1970. In the past twenty years, less than five thousand Japanese per year have immigrated to the United States. Creating generational proxies by age distribution for Chinese, Koreans, Vietnamese, and Asian Indians is not possible because successive waves of immigration and the recent influx of refugees make age a poor proxy for generation among these populations. See U.S.I.N.S. *Annual Report on Immigration and Naturalization* (Washington, D.C.: U.S. Government Printing Office, 1970-1986).

31. Darrel Montero, "The Japanese Americans: Changing Patterns of Assimilation Over Three Generations," *American Sociological Review* 46(1981): 829-839; Douglas T. Gurak and J.F. Fitzpatrick. "Intermarriage among Hispanic Ethnic Groups in New York City," *American Journal of Sociology* 87 (1982): 921-934; Kitano et. al., "Asian American Interracial Marriage," 181.

32. As Porterfield argues in his study of black American intermarriage patterns, it is debatable whether the "symbolic family estate" (i.e., the development of a racial peoplehood) tendencies of the 1960s will mark a permanent change toward marriages within the race. Porterfield believes the general trend will show that the movement toward such within-race marriages is temporary. See Ernest Porterfield, "Black-American Intermarriage in the United States," *Marriage and Family Review* 5 (1982): 31. We believe that the

Yonsei patterns will not be as heavily influenced as those of the *Sansei* by the cultural nationalist and civil rights movements of the 1960s and 1970s that have emphasized empowerment within the Asian American community.

33. Robert W. Gardner, Bryant Robey, and Peter C. Smith, "Asian Americans: Growth, Change, and Diversity," *Population Bulletin* 40 (1985): 24-27. See also, Charles Hirschman and Morrison Wong, "Trends in Socioeconomic Achievement Among Immigrant and Native-born Asian Americans, 1960-1976," *Sociological Quarterly* 22 (1981): 495-514; Victor Nee and Jimy Sanders, "The Road to Parity: Determinants of the Socioeconomic Achievement of Asian Americans," *Ethnic and Racial Studies* 8 (1985): 75-93; and Charles Hirschman, "America's Melting Pot Reconsidered," *Annual Review of Sociology* 9 (1983): 397-423.

34. Among Asian American men, as opposed to Asian American women, differences in the educational attainment of intramarried and intermarried are less marked. This may be due to the patriarchal nature of American society, which gives men gender advantages regardless of their racial background. Since Asian American men have the advantage of their gender, the socioeconomic status and educational levels of a possible marriage partner are not as important a considerations as they are for Asian American women.

35. These findings concur with those of Harley Browning et. al., who observed that white men who are veterans tend to have lower educational levels than non-veteran white men, while racial minority men who are veterans tend to have a higher educational level than the average non-veteran member of their respective minority group. See Harley L. Browning, Sally C. Lopreato, and Dudley L. Poston, Jr., "Income and Veterans Status: Variations among Mexican Americans, Blacks and Anglos," *American Sociological Review* 38 (1973): 74-85.

36. A cursory look at the marriage patterns of highly educated interracially married white men would lead us to assume that these men marry Asian American women who have similar educational and class backgrounds as themselves. One wonders, then, why so many white men opt to marry women who clearly have lower racial status than themselves, given that white men have a choice between marrying white women who have a high racial status similar to their own and Asian American women who have lower racial status. The difference may be accounted for by the educational and class background of the women available as marriage partners for white men. White men who marry Asian American women marry those who are more highly educated and at higher socioeconomic levels than the average Asian American and white women.

37. See Van Den Berghe, "Hypergamy, Hypergenation, and Miscegenation," 83-91; and Robert K. Merton, "Intermarriage and the Social Structure: Fact and Theory," *Psychiatry* 4 (1941): 361-374. For specific references to class factors, see John H. Burma, G. A. Cretser, and T. Seacrest, "A Comparison of the Occupational Status of Intramarrying and Intermarrying Couples: A Research Note," *Sociology and Social Research* 54 (1970): 508-519.

38. Gordon, *Assimilation in American Life*, 40-49, 61-83.

39. The current literature on Asian American intermarriages assumes either that marital assimilation does not require a prior structural assimilation, or views it as a step toward the structural assimilation of Asian Americans. Characteristically, most of the research on Asian American intermarriage argues that: (1) assimilation occurs when intermarriage is high; (2) one finds high rates of intermarriages among Asian Americans; and (3) therefore,

one can conclude that Asian Americans are assimilated or are well on their way towards total assimilation.

40. Davis, 388-390; and Merton, "Intermarriage," 364-374.

41. Labor force status refers to the employment status of individuals in the labor market as defined by the U.S. Census Bureau. This is differentiated from labor force participation, which is the number of individuals who are employed divided by the number of individuals who are available to work. People available to work include those who are currently working and those who are seeking gainful employment in any given period.

Perceptions of Intergroup Relations: A Comparison of Anglo American and Mexican American University Students

Silvia J. Santos, Raymond T. Garza, and Lisa M. Bohon-Hock

The unique sociohistorical context within which Anglo Americans and Mexican Americans have interacted in the United States provides an excellent milieu for the social psychological study of interethnic relations. Anglo Americans and Mexican Americans are the two predominant ethnic groups in California and the Southwest. There has been a long history of tensions between them that can be traced to their historical competition for the control of economic resources and political power. The displacement of Mexican Americans from their land historically has probably been the most important source of conflict between the two groups.[1] The 1848 Treaty of Guadalupe Hidalgo, despite provisions to the contrary, accorded the Mexican population residing in the Southwest a second-class status in an area that was once their own and made them victims of Anglo domination.[2]

At present, the conflict between Anglos and Mexican

Americans revolves primarily around three issues: political representation, economic opportunity, and social segregation. Political representation has been an ongoing source of tension because compared to their numbers in the general population, the political representation of Mexican Americans is dismally small. Even in localities where Mexican Americans enjoy a commanding numerical majority, the Anglo group exercises political control. With a few notable exceptions--particularly the case of Henry Cisneros, the very popular mayor of San Antonio, Texas--the underrepresentation of Mexican Americans has not changed appreciably in the last three or four decades.

Because of the long-standing control of resources by Anglo Americans, Mexican Americans have a limited range of economic opportunities. People of Mexican heritage are grossly underrepresented among white-collar employees and overrepresented within the ranks of blue-collar and unskilled workers,[3] whereas Anglo Americans have exactly the opposite employment distribution. The disparity is particularly acute in agriculture, where the labor force is composed almost entirely of people of Mexican ancestry, many of whom have entered the United States illegally.[4] Despite special legislation to bring about ethnic parity in the work force, the overall situation remains inequitable. Moreover, efforts to implement equal opportunity legislation passed in the mid-1960s have led to a backlash, with charges of "reverse discrimination" against whites.[5]

At the social and interpersonal levels, social segregation best describes the relationship between Anglo and Mexican Americans. Most communities are still marked by ethnically segregated neighborhoods. For example, in the city of Los Angeles, the bulk of the large Mexican-ancestry population resides in or near the area known as East Los Angeles. Although much of this segregation has been self-imposed, the net effects have been decreased upward mobility and limited participation in the mainstream of American society. Those of Mexican descent clearly continue to have a subordinate position within American society.[6]

The Relevance of Social Identity Theory

The present study is an attempt to apply Tajfel's social identity theory to the study of relations between Mexican Americans and Anglo Americans. According to Ward and Hewstone, this theory is particularly applicable to real-world intergroup relations between groups with different statuses.[7] The underlying assumption in Tajfel's theory is that individuals define themselves, to a large extent, through their membership in social groups. This membership is known as an individual's social identity. A highly valued social identity is presumed to affect the individual's self-esteem positively. Conversely, a negative social identity is hypothesized to be detrimental. The low socioeconomic position of Mexican Americans, coupled with several other indicators of disadvantage and discrimination, support the widely held perception that Mexican Americans are much lower in status than Anglos.[8] A negative social identity is thus associated with membership in the Mexican American group--a fact that has an adverse impact on the self-esteem of the group's members.

Tajfel believes that people strive to define themselves positively in an effort to boost their self-esteem through membership in groups with a positive social identity.[9] Members of subordinate groups can pursue two alternative options in order to enhance their self-esteem or social identity: they can strive for individual mobility by leaving their low status group for a higher status one, or, if this is not possible, they can struggle to change the social system in order to enhance the status of their entire group.

The strategy of individual mobility is based on the belief that society is flexible and permeable, i.e., movement between status groups is possible. Therefore, if an individual is not satisfied with the conditions imposed upon his/her life due to membership in a particular social group, he/she can move into a more satisfactory group through talent, hard work, or good luck. On the other hand, advocates of social change believe that society is rigid. According to this view, it is difficult for individuals to remove themselves from an unsatisfactory, underprivileged, or stigmatized group. Hence, in order to improve a negative social identity while remaining a member of the group an individual must strive to enhance the status of the group as a whole. The catalyst for changing the system is the perception of injustice. Indeed, according to Tajfel, the development of competitive ethnocentrism and intergroup conflict between groups of different statuses is contingent upon a perception that the status differential is illegitimate and unstable.[10] Tajfel believes that the perception of an illegitimate status relationship between groups leads to increased perceptions of underlying similarity or comparability between groups, encompassing many dimensions such as status, power, or dominance.[11] Such perceptions by members of subordinate groups may trigger social action and competition in intergroup behavior.

Turner and Brown have stated that "subordinate groups will seek positive distinctiveness (dimensions on which they are superior) to the degree that their inferiority is not perceived as inherent, immutable or fully legitimate."[12] Given the long history of conflict between Mexican Americans and Anglos, the former would not be expected to perceive existing status differences between themselves and Anglos as stable and legitimate. Therefore, Mexican Americans are likely to consider Anglo Americans as a relevant group for social comparison. Since perceived illegitimacy theoretically increases the comparability of different status groups, such increased comparability will probably be reflected in intensified levels of social competition (ingroup favoritism) among Mexican Americans when they have the opportunity to compare themselves to Anglos on various relevant dimensions.[13]

Turner and Brown conducted the first study to measure the impact of variations in legitimacy, stability, and status on intergroup relations.[14] Generally speaking, their study provided empirical support for Tajfel's predictions within a controlled laboratory setting. The present study explores similar issues in the context of "real world" intergroup relations and interethnic conflict between Mexican Americans and Anglos in American society.

The following predictions are based on social identity theory and the social history of Anglo and Mexican American interethnic relations. Because of the long history of conflict between the two groups, we expected Mexican Americans to perceive the current status differences as more illegitimate and unfair than would Anglos. Subordinate groups who cannot engage in individual mobility and perceive the system as illegitimate will generally opt for a strategy in which the status of the group as a whole is increased. In light of the many social barriers keeping Mexican Americans from advancing in our society, we expected them to espouse a greater social change orientation than Anglo Americans. Conversely, Anglo Americans were expected to advocate individual mobility. Because American society *is* more flexible for Anglos and allows them individual mobility, it is the most adaptive strategy for them to pursue. Finally, based on social identity theory, we also expected Anglo Americans and Mexican Americans to display ingroup favoritism and to harbor discriminatory attitudes toward one another when asked to compare the two groups on specific dimensions.

Method

Subject Population

Subjects were 169 students attending the University of California, Riverside. Seventy-five subjects identified themselves as Anglo Americans, and ninety-four as Mexican Americans, Chicanos or Hispanics. Since the majority of the Hispanic students identified themselves as Mexican Americans, we opted to use only the data that comprised the majority of our sample. (Hereafter, "Hispanic" and

"Mexican American" will be used interchangeably.) The two ethnic groups were comparable in terms of age and major field of study.

Procedure

Questionnaires were distributed to students during class. Subjects were informed that the purpose of the survey was to gather data about opinions concerning the status relations between Anglos and Hispanics in society. Subjects choosing to participate were asked to read standardized instructions and fill out the questionnaire carefully.

Instrument

A fifteen-item questionnaire was developed to obtain a measure of perceived status relations between Anglo Americans and Hispanic Americans. A detailed item analysis of the questionnaire, followed by a close examination of simple correlations among the items, and finally a confirmatory factor analysis was conducted to substantiate conceptually-driven item groupings. The factor analysis yielded four factors (eighen values > 1) corresponding to the dimensions of (1) social change, (2) individual mobility, (3) legitimacy versus illegitimacy, and (4) ingroup favoritism.

Results

The data were analyzed by means of four two-way Multivariate Analysis of Variance (MANOVA) using ethnic background and gender as independent variables. A separate MANOVA was performed on the individual items (scores) under the following conceptual groupings: social change, individual mobility, legitimacy versus illegitimacy, and ingroup favoritism.

The social change grouping consisted of four items. Two of them tapped into individuals' beliefs concerning the perception of status differences between Anglos and Hispanics in terms of power, prestige, and economic means. The other two items concerned the perception of barriers to personal success as well as obstacles to the success of Hispanics. The MANOVA on the social change items indicated a significant main effect for ethnic background $F(4,160) = 8.02$, $p<.0001$. The univariate analysis of the four social change items indicated that both groups agreed the overall status of Hispanics is lower than that of Anglos $F(1,164) = <1$, ns. However, Mexican American subjects perceived a significantly larger difference in power, prestige, and economic means than did Anglo subjects $F(1,163) = 7.14$, $p<.01$. They also perceived more barriers $F(1,163) = 3.62$, $p<.05$, and obstacles to their success based on ethnicity than did Anglo subjects $F(1,163) = 27.71$, $p<.0001$. These results indicated a greater social change orientation among Mexican Americans than among Anglo Americans. The cell means for these effects are shown in Figure 1.

Three items were associated with the individual mobility grouping. Two of them suggested that a positive change had occurred in the perception of Hispanics. The third item stated that only individual effort will permit Hispanics to succeed. The individual mobility grouping provided significant MANOVA main effects for ethnic background $F(3,162) = 3.48$, $p<.0174$, and gender $F(3,162) =$

Figure 1. Means for items on the social change grouping as a function of subject ethnicity.

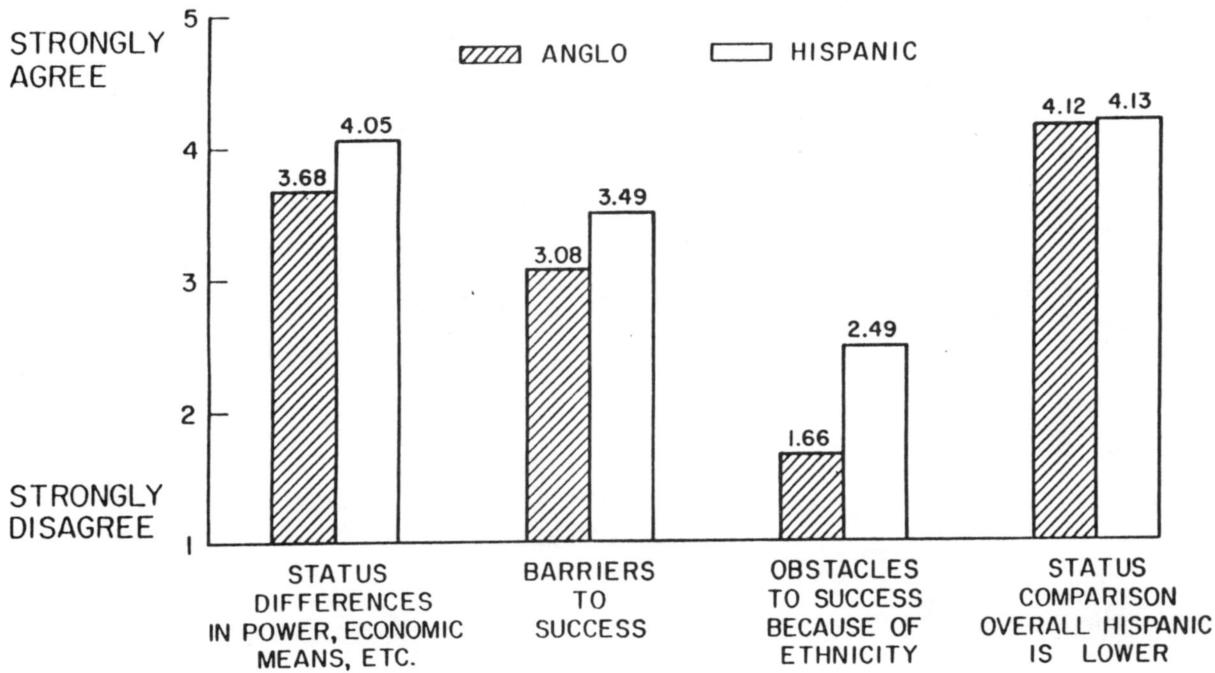

Figure 2. Means for items on the individual mobility grouping as a function of subject ethnicity

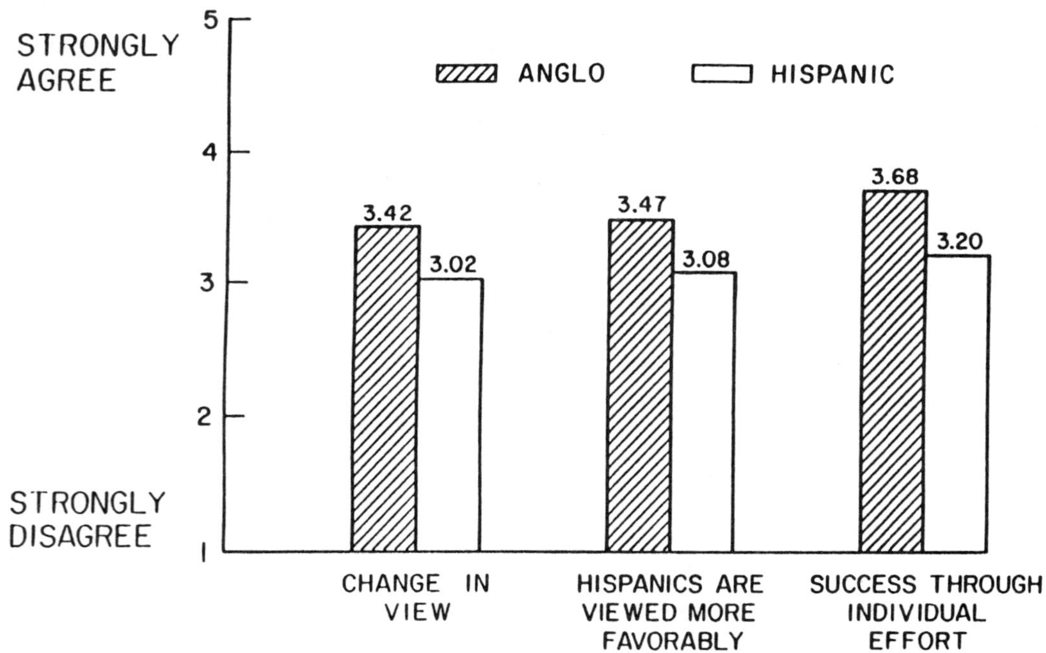

2.69, $p<.0484$. The univariate analysis of the three individual mobility items showed that Anglo subjects and women reported a significant change in the Anglo view of Hispanics. However, Mexican Americans $F(1,164) = 4.44$, $p<.03$ and men $F(1,164) = 3.58$, $p<.05$ did not perceive such an appreciable change in view. Anglo subjects also perceived their views of Hispanics as being more favorable than Mexican-American subjects did $F(1,165) = 4.06$, $p<.04$. Finally, Anglo subjects believed more firmly than did Mexican Americans that individual effort is the only avenue available for Hispanics who wish to succeed $F(1,161) = 5.76$, $p<.01$. It is clear that Anglos espoused a stronger individual mobility belief structure than did Mexican American subjects (Figure 2). Females, as well, were more oriented toward individual mobility than were males.

The legitimacy versus illegitimacy grouping consisted of three items tapping the perceived fairness and justification of status differences between Anglos and Hispanics. Included in this grouping was an item concerning the perception of conflict between Anglos and Hispanics. The legitimacy versus illegitimacy grouping was significant by both ethnic background $F(3,163) = 2.71$; $p<.0471$ and gender $F(3,163) = 3.04$; $p<.0307$. The univariate analysis of the three items showed that while both groups agreed that status differences between Anglos and Hispanics are unjust $F(1,165) = 1$, ns; more men and Anglos saw the treatment of Hispanics in society as fair $F(1,165) = 8.03$, $p<.01$ than did women $F(1,165) = 2.85$, $p<.05$ and Mexican American subjects. More women also perceived the status differences between Anglos and Hispanics as unjust $F(1,165) = 8.18$, $p<.05$, in

Figure 3. Means for items on the legitimacy versus illegitimacy grouping as a function of subject ethnicity

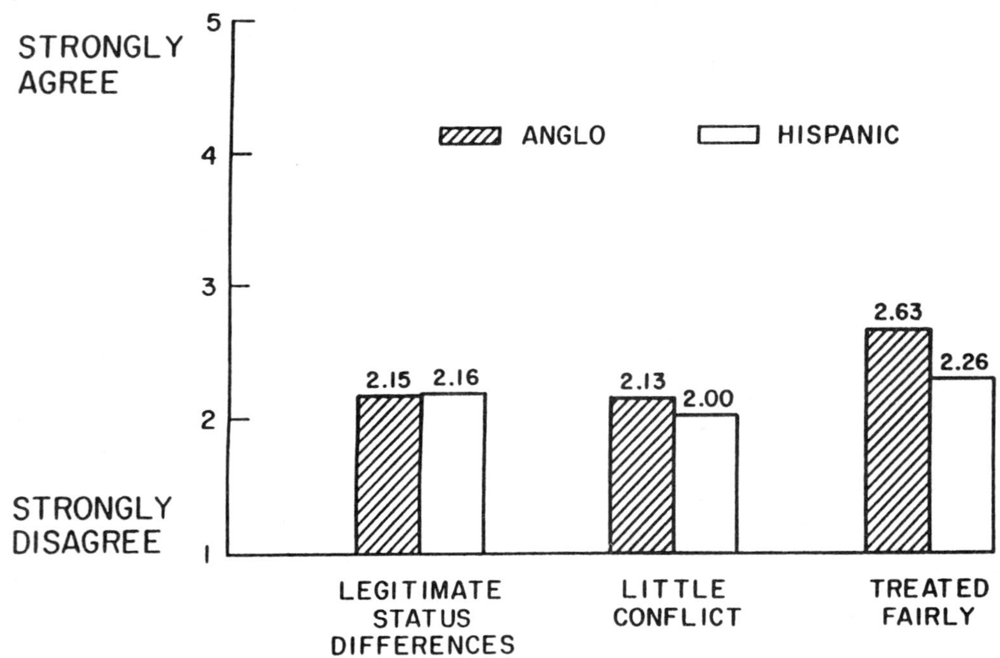

Figure 4. Means for items on the legitimacy versus illegitimacy grouping as a function of subject gender.

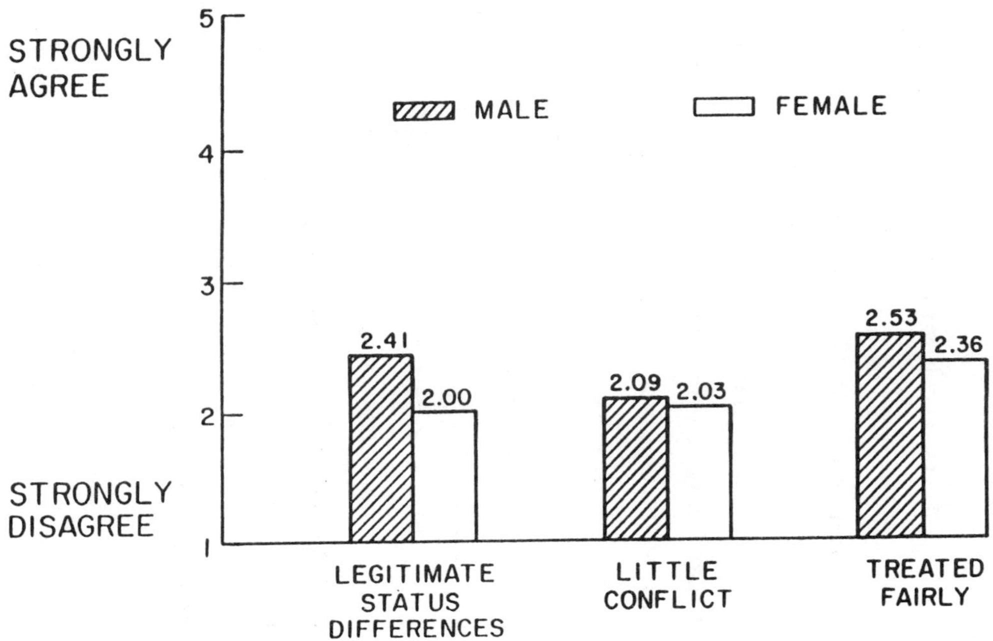

comparison to men. More Mexican Americans than Anglos believed that status differences between Anglo and Hispanics are illegitimate (means for these effects are shown in Figure 3). Furthermore, more females than males perceived the status differences as illegitimate (see Figure 4).

The ingroup favoritism grouping consisted of five comparative items of Anglo versus Hispanic performance on mental work, sports, physical work, math problems, and verbal problems. The multivariate analysis revealed a significant ethnic effect only $F(5,156) = 8.55$, $p<.0001$. An examination of the univariate effects for ingroup favoritism showed significant differences in four of the five dimensions: mental work $F(1,160) = 5.68$, $p<.02$; sports $F(1,160) = 10.65$, $p<.001$; physical work $F(1,160) = 33.47$, $p<.0001$; and math problems $F(1,160) = 10.85$, $p<.001$. Overall, both groups displayed ingroup bias. (Subjects rated the performance of Hispanics relative to Anglos; scores above 3 indicate Hispanic superiority.) As can be seen in Figure 5, Hispanic performance on these dimensions was upgraded by Mexican Americans and downgraded by Anglos. Although physical work performance by Hispanics was given high marks by both groups, Mexican Americans showed extreme ingroup bias on this dimension. Finally, Hispanics were rated lower than Anglos on verbal problem solving by both groups $F(1,160) = < 1$, ns.

Discussion

In general, the data from the scales validate Tajfel and Turner's theoretical framework and provide support for the prediction that

Figure 5. Means for items on the ingroup favoritism grouping as a function of subject ethnicity.

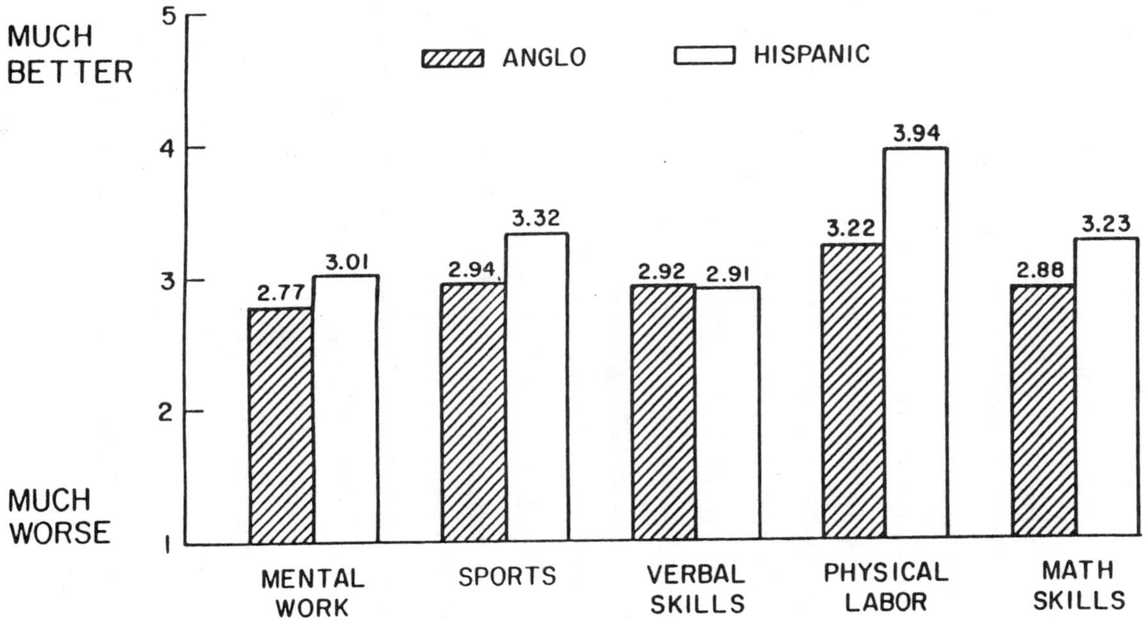

group membership (dominant versus subordinate, including the positive or negative social identities inherent in such group memberships) influences a person's orientation towards individual mobility or social change.[15] Furthermore, it also seems clear that Mexican Americans perceive the social system to be more illegitimate than do Anglo Americans. Finally, both groups exhibited ingroup favoritism on several dimensions of comparison.

As expected, Mexican American subjects exhibited a more social change oriented belief structure than did Anglo subjects. Conversely, Anglos exhibited a greater orientation toward an individual mobility belief structure than did Mexican Americans. Tajfel and Turner's social identity theory predicts that minority groups are more likely to experience a negative social identity as a result of low status.[16] Mexican Americans belong to a stigmatized group and experience the consequences of a negative social identity. Perhaps because of this, they see the social system as more rigid and illegitimate than Anglos do. In this case, enhancing the group's social identity as a whole is the most effective way to raise the individual's social identity. This is true particularly in the absence of opportunities for individual mobility. Indeed, social identity theory predicts that individual mobility is the preferred strategy if the opportunity is present, as it should be in a flexible and permeable society. This is consistent with the Anglo subjects' belief that through their own effort and talent they can climb the ladder of success. Such a philosophy is based on the traditional American ideal of the rugged individualist who succeeds by his own merit against all odds.

We also found that females exhibited a greater individual mobility orientation than males. Traditionally, women have assumed the status of their husbands when they marry, and they have usually been socialized to marry men of equal or greater status--hypergamy being a socially sanctioned strategy for upward mobility. Recent findings by Shinagawa and Pang show that even today, women still tend more than men to strive for upward social mobility through marriage.[17] For that reason, women are more likely than men to perceive society as flexible, due to their greater access to upward mobility through marriage.

In general, although Anglo subjects perceived the status differences between Anglos and Hispanics as basically illegitimate, Mexican American and female subjects were significantly more extreme in their perceptions. These findings, in conjunction with Mexican Americans' greater social change orientation, support Tajfel's notion that a social change perspective is closely related to the perception of an illegitimate and unjust social system.[18] The fact that women see the system as more illegitimate than men do may reflect their greater consciousness of the inequalities within the social system, probably due to the victimization and stigmatization that women experience by virtue of their lower status.[19]

Finally, the data provide support for the prediction of ingroup favoritism. Both Anglo and Mexican American subjects exhibited ingroup bias in their comparison of Anglo and Hispanic performance of mental work, athletic activities, and mathematical abilities. Hispanics' performance on these dimensions were upgraded by

Mexican Americans and downgraded by Anglos. On the dimension of physical work, Hispanics were given high marks by both groups, with Mexican Americans showing extreme ingroup favoritism. This finding may reflect the overrepresentation of Mexican Americans in the agricultural labor force. However, both groups rated Hispanics lower than Anglos on verbal problem solving, which may be a reflection of the belief that Anglos are superior in terms of language.[20] According to Tajfel and Turner, upgrading the ingroup through social competition is a means to boost positive distinctiveness and thus social identity. This makes ingroup favoritism an accessible and salient vehicle with which to enhance self-esteem.[21]

Our findings show that Tajfel and Turner's theory seems appropriate for studying interethnic relations between Mexican Americans and Anglos.[22] We hope that real world relations will be explored in more detail so that a greater understanding of interethnic conflict and tension between Mexican Americans and Anglos in American society can be reached.

Notes

1. Mario Barrera, *Race and Class in the Southwest: A Theory of Racial Inequality* (Notre Dame: University of Notre Dame Press, 1979).

2. Robert Rosenbaum, "Mexicano Resistance in the Southwest," in Robert Rosenbaum, *The Sacred Right of Self-Preservation* (Austin, TX.: University of Texas Press, 1984).

3. Barrera, *Race and Class*.

4. Ibid.

5. Gloria Romero and Raymond Garza, "Attribution for the Occupational Success/Failure of Ethnic Minority and Nonminority Women," *Sex Roles* 14 (1986):445-452.

6. Refugio Rochin, "The Socioeconomic Status of the Hispanic Population," in this volume.

7. Colleen Ward and Miles Hewstone, "Ethnicity, Language and Intergroup Relations in Malaysia and Singapore: A Social Psychological Analysis," *Journal of Multilingual and Multicultural Development* 6 (1985):271-296; Henri Tajfel and John Turner, "An Integrative Theory of Intergroup Conflict," in *Psychology of Intergroup Relations,* ed. W. G. Austin and S. Worcher (Chicago: Nelson-Hall, 1985), 7-24.

8. Rochin, "Socioeconomic Status"; Rosenbaum, "Mexicano Resistance."

9. Henri Tajfel, "Social Categorization, Social Identity and Social Comparison," *Differentiation Between Social Groups: Studies in the Social Psychology of Intergroup Relations,* ed. H. Tajfel (London and

New York: Academic Press, 1978), 33-47.

10. Ibid.

11. Henri Tajfel, "The Exit of Social Mobility and the Voice of Social Change: Notes on the Social Psychology of Intergroup Relations," *Social Science Information* 14 (1975):101-118.

12. John Turner and R. Rupert Brown, "Social Status, Cognitive Alternatives and Intergroup Relations," in *Differentiation Between Social Groups,* ed. Tajfel.

13. Tajfel, "Exit of Social Mobility."

14. Turner and Brown, "Social Status."

15. Tajfel and Turner, "Integrative Theory."

16. Ibid.

17. Larry Shinagawa and Gin Yong Pang, "Marriage Patterns of Asian Americans in California, 1980," in this volume.

18. Tajfel, "Social Categorization."

19. John Williams and Howard Giles, "The Changing Status of Women in Society," in *Differentiation Between Social Groups,* ed. Tajfel, 431-446.

20. Howard Giles, *Language, Ethnicity, and Intergroup Relations* (London and New York: Academic Press, 1977); Howard Giles and P. Johnson, "The Role of Language in Ethnic Group Relations," in *Intergroup Behavior,* ed. J. C. Turner and H. Giles (Oxford: Basil Blackwell, 1981), 199-243.

21. Tajfel and Turner, "Integrative Theory."

22. Ibid.

Interactions Between Latinos and Anglos on Prime-time Television: A Case Study of "Condo"

Federico A. Subervi-Velez

During the last three decades, a number of studies have analyzed the frequency and/or characteristics of the roles in which minorities have been portrayed on television. Most of these have focused on Afro-Americans, but recently some studies and critical essays have dealt with television portrayals of Latinos, Asians, and Native Americans.[1] Altogether, the research shows that although the number and quality of roles played by some minorities, particularly blacks, have improved significantly since the 1960s, these roles still do not represent adequately the socioeconomic and cultural diversity of the ethnic minority populations.[2]

An important aspect of minority portrayals that the research has virtually ignored is the amount and kind of interaction between characters of different ethnic backgrounds. Of the numerous studies that analyze the representations of minorities on television, less than a handful have focused specifically on interethnic interactions among nonanimated characters.[3] In spite of the increasing numerical representation of ethnic minorities, these studies reveal a dearth of significant and positive communication between minority and Anglo characters on television.

This study investigates interactions between Latinos and Anglos in the context of family relations on television shows and explores new quantitative and qualitative approaches to the analysis of ethnic minority portrayals on television. Most importantly, it applies tenets of assimilation and pluralism theories to analyze whether those television interactions represent: (a) Latinos' assimilation or pluralism in relation to the dominant society, and (b) how Anglos accept or reject Latinos' efforts to integrate or to maintain some of their distinctive family, cultural, and social characteristics.

Although there have been some analyses of black families on the small screen, these have neglected the issue of relations with Anglos.[4] Research on Anglo families on television has not analyzed Anglo-black interactions, either.[5] The few studies of Latinos on television have not discussed interactions or family relations and, for the most part, are atheoretical descriptive analyses of stereotyped roles or functions. One reason for the scant attention given to Hispanics could be that, as stated in a study of the demography of fictional television characters, they "still do not exist in sufficient frequency to enable an intensive quantitative analysis."[6]

Changing Ethnic Milieu and a Special Role for Television

Today there are compelling reasons to analyze television portrayals of interactions between Anglos and other ethnic groups, particularly Latinos. First, Hispanics and other immigrant and minority populations should be dealt with more effectively by the media, if for no other reason than their dramatic growth in numbers. Nationwide the Latino population was estimated at over 18 million in 1987, representing 7.5 percent of the total U.S. population.[7] Forecasts expect it to double by the year 2020.[8] According to Willis, by the year 2005, "California's Latino, Asian and black population will outnumber non-Latino whites statewide."[9] In some localities, the population change is particularly notable. In Los Angeles, at the start of the 1985 school year, 62 percent of the children in public kindergarten were Latino. Because of this growth in numbers, the U.S.-born ethnic minorities, along with the new waves of immigrants, are expected to make significant political, cultural, and economic changes in America.[10] Therefore, majority society members will have to learn to interact with, and adapt and relate to, the diverse ethnic populations. Minorities will have to do likewise and perhaps each group will vary in the degree to which they assimilate or stay pluralistic vis-à-vis the dominant society. In other words, the process of mutual learning, interaction, and adaptation will have to occur among all segments of society.

Secondly, the media can and should play a more significant and positive role in disseminating notions about the growing multiethnic populations. Television should have a special responsibility in this process, because by watching television representations of minority characters, audiences will absorb and learn a great deal about minorities, which in turn, will affect their attitudes toward the minorities in real life.[11] And, at least among children, television programming could encourage interaction with members of different ethnic groups.[12] The responsibility of this medium is great because under certain conditions its socialization impact is intensified, e.g., when "the values or views recur from program to program."[13] The recurrence is especially evident in representations of Latinos. Greenberg, Burgoon, Burgoon, and Korzenny conclude that there has been, among other problems, "an absence of positive images in television and a virtual absence of any images" and "an emphasis on the portrayal of Hispanics as crooks, cops, and comics."[14] The symbolic media also influence viewers who do not have other sources of information or experiences that "provide a standard against which to assess the views offered by television."[15] The number of people who rely mostly on television to develop their notions about Latinos and other ethnic groups is not known, but one study found that among 300 white elementary school children in Michigan, 40 percent cited television as their best source of information about how blacks look, talk, and dress.[16] Therefore, television not only should diversify its ethnic representations, but also should incorporate more positive images as well as frameworks for interpreting the growing variety of ethnic life in this country. Attention should be given to all population groups because, as Dorr indicates, the learning process from television occurs among people of all ethnic/racial backgrounds and there is "no evidence that it differs in any substantial way, as a process, among those groups."[17]

Recognizing that interactions of Anglos with Hispanics and other ethnic groups are bound to increase, and that there is a need to produce more diverse and positive images, this essay explores an integrated and theoretically based approach for analyzing television's portrayals of interactions between Latinos and Anglos.

What Is Known About Television Portrayals of Ethnic Relations?

The previous studies of interethnic relations on television, which have primarily looked at prime-time situation comedies and drama, call attention to the disjunction between improved role images and interaction portrayals. For example, Weigel, Loomis and Soja found that "all types of black-white interactions constituted less than 2 percent of prime-time programming."[18] On the qualitative side, their analysis showed that although relations between these ethnic groups often involved cooperative interdependence, they also were characterized by greater formality and less individualism than interactions among white characters, which were rated as being more intimate, multifaceted, and likely to involve shared decision-making. Baptista-Fernandez and Greenberg also documented the infrequent number of cross-ethnic relations, revealing that "blacks averaged three interactions with whites for every one that whites had with blacks."[19] However, these authors found no significant differences between black and white characters in terms of giving, seeking, or receiving advice, information, or orders.

Lemon investigated intersex and interrace dominance patterns and concluded that blacks were more dominant, more equal, and less frequently dominated in situation comedies than in dramatic shows. According to her, "the situation comedies which deal with family situations, interpersonal problems, and casual plot lines seem to lend themselves to egalitarian interactions. . . ."[20]

In a more recent study, Auletta and Hammerback integrated the socioeconomic dimension of dominance and the interpersonal dimension of dependency to analyze interracial communication.[21] Although they found blacks being portrayed as equals, the authors state that "Blacks and Whites are depicted as being apart and independent rather than together and interdependent. The equal but separate relationship prohibits close friendships, accurate and deep understanding of one another, and collaborative working relationships."[22]

These studies reveal the characteristics of black-white communication patterns on television and are possibly also representative of interaction patterns between Anglos and other minority groups on the small screen. Unfortunately, Hispanics, Asians, and Native Americans are portrayed in too few significant roles for sufficient data to be aggregated and analyzed to replicate the studies that have been conducted with blacks. Thus, a case study was required in which theory, specifically, the concepts of assimilation and pluralism, could be applied.

Foundations for the Assimilation/Pluralism Framework

Abramson indicates that the many terms used to denote the dynamics of ethnic relations with the dominant society "fall into two broader categories: those of assimilation, the processes that lead to greater homogeneity in society, and those of pluralism, conditions that produce sustained ethnic differences and continued heterogeneity."[23] A common view among the many interpretations of these concepts is that changes take place in various dimensions, levels, and stages.[24] Three of the most significant dimensions are family affairs (e.g., interethnic/racial visiting and marriage), cultural affairs (e.g., language, food, music, and religion), and social affairs (e.g., recreational practices and membership in clubs). It can be postulated that a person has been assimilated when, in any of these or other dimensions (e.g., politics), he/she has attitudes and behaviors that resemble those of the majority society more than those of his/her own ethnic group. The converse would be true for pluralism, i.e., preference and action in line with the ethnic group instead of the majority society. However, as Subervi-Velez has proposed, changing attitudes or behavior in one dimension may not necessarily be related to the attitudes or behavior in other dimensions.[25]

A complimentary aspect of ethnic group dynamics is the reaction of the members of the dominant society--the attitudes and behaviors that denote how the "mainstream" population accepts or rejects the minorities' efforts to assimilate or maintain their differences. On the one hand, Anglos may contribute to Latinos' assimilation by accepting their efforts to partake in the former group's familial, cultural, or societal affairs, while on the other hand, Anglos may contribute to Hispanics' pluralism, either by accepting their maintenance of their own language, values, etc., or by rejecting Latinos' assimilation efforts, which may imply to Latinos that they should keep their ways for lack of viable alternatives. A third way Anglos may help to perpetuate Latinos' pluralism is by adopting some Hispanic tastes, such as in music, art, food, architecture, or holiday celebrations. Here, too, attitudinal and/or behavioral acceptance or rejection in one dimension may or may not be related to acceptance or rejection in another dimension. In either case, the reaction of members of the majority society can greatly influence the changes made by the members of the minority group.

Recent studies of minority groups and the mass media show increasing interest in the topic of ethnic assimilation and pluralism.[26] However, most of these studies have looked at how minorities are similar to or different from the dominant society in their communication patterns or how minorities' assimilation or pluralism is affected by their media use or exposure. These communication studies seriously neglect the influence of the dominant society's acceptance or rejection of the ethnic minorities' assimilation or pluralism efforts.

Analyses of media content rarely use the theoretical concepts discussed above, but in one study, McGee-Banks used assimilation theory to analyze images of black Americans on television.[27] In assessing differences in the portrayals of blacks in shows with integrated versus nonintegrated casts, she found that the former programs had significantly fewer theme units with stereotypic black characteristics: low social status of blacks, community problems, and personal problems. McGee-Banks concluded that blacks portrayed in integrated settings were shown to be more assimilated than blacks in nonintegrated settings.

Since there are no commercial television programs with nonintegrated casts of Latinos, the present study could only explore the degree of assimilation (or pluralism) of Hispanics in an integrated setting.[28] The situation comedy, "Condo," aired by the ABC television network in 1983, provided a rare opportunity to analyze systematically extensive interactions between Latino and Anglo family members in a prime-time series.[29] A descriptive "one-sheet" provided by Richard Kozak, ABC's vice-president of affiliate relations, states that the show featured a textbook WASP and an upwardly mobile Hispanic who find themselves as condominium neighbors on opposite sides of almost every question, yet who are faced with impending family ties. The Anglo character, James Kirkridge, has been forced by uncertain economic times to forgo his rambling old house in favor of a new condo. Jesse Rodriguez, on the other hand, has moved up from the barrio as the result of his expanding business. This study focuses on how family and social and cultural affairs between Latinos and Anglos were portrayed in the show, and how these portrayals represent or reflect assimilationist versus pluralistic adaptation.

Methodology

Sample. I recorded on video tape eleven of the thirteen episodes of "Condo" shown during the season; two episodes could not be recorded due to technical difficulties. I reviewed all taped episodes, took extensive notes on the principal themes of each program, and then selected five for detailed analysis. The programs were selected because they dealt explicitly with family, cultural, and/or social affairs during most of the episode.

Measures. The unit of analysis was the whole program, but to explore new quantitative and qualitative approaches to the analysis of ethnic portrayals on television, I analyzed three aspects of Anglo-Latino interaction. First, I measured the appearance time of Latinos and Anglos together, Latinos alone, and Anglos alone. Previous studies have analyzed how much time minority characters appear on the screen but have not used this measure as an overall indicator of interethnic interaction potential. Second, I coded utterances relating to assimilation or pluralism made by each major character. For the most part, I examined complete sentences, but I also noted fragments of sentences that clearly expressed a value about assimilation or pluralism. I also coded scenes related to assimilation and/or pluralism. For this unit of observation, analyses are based predominantly on visual cues that allow for inferential classifications, but I included some combinations of visual and verbal statements which, when discussed together, provide a much richer analysis of the interethnic interactions. This means that coding and analysis of utterances and scenes is not a mutually exclusive but a complementary process. I did not analyze scenes and statements unrelated to assimilation/pluralism. Following the analytical distinctions outlined above, I coded and classified selected statements and scenes under three interrelated schemas: the ethnicity of the source, the type of assimilation/pluralism expressed, and the topic category. The first specified if the statement/scene was uttered by or involved a Latino and/or Anglo character, the second assessed whether it reflected acceptance or rejection of the other group, while the third determined if the acceptance/rejection pertained to family, cultural affairs, or social affairs.[30]

Assimilation is inferred when a Latino character is a participant in, is positive towards, praises, likes, or accepts Anglo family, culture, or society. Assimilation is also inferred when an Anglo character accepts, agrees with, supports, or encourages the assimilation overtures or efforts of Latinos. Pluralism is inferred in four different ways: first, if a Latino character is pro-Latino (e.g., is a participant in, is positive towards, praises, likes, or accepts his/her own family, culture, or society, or shows attachment to Latino roots); second, if a Latino character is anti-Anglo (e.g., is negative towards, critical of, insulting or indifferent to, or rejects Anglo family, culture, or society); third, if an Anglo character is pro-Latino as Latino (e.g., positive toward Latinos for being Latinos); and fourth, if an Anglo character is anti-Latino (e.g., is negative towards, critical of, insulting or indifferent to, or rejects Latino family, culture, or society). Anglo rejection of Latino assimilation efforts is also coded in this latter category.

This coding scheme is basically founded on the aforementioned theory and research, but coding and classification of assimilation and pluralism utterances and scenes is inferential because neither the Latino nor Anglo characters ever state explicitly that they are pro- or anti- assimilation or pluralism.[31] Also, I did not interview the program's script writers to discover if they wished to convey--in addition to humor to obtain high ratings--any particular messages about interethnic relations. Nevertheless, to assure some qualitative degree of reliability, I viewed each episode repeatedly (pausing and rewinding the videotape as often as necessary) while making notations and oftentimes full transcriptions of the pertinent statements and scenes. Classificatory decisions were made only when sufficient information and cues allowed for reasonable judgments. Still, the findings in the next section are based only on my own interpretations of the show. As discussed below, the exploratory nature of this study requires further replications and specifications for improved reliability in the analysis of interethnic interactions on television, using the theoretical framework of assimilation and pluralism.

Finally, it should be noted that the interactions were not coded for other characteristics (e.g., domination, interdependence, direction, mode, initiator or recipient of acts) because the purpose of the study was to explore the application of assimilation/pluralism theories, and the context and setting of the program rigidly established the boundaries within which the actors had to relate to each other. Nevertheless, some notes were made of such interactions when they were found within the aforementioned theoretical context.

Findings

Presentation and interpretation of the findings requires a brief summary of the program setting. The findings are then divided into three parts: frequency of interethnic interactions, statements, and scenes.

The program setting. The Latino family was composed of Jesse Rodriguez (a former gardener and current owner of a landscaping business), his wife Maria (employed but occupation unspecified), their daughter Linda (eighteen years old and college-bound), and Maria's father, Jose Montoya (retired but uppity). The Anglo family was composed of James Kirkridge (a self-employed insurance salesman), his wife Kiki (occupation unspecified), their oldest son Scott (nineteen years old and a college freshman), and younger son Billy (a junior high school student).

During the premiere episode, Jesse and James walk out to their adjoining terraces and, upon finding out that they are going to be neighbors, begin the first of numerous verbal clashes in which they often treat each other with some bigotry and disdain.[32] In contrast, their wives are very friendly and cordial, while Linda and Scott fall madly in love at first sight. Cognizant of their fathers' disapproval of their growing romance, Linda and Scott elope and secretly marry. Several of the following episodes are based on Linda and Scott's relationship, their child, and their families' reactions to them, but the majority of the plots and sub-plots also involve the older characters.

Frequency of interethnic interactions. Table 1 presents the distribution of ethnic appearance time in each episode. Adding the total times for the five episodes suggests that Latinos and Anglos are engaged in interethnic interactions 61 percent of the time. Latinos are shown interacting only among themselves 18 percent of the time, Anglos 21 percent. Thus, Latinos appear during 79 percent of the program time when the integrated settings are combined with the all-Latino settings. Appearance time for each character varies by episode, but of the approximately twenty-two minutes of each episode, at least one character from each ethnic group appears together close to 13.5 minutes. During a good portion of the interethnic interaction time, most members of both families are present, but the verbal exchanges are predominantly between the two main male characters (Jesse and James). Altogether, the presentation of interethnic interactions is a major feature of "Condo." Although this time measurement is a crude indicator of the prominence of ethnic portrayals on television, it can

Table 1

Distribution of Ethnic Appearance Time in Minutes

Episode number	Latinos & Anglos	Latinos Alone	Anglos Alone
1	14.10	4.06	3.44
2	15.23	3.16	1.43
3	13.15	3.47	3.53
4	8.21	6.33	7.32
5	13.25	1.52	6.40
Total time	64.34	19.34	22.32
Average time per episode (%)	(61)	(18)	(21)

serve for at least general comparisons with other television programs.

The statements. Tables 2, 3 and 4 show a summary distribution of the coded statements. Overall, there are significantly fewer assimilationist than pluralistic utterances (28 vs. 145; $p<.001$).[33] Thus, Latino characters as a whole are not portrayed as assimilationist. And, although Latinos and Anglos are both shown making an equal number of statements related to assimilation (Table 2), the distribution of these by topic reveals an interesting contrast: Latinos' assimilation overtures are generally about social affairs while those of the Anglos are all about family affairs.

The summary tables of the pluralistic statements reveal a different perspective of the Latino-Anglo interactions. Most of the pluralistic statements made by Latinos were anti-Anglo (Table 3-B). These significantly outnumber their assimilationist statements (41 vs.

Table 2

Number of Assimilation Statements by Ethnic Group and Topic

	A. by Latinos					B. by Anglos					
Topic	JR	M	L	JM	t	JK	K	S	Othr	t	Totals
Family	1	1	2	-	4	7	4	1	2	14	18
Culture	1	-	-	-	1	-	-	-	-	-	1
Society	9	-	-	-	9	-	-	-	-	-	9
Totals	11	1	2	-	14	7	4	1	2	14	28

Table 3

Number of Pluralistic Statements by Type and Topic for Latinos

	A. pro-Latino					B. anti-Latino					
Topic	JR	M	L	JM	t	JR	M	L	JM	t	Totals
Family	-	-	2	-	2	13	2	2	-	17	19
Culture	19	2	2	4	27	7	-	-	1	8	35
Society	1	1	-	-	2	5	6	2	3	16	18
Totals	20	3	4	4	31	25	8	4	4	41	72

Table 4

Number of Pluralistic Assertions by Type and Topic for Anglos

	A. pro-Latino as Latino					B. anti-Latino					
Topic	JK	K	S	Othr	t	JK	K	S	Othr	t	Totals
Family	3	1	4	-	8	18	1	-	2	21	29
Culture	2	2	-	1	5	12	-	1	-	13	18
Society	3	1	-	-	4	14	-	-	8	22	26
Totals	8	4	4	1	17	44	1	1	10	56	73

Legend: JR: Jesse, M: Maria, L: Linda, JM: Jose, JK: James, K: Kiki, S: Scott, Othr: Other Anglo/Latino Characters.

14; $p<.001$) but not their pro-Latino statements (41 vs. 31; n.s.). In addition, most of the pluralistic statements made by the Anglos are anti-Latino (Table 4-B). These also outnumber their positive statements about Latinos of either the pluralistic type (56 vs. 17; $p<.001$) or the assimilation type (56 vs. 14; $p<.001$).

The focus of Latinos' negative statements about Anglos is on family and social affairs; the test for differences between topics is significant at $p<.05$. The same focus is evident in Anglos' anti-Latino statements, but their topic differences are not significant. The most alluded-to topic of Hispanics' pro-Latino statements concern cultural affairs (the statistical difference in topic codes for Table 3-A is significant at $p<.001$). No significant difference is found in the topic distribution of Anglos' pro-Latino statements.

An analysis of which characters make the various types of statements is also very revealing about cross-gender interactions. For both ethnic groups, the two principal adult males make more negative than positive statements about each other, their respective cultures and societies. For example, Jesse is coded making eleven assimilationist statements versus twenty-five pluralistic ones of the anti-Anglo type, while James makes seven assimilationist statements compared to fifty-two pluralistic ones, forty-four of which are of the anti-Latino type (intra-character differences by type are significant at least at $p<.05$). This imbalance is also evident for the few secondary ("other") Anglo characters (all male) who in their brief appearances make numerous anti-Latino statements.

Typical negative comments by Jesse allude to James' multicolored plaid pants, or his family. The word "gringo" is pejoratively used by Jesse and Jose, his father-in-law, at least four times. Most of Jesse's assimilationist statements are inferred from an episode in which he wants to join the exclusive Anglo country club. Most of his pro-Latino pluralistic statements reflect his attachment to his Hispanic roots, particularly his Catholicism. For example, he demands that Scott and Linda have a Catholic wedding, and during a moment of family stress, he exclaims the name of several saints in Spanish. James frequently criticizes Latino food and society in general.[34] He often uses the words "you people" to negatively refer to some aspect of Latino society (e.g., "your Aztec ancestors...sacrificing virgins") or culture (e.g., "you people show up at weddings dressed like matadors"). The few instances of James' pro-Latino assertions occur mainly during two events: his reluctant defense of Jesse's membership at the country club and his admission (in the face of a prospective client whose bigotry exceeds his tolerance) that Linda is his daughter-in-law. Thus, the family, cultural, and social relations between the adult males are generally negative.

In contrast, the adult females are shown generally more cordial and accepting of each other. For example, Kiki makes four statements supporting Jesse's membership at the exclusive Anglo country club. And, although Table 3-B indicates that Maria makes eight anti-Anglo versus only one assimilationist statements, five of these are in one program, when she expresses reluctance to join the country club because of its ethnic/racial discrimination policies. Thus, most of Maria's and Kiki's interactions are generally positive, neither anti- nor pro- Anglo or Latino, just funny or supportive and understanding of their families and one another.

Table 5

Summary of Scenes Related to Assimilation and Pluralism

Assimilation by Latinos
A. The Rodriguez family has moved from a small house in the Latin barrio to a condo in a middle class, predominantly Anglo neighborhood.

B. Jess greatly likes the status of the exclusive Anglo country club and seeks admission as a member.

Assimilation by Anglos
C. Kiki supports Jesse's membership at the club during her meeting with the club's admission committee.

Pluralism by Latinos (pro-Latino)
D. When the Kirkridge family visits the Rodriguezes to celebrate Jose Senior's birthday, *menudo,* a traditional Mexican dish made of tripe, is served.

E. The Rodriguezes put up Latino-style decorations when they celebrate the 10th anniversary of Jesse's landscaping business.

F. Later, the music at that party is Mexican--a live mariachi band was hired to play.

G. Various guests shown in the background at the anniversary party have Latino physical features; in addition, two of the guests are black.

Pluralism by Latinos (anti-Anglo)
H. Linda does not like Scott's rich Anglo high school friends who are not too fond of her, either.

I. It is implied that Linda's and Scott's son was named Joselito in honor of Linda's grandfather, Jose.

J. James and Kiki dance and laugh at the Rodriguezes' business anniversary party.

K. James embraces Linda and admits she is his daughter-in-law as he defends her from a prospective insurance client who has been insulting with his racism and bigotry against Mexicans. James also embraces Jesse and shows affection for the latter's extended family.

Pluralism by Anglos (anti-Latino)
L. James expresses intense dislike and feigns illness when he is informed of the main ingredient of menudo.

M. When Jesse asks James to sponsor him for membership at the country club, James shows nonverbal (and verbal) displeasure with the request and moves away from Jesse to avoid giving an answer.

Mutual Accommodation
N. Linda and Scott, after having married secretly, decide to get married again, this time in a church to please their parents (particularly Jesse).

O. Scott decides to please both sets of parents by having the wedding at a Catholic chapel (not a cathedral where the Rodriguezes' wanted it nor at a Protestant church where his mother wanted it).

P. Both a priest and a minister officiate the ceremony at the chapel.

Q. The best man at the wedding is an Anglo while the maid of honor has Latino features. Also, both Latino and Anglo people are shown in the pews.

R. Linda's grandfather breaks a hole in the wall between two adjacent bedrooms of the Rodriguezes' and Kirkridge's condo apartments in order to build a door between them, because Scott and Linda have decided to live in a room in one apartment and provide their child his own room in the other.

S. Both the Rodriguezes and Kirkridges express affection for their children-in-law.

T. It is implied that Scott has been employed by Jesse to work in his landscaping business.

The youth of both genders and ethnic groups make few identifiable statements about assimilation or pluralism. In fact, the relationship between Linda and Scott primarily reflects mutual accommodation. Through their marriage, child, and apparent acceptance of each other, they represent the merging of the two cultures. This is best reflected in the scenes.[35]

The scenes. Table 5 summarizes twenty scenes related to family, cultural, and social affairs within the context of assimilation and pluralism. Only three are classified as reflective of ethnic assimilation, while ten are classified as reflective of pluralism in its various types. In an additional, unexpected finding, seven scenes require a third classification: mutual accommodation between Latinos and Anglos.

Latino assimilation efforts are represented in the first two scenes--the move to the Anglo middle class condo and Jesse's overture to join the country club--while scene C suggests a positive Anglo reaction (by Kiki) to the latter effort. On the other hand, ten scenes reflect some type of pluralism. Scenes D-F summarize how Latinos are portrayed as valuing some aspect of their culture and, in scene G, their society. Latinos' pluralism in the form of rejection of Anglos is most evident in the statements, particularly from Jesse, but in one scene (H), Linda's displeasure with her husband's Anglo friends is best inferred from her nonverbal expressions.

Anglos' pluralism in acceptance of Latinos is represented in three scenes, one related to culture (I), another to society (J), the third to family (K). They react negatively to Latinos in two others; one is specific to culture (i.e., the food scene, L), the other to a Latino societal assimilation effort--Jesse's wish to join the club (M).

The most interesting and unexpected findings are related to the seven scenes (N-T) representing mutual accommodation--that is, changes in the behavior of both Latinos and Anglos. Three scenes relate to family affairs (N, R, S), two to culture, specifically religion (O and P), and two to social affairs (Q and T). The majority of these scenes concern Linda's and Scott's relationship, particularly the wedding arrangements (N-R). A common characteristic of the scenes selected for summary is that the end result of the accommodation is portrayed in a positive way: both Latinos and Anglos accept something of the other's family or culture; they all agree with the arrangements.

Finally, throughout the studied episodes, the Rodriguezes visit the Kirkridges on two occasions while the Kirkridges visit the Rodriguez four times. Even though the specific statements and scenes from these visits have already been assessed, the overall message based on the differential frequency of the visits suggests that Anglos are portrayed as moving toward Latinos, instead of Latinos toward Anglos.

Discussion

This exploration of an integrated and theoretically based approach for analyzing interethnic interactions on television reveals the potential for insights overlooked in past studies of ethnic minorities on television. Although possibly requiring improvement, the approach suggests that combined, theoretically based analyses allow for a more comprehensive understanding of the messages being broadcast about how people of different ethnic backgrounds interrelate.

Specifically, "Condo," in contrast to other programs, portrayed Latinos as central, and not just background, characters. Neither did it show them as buffoons, cops, or lawbreakers. Although they were shown in comic situations (often as the main object of James' cynical assertions), the Latino actors appeared in few negatively stereotyped scenes. Even though the main Anglo male actors (James, his country club friends, and bigot client) made numerous anti-Latino statements, the pro-Latino statements and scenes counterbalanced them with some positive views. The anti-Anglo statements by the main Latino character (Jesse) were equally counterbalanced with some accommodation scenes. As Bark points out, the insults were supposed to "lead to some sort of enlightened understanding on the part of both lead characters."[36] He later adds, "Hispanics get some role models amid the carnage."[37] The statements and scenes about traditional aspects of Latino culture and society (e.g., religion, party decorations and music) were shown from relatively positive perspectives rather than ridiculed. An underlying message across the five episodes that I analyzed was that the Rodriguezes were a normal middle-class family with some variations in their cultural behaviors.

Yet, in "Condo" the dynamics of Latino and Anglo relations imply more heterogeneity than homogeneity. The program did not portray Latinos with major assimilationist orientations; rather, it emphasized pluralism and accommodation. "Condo" carried a general message that Latinos can be upwardly mobile, relate to Anglo neighbors, and still retain aspects of their own culture. For example, Linda's marriage to an Anglo, otherwise classifiable as a case of assimilation, involves accommodation when both families compromise for the wedding and pluralism when she shows her discomfort with Scott's Anglo friends. "Condo" concomitantly showed Anglos relating to Latinos and accommodating to some of their social and cultural norms. Thus, one of the unexpected findings was the various examples of accommodative relations, i.e., compromised mutual acceptance by both Latinos and Anglos. Nevertheless, depending on one's interpretation, these examples could also be seen as indicating some assimilation or pluralism.

If I had used the frameworks proposed by Auletta and Hammerback, Lemon or Weigel, Loomis, and Soja, a major conclusion of the study might have been that the adult males exhibit mostly independent interactions.[38] Although neither is dominant over, or dominated by, the other, and they are usually uncooperative, they do manage to reach some agreement on family affairs. Those approaches would also have shown that although the interactions between the adult females reflect some degree of independence, they also exhibit cooperation and no domination by one over the other. In addition, a high degree of interdependence is evident between Linda and Scott in practically all of their interactions. Interesting as these interpretations may be, they are less revealing than the approaches used here.

Some Institutional Underpinnings

One of the major limitations on the application of the new approaches and the theoretical framework may lie not so much in the methodology, but in the few opportunities television programming provides to study ethnic minority characters engaged in a broad range of interactions. Because this has been particularly true for Latinos, Native Americans, and Asian Americans in the context of family relations, an assessment was made of some of the factors related to the ratings and other institutional aspects pertinent to the life and death of this unique series. This structural data may help others analyze future developments relating to programs with minority characters.

Given television producers' limited sensitivity to minorities,[39] and given the findings discussed above, one of the first questions to ask is whether the heavy emphasis on acceptance of Latinos as such and on mutual accommodation between the ethnic groups led some network executives to cancel the show. According to Larry Hymes of the ABC Network, demographics were to blame for the show's termination. He indicated in a telephone interview that the program reaction scores were low in studio tests with sample audiences. He also stated that although the ratings during the first weeks were average (about 15.5, with a 24 share), the program's audience profile was women over fifty years of age; few young adults and males watched. Thus, like many other shows that seem socially valuable but have limited profit potential, "Condo" was canceled.

Did the network do anything to improve the show and increase the ratings? Probably not, at least according to the evidence gathered during this research. On the contrary, there were many barriers to the success of "Condo." First, it was aired during the most challenging slot of the evening: 8 p.m. (Pacific time), opposite "Magnum, P.I." (CBS), which was among the top five rated shows that spring, and "Fame" (NBC), which also had very high ratings. Second, it was preempted several times: after the fifth and eighth episodes and after the tenth episode, when it was off the air for three consecutive weeks. Halfway through the season, four episodes were broadcast at a different time (8:30 p.m.), while the last four shows were again aired at 8 p.m. Thus, not only was the show aired at a time when it could not develop a steady following, but the young adult male audience ABC was targeting was tuned in to the adventure and human drama on the other networks.

Another barrier to the success of the show may have been the limited interest of the creators and producers themselves. Sheldon Bull, the creator of "Condo" and the writer of the first four episodes, was subsequently replaced by other writers. In a telephone interview, Susan Palladino (an employee of the program's production company, Witt/Thomas) indicated that "Condo" had been based on Bull's personal experience but that he did not continue writing the scripts because he went on to other projects.

The demise of "Condo" and later "a.k.a. Pablo," which had a shorter run and worse ethnic humor, has not led to new efforts to improve portrayals of Hispanic families or Latino-Anglo relations. At the time of this writing, some prime-time programs feature Latinos (e.g., "L.A. Law," "Miami Vice," "I Married Dora"). But programs with Hispanic families, which have yet to last as long as those featuring Afro-American families, are currently nonexistent in the three major networks. To change these institutions will require dramatic improvement in the way their executives, screenwriters, and producers are sensitized to the effects of their programming. The activities and pressures of interest groups are also important for bringing about change.[40] Recently, the National Hispanic Media

Coalition has formed to address the problems of portrayals and the employment of Latinos in the media.[41] Future improvements on the portrayals of Latinos and other ethnic groups will require greater interest on the part of television decision-makers and possibly significant action by interested members of the ethnic populations.

Conclusion

The effects of ethnic portrayals on television is another area in need of exploration. Although research on the effects of television viewing on children is scarce and inconclusive,[42] some studies suggest that increased positive portrayals of ethnic minority characters could at least indicate to some viewers that they are a legitimate part of our society.[43] By seeing more positive role models of their own ethnic groups, minorities may enhance their self-esteem. Concomitantly, viewing positive minority characters could help improve Anglos' understanding of and relationship to them. This could lead to better interethnic interactions and to mutual adaptation and accommodation. In sum, it is imperative that efforts be made to better understand and to improve television images and their effects on our ever growing multiethnic society.

Notes

1. For literature, reviews, and annotated bibliographies on Afro-Americans see Gordon Berry and Claudia Mitchell-Kernan, "Television as a Socializing Force Within a Society of Mass Communication," in *Television and the Socialization of the Minority Child*, ed. Gordon Berry & Claudia Mitchell-Kernan (New York: Academic Press, 1982); George Hill, *Black Media in America: A Resource Guide* (Boston: G.K. Hall, 1984); Ernest Kaiser, "Blacks and the Mass Media: A Bibliography," *Freedomways* 22 (1982) 193-209; Paula Poindexter and Carolyn Stroman, "Blacks and Television: A Review of the Research Literature," *Journal of Broadcasting* 25 (1981):103-121; J. William Snorgrass and Gloria Woody, *Blacks and Media: A Selected, Annotated Bibliography, 1962-1982* (Tallahassee, Fl.: A.& M. University Press, 1985).

For studies of Latino images on television, see Norman Friedman, "A.k.a. Pablo: Mexican American Images for Television," *Exploration in Ethnic Studies* 8 (1985):1-10; Bradley Greenberg and Pilar Baptista-Fernandez, "Hispanic Americans: The New Minority on Television," in *Life on Television,* ed. Bradley Greenberg (Norwood, N.J.: Ablex Press, 1980):3-12; Carrie Heeter, Bradley Greenberg, B. Mendelson, Judee Burgoon, Michael Burgoon, and Felipe Korzenny, "Cross Media Coverage of Local Hispanic American News," *Journal of Broadcasting* 27 (1983):395-402; S. R. Lichter, L. S. Lichter, S. Rothman, and D. Amundson, "Prime-time Prejudice: TV's Images of Blacks and Hispanics," *Public Opinion* (July/August 1987):13-16; Public Advocates, Inc., "The Network Brownout: A National Hispanic Network Audit" (Unpublished paper prepared upon request by The League of United Latin American Citizens, Washington, DC., 1983); Luis Reyes, "The Hispanic Image on Network Television: Past and Present," Caminos (March 1983):10-16.

For studies of other minorities on television, see Yayoi Anzai, Juliet Dee, and Federico Subervi, "Mutual Images: Americans and Japanese in TV Commercials," *Human Communication Studies* 13 (Spring 1986):1-33; U.S. Commission on Civil Rights, *Window Dressing on the Set: Women and Minorities in Television* (Washington, D.C.: Government Printing Office, 1977); idem, *Window Dressing on the Set: An Update* (Washington, D.C.: Government Printing Office, 1979); Clint Wilson and Felix Gutierrez, *Minorities and Media* (Beverly Hills, Calif.: Sage Press, 1985).

For studies of Latino images in media other than television, see Ricardo Chavira, "A Case Study: Reporting of Mexican Emigration and Deportation," *Journalism History* 4 (1977):59-61; Carlos Cortez, "Chicanas in film," in *Chicano Cinema,* ed. G. Keller (Binghamton, N.Y.: Bilingual Review/Press, 1985), 94-108; Joshua Fishman and Herbierto Casiano, "Puerto Ricans in Our Press," *Modern Language Journal* 53 (1969):157-162; Gary Keller, "The Image of the Chicano in Mexican, United States, and Chicano Cinema: An Overview," in *Chicano Cinema,* ed. Gary Keller (Binghamton, N.Y.: Bilingual Review/Press, 1985), 13-58; Leo Sanchez, "Treatment of Mexican Americans By Selected U.S. Newspapers, January-June 1970" (M.A. thesis, Pennsylvania State University, 1973); Linda Williams, "Type and Stereotype: Chicano Images in Film," in *Chicano Cinema,* ed. Gary Keller (Binghamton, N.Y.: Bilingual Review/Press, 1985), 59-63; Allen Woll, *The Latin Image in American Film,* Revised Edition (Los Angeles: Latin American Center Publications University of California, 1980).

2. The terms black and Afro-American are used interchangeably, as are the terms Latino and Hispanic.

3. Gale Auletta and John Hammerback, "A Relational Model for Interracial Interactions on Television," *The Western Journal of Speech Communication* 49 (Fall 1985):301-321; Pilar Babtista-Fernandez and

Bradley Greenberg, "The Context, Characteristics and Communication Behaviors of Blacks on Television," in *Life on Television,* ed. Bradley Greenberg (Norwood, N.J.: Ablex, 1980), 13-21; Judith Lemon, "Women and Blacks on Prime-time Television," *Journal of Communication* 27 (1977):70-79; Russel Weigel, James Loomis, Mathew Soja, "Race Relations on Prime Time Television," *Journal of Personality and Social Psychology* 39 (1980):884-893.

For a study of interethnic interactions among cartoon characters, see Russel Wiegel and Paul Howes, "Race Relations on Children's Television," *Journal of Psychology* 3 (1982):109-112.

4. Anthony Jackson, *Black Families and the Medium of Television* (Ann Arbor, MI: Busch Program in Child Development and Social Policy, 1982); Bradley Greenberg and Kimberly Neuendorf, "Black Family Interactions on Television," in *Life on Television,* ed. Bradley Greenberg (Norwood, N.J.: Ablex, 1980), 173-181; William Edwards, "Programming the Black Family on Television: A Case of Distorted Imagery" (Paper presented at the annual conference of the Association of Black Sociologists, Detroit, 1983); George Sweepwer, "The Image of the Black Family and the White Family in American Prime-Time Television Programming, 1970 to 1980" (Ph.D. Dissertation, New York University, 1983).

5. See, for example, Bradley Greenberg, Nancy Buerkel-Rothfuss, Kimberly Neuendorf and Charles Atkin, "Three Seasons of Television Family Role Interactions," in *Life on Television,* ed. Bradley Greenberg (Norwood, N.J.: Ablex, 1980), 161-172; Bradley Greenberg, Mary Hines, Nancy Buerkel-Rothfuss, and Charles Atkin, "Family Role Structures and Interactions on Commercial Television," in *Life on Television,* ed. Bradley Greenberg (Norwood, N.J.: Ablex, 1980), 149-160.

6. Bradley Greenberg, Katrina Simmons, Linda Hogan and Charles Atkin, "The Demography of Fictional TV Characters," in *Life on Television*, ed. Bradley Greenberg (Norwood, N.J.: Ablex, 1980), 35-46.

7. Thomas Exter, "How Many Hispanics?" *American Demographics* (May 1987):36-59.

8. Kenneth Reich, "Doubling of U.S. Latinos by 2020 Forecast," *Los Angles Times* (26 September 1986), Part I, pp. 1, 26.

9. Doug Willis, "Minorities to Swell State's Population," *Los Angeles Times*, 17 February 1985, Part II, p. 1.

10. Ibid.; Kevin Phillips, "New Americans for the Next America," *Los Angeles Times* (11 May 1986), Part V, pp. 1-2; Time, "Immigrants: The Changing Face of America," Special issue (8 July 1985).

11. Aimée Dorr, "Television and the Socialization of the Minority Child," in *Television and the Socialization of the Minority Child*, ed. Gordon Berry & Claudia Mitchell-Kernan (New York: Academic Press, 1982), 15-35; Sherryl Graves, "Psychological Effects of Black Portrayals on Television," in *Television and Social Behavior: Beyond Violence and Children*, ed. Stephen Withey & Ronald Abeles (Hillsdale, N.J.: Lawrence Erlbaum Assoc., 1980), 259-289; idem, "The impact of Television on the Cognitive and Affective Development of Minority Group Children," in *Television and the Socialization of the Minority Child,* ed. Gordon Berry & Claudia Mitchell-Kernan (New York: Academic Press, 1982), 37-67; Gloria Powell, "The Impact of Television on the Self-concept Development of Minority Group Children," in *Television and the Socialization of the Minority Child*, ed. Gordon Berry & Claudia Mitchell-Kernan (N.Y.:

Academic Press, 1982), 105-131; Carolyn Stroman, "Television Viewing and Self-concept among Black Children," *Journal of Broadcasting and Electronic Media* 30 (1986):87-93.

12. Gerald Gorn, Marvin Goldberg and Rabindra Kanungo, "The Role of Educational Television in Changing the Intergroup Attitudes of Children," *Child Development* 47 (1976):277-280.

13. Berry and Mitchell-Kernan, "Television as a Socializing Force," 4.

14. Bradley Greenberg, Marvin Burgoon, Judee Burgoon, and Felipe Korzenny, *Mexican Americans and the Mass Media* (Norwood, N.J.: Ablex, 1983), 33-34.

15. Berry and Mitchell-Kernan, "Television as a Socializing Force," 4.

16. Bradley Greenberg, "Children's Reactions to T. V. Blacks," *Journalism Quarterly* 49 (1972):5-14.

17. Dorr, "Television and Socialization," 19.

18. Weigel, Loomis and Soja, "Race Relations."

19. Baptista-Fernandez and Greenberg, "Context, Characteristics and Communication," 18.

20. Lemon, "Women and Blacks," 75.

21. Auletta and Hammerback, "A Relational Model."

22. Ibid., 318-319.

23. Harold Abramson, "Assimilation and Pluralism," in *Harvard Encyclopedia of American Ethnic Groups*, ed. Stephan Thernstrom (Cambridge, Mass.: Harvard, 1980), 150.

24. John Berry, "Acculturation as Varieties of Adaptation, in *Acculturation: Theory, Models and Some New Findings*, ed. Amado Padilla (Boulder, CO: Westview Press, 1980), 9-26; Milton Gordon, *Assimilation in American Life* (London: Oxford University Press, 1964); Edward Murgia, "Assimilation, Colonialism and the Mexican American People," *Mexican American Monograph Series #1* (Austin, Tex.: University of Texas Press, 1975).

25. Federico A. Subervi-Velez, "Ethnic Assimilation and Pluralism: The Role of the Mass Media," *Communication Research*, 13 (1986):71-96.

26. For a comprehensive review, see Ibid.

27. C. McGee-Banks, "A Content Analysis of the Treatment of Black Americans on Television," *Social Education* (April 1977):336-339.

28. There have been programs with mostly Latino casts on public television and, of course, on the Spanish-language television stations and networks. The only commercial television program with a mostly Latino cast was "Sanchez of Bel-Air," which aired on USA Cable TV for thirteen weeks in 1987.

29. "Condo" was aired Thursday evenings from February 10 to June 16, 1983. Prior to "Condo," Hispanic families had been prominently portrayed only in "The High Chaparral" (NBC 1967-71) and "Viva Valdez" (ABC 1976); there are no studies of these portrayals.

30. The coding scheme also specified the subdivisions of cultural affairs, family affairs, and social affairs, examples of which were listed previously in this text. But the analysis showed that individual frequencies for each were too low to merit presentation in the tables.

31. Abramson, "Assimilation and Pluralism"; Berry, "Acculturation"; Gordon, "Assimilation"; Murgia, "Assimilation, Colonialism."

32. Technical problems impeded the coding of the first episode, which, because of its content, would have been included in the formal analysis.

33. For computing differences between the proportions, the binomial test was used (Sidney Siegel, *Nonparametric Statistics for the Behavioral Sciences* [New York: McGraw-Hill, 1956]).

34. James' remarks about Jesse's baldness and height were not coded as anti-Latino because they were more personal than ethnic. The same rule was applied to Jesse's negative remarks about James as a person.

35. Scott twice expressed dislike for his parents' country club, thus rejecting an important aspect of his own society. James also made critical comments of the bigotry of some of the "other" Anglos. Kiki was the only one asserting a weak defense of her Protestant religion. These statements do not fall under any of the established coded classifications. Future studies of interethnic interactions may find these types of statements worthy of more analysis if they occur with sufficient frequency.

36. Ed Bark, "'Condo' Starts Off Crudely, but Treats Hispanics Well," *Dallas Morning News* (10 February 1983).

37. Ibid.

38. Auletta and Hammerback, "A Relational Model"; Lemon, "Women and Blacks"; Weigel, Loomis, and Soja, "Race Relations."

39. Katheryn Montgomery, *Target: Prime-time* (London: Oxford University Press, forthcoming); Wilson and Gutierrez, "Minorities and Media."

40. Montgomery, *Target: Prime Time.*

41. The National Hispanic Media Coalition was organized in mid-1987 and is based at 205 South Broadway, Suite 1020, Los Angeles, California, 90012. Telephone (213) 613-0235.

42. Berry and Mitchell-Kernan, "Television as a Socializing Force"; Stroman, "Television Viewing"; Federico A. Subervi-Velez and Juan Necochea, "Television Viewing and Self-concept Among Latino Children" (Unpublished paper, University of California, Santa Barbara, 1987).

43. Dorr, "Television and Socialization"; Greenberg, "Children's Reactions."

Studies of Minority Groups in Community Psychology Journals, 1965-1985*

Chalsa Loo, Kenneth T. Fong, and Gayle Iwamasa

Over twenty years have passed since the birth of community psychology, a period of sufficient length to evaluate how well the field has accomplished its original goals. Researchers have endeavored to assess the accomplishments of the field through examination of past research published.[1] Most scholars who had participated in the 1965 Swampscott Conference have thought that the original hopes for community psychology have not been realized despite the growth of the field.[2] Similarly, Novaco & Monahan concluded that a gap exists between stated objectives in the field and its published research:

> If one accepts the definitions of community psychology given in the field's leading texts--with their focus on prevention, institutional change, and ecological analysis--the majority of research published in the field's leading journal [*American Journal of Community Psychology*] has little to do with the stated objectives of the discipline.[3]

---

* A slightly different version of this article has appeared under the title, "Ethnicity and Cultural Diversity: An Analysis of Work Published in Community Psychology Journals, 1965-1985," *Journal of Community Psychology* 16 (1988): 332-349.

To this list of community psychology's stated objectives, we add research on cultural diversity and ethnic minority populations.

Recognizing that the mental health needs of the lower socioeconomic classes and ethnic minority groups were not being met by traditional approaches, the fields of community psychology and community mental health sought to provide better mental health services to ethnic minorities as well as to conduct more research on these underserved populations.[4] Sarason addressed this issue in the following manner:

> There was a growing awareness that there were large segments of the population for whom mental health services did not exist or if they did exist were beyond their financial means or inappropriate in a cultural sense. It was not only that mental health services were inequitably distributed in the society but that mental health professions were dependent on a very narrow band of treatment possibilities that were not sensitive to cultural and racial variations.[5]

There was hope that community psychology, because of its commitment to rectifying past inequities in service delivery and its support of cultural pluralism, would lead in the movement to legitimize cultural diversity within the psychology profession.[6] But there was also skepticism. As Moore put it, "Minority people are also aware that as the movement grows, it forgets earlier commitments,"[7] while Snowden expressed "frustrating dissatisfaction" that community psychology has not succeeded in working with groups lying outside of the social mainstream and therefore has not accomplished its aims.[8] Rickel argued that community psychology must articulate its perspective if it is to solve its present identity crisis and "sensitivity to minorities and underrepresented groups is critical in defining this perspective."[9]

In this article, we examine the extent to which community psychology has committed itself to one of its original missions: incorporating and fostering cultural relativity and diversity. We used the number of published articles dealing with culture or ethnicity as a measure of the field's commitment to these values. We studied systematically how well cultural diversity and ethnicity have been reflected in the field of community psychology over its twenty-year history by analyzing the articles published in three major journals on community psychology and/or community mental health.

We used content analysis as our method of inquiry. Content analysis of academic journals had been previously used to define and identify topic trends in the field,[10] but no detailed content analysis has been conducted on cultural diversity and ethnic minorities in the field of community psychology. Lounsbury, Roisum, Pokorny, Sills, and Meissen analyzed the content of all published articles in the *Community Mental Health Journal* from 1965 through 1977 in order to provide a cross-sectional view of the community mental health field and to identify topic trends over time; they found that articles on "minority problems and concerns" in thirty-eight topic areas represented only 1.7 percent of the total number of articles (604) published, "with virtually no change in relative emphasis over the three four-year periods."[11] However, Lounsbury et al.'s study did not include two other community psychology journals and failed to examine aspects of cultural diversity other than minority problems and concerns.

In our opinion, the proper benchmark for measuring the field's accomplishments in meeting its commitments to cultural diversity and ethnic minorities should be, at a minimum, the proportion of the total U.S. population that ethnic minorities comprise, which in 1980 was roughly 20 percent. We believe that a population-based benchmark is appropriate because community psychology topics (e.g., prevention, consultation, mental health treatment) when applied to ethnic minority populations (e.g., mental health among Native Americans or consultation to Southeast Asian refugees) qualify as research that fosters cultural diversity. The words "at a minimum" imply that cultural diversity refers to the study of cultures outside the U.S. as well.

We analyzed each journal separately as well as the three collectively. We also analyzed non-U.S. cultures, counting articles on Asian Indians, Lebanese, Mexicans, Israelis, and Southeast Asians outside of the U.S. as indicators of "cultural diversity." In order to ascertain whether greater attention was paid to some U.S. ethnic minority groups than to others, we content-analyzed all articles according to specific ethnic/racial categories: Asian American/Pacific Islander, black, Hispanic/Puerto Rican, Native American/Alaskan, and white. To explore whether published articles were quantitative or qualitative, we categorized the articles according to whether they were issue-oriented (descriptive) or empirical. As a new field develops, the proportion of published articles that are empirical normally increases. To ascertain whether the body of knowledge concerning ethnic minorities and cultural diversity has increased over the field's twenty-year existence, we conducted a trend analysis. Lastly, we compared articles exclusively on ethnic minorities with articles that compared a sample of ethnic minorities to a white sample (or control group). We hypothesized that in the early stage of research in the new field, studies comparing ethnic minorities to whites might more likely have been accepted for publication, given traditional psychology's "[adoption of] an implicit faith that the single standard of white, middle-class society is, on an absolute basis, superior to all others."[12]

Method

All articles published in the *American Journal of Community Psychology* (*AJCP*), the *Community Mental Health Journal* (*CMHJ*), and the *Journal of Community Psychology* (*JCP*), from the journals' inception through 1985, were content-analyzed. Precedent dictated the inclusion of *AJCP* and *JCP* as journals reflective of the field of community psychology; Novaco and Monahan and Lounsbury et al. had analyzed both journals.[13] We included *CMHJ* as well because its contents had been used previously as an indicator of trends in community mental health, and we consider community mental health to be an important aspect of community psychology.[14] The last issue tallied for these journals was 13:6(1985) for *AJCP*; 21:4(1985) for *CMHJ*, and 13:4(1985) for *JCP*.

Book reviews, rebuttals, editorial statements, film reviews, commemorative award speeches, tributes, brief reports and anything less than three pages in length were excluded from our analysis. In total, 1,883 articles were analyzed: 545 articles in *AJCP* (covering 1973-1985), 787 articles in *CMHJ* (covering 1965-1985), and 551 articles in *JCP* (covering 1973-1985).

All articles were coded into one of the following categories: "single ethnic," "interethnic or multiethnic," "ethnic-white comparison," "international," "white," and "other." An article was classified as "ethnic" if, in the title or abstract of the article, there was mention of ethnicity, culture, a specific ethnic minority group or groups, or a comparison between white and one or more ethnic minority groups. If the article did not have any of the above, we looked at the methods and results sections; if 50 percent or more of the sample or 50 percent or more of the article (nonempirical in nature) dealt with ethnic minorities or nonwhites, the article was coded as "ethnic." Basically, regardless of the size of the sample, if the authors planned to study ethnic minorities or cultural diversity, this intention was normally reflected in their title or abstract, in which case, the article was coded as "ethnic."

An article was coded as "single ethnic" if only one U.S. ethnic minority group was studied. Single ethnic sub-categories included "Asian American/Pacific Islander," "black," "Hispanic/Puerto Rican," and "Native American/Alaskan." An article was coded "interethnic or multiethnic" if more than one U.S. ethnic minority group was studied. An article was coded as "ethnic-white comparison" when the article compared one or more ethnic minority groups with a white sample. An article dealing with a cultural group outside the United States and its territories (which may or may not involve a comparison with a white group) was coded as "international."

An article was coded as "other" if the authors mentioned an ethnic minority or minorities within a graph or table that represented a breakdown of the sample, but this mention only occurred in the results section. An article was also coded as "other" if ethnic minorities were part of the sample but comprised less than 50 percent of it, or were only mentioned in the methods section with no breakdown of findings for these ethnic minorities in the results or discussion sections, and with no mention of ethnicity, culture, or the ethnic group in the abstract or title. In other words, an article coded as "other" was one in which the authors did not intend to study ethnic minorities or cultural diversity but it so happened that their sample contained a few minorities.

An article was coded as "white" if none of the above categories applied, i.e., if no intent to study ethnic minorities in the U.S. or cultures outside of the U.S. and its territories was evident, and the proportion of ethnic minorities in the sample was less than 50 percent.

In this study, we define "single ethnic," "interethnic/multi-ethnic," "ethnic-white comparison," and "international" articles as contributions to cultural relativity and diversity, whereas articles coded as "white" or "other" are not so considered.

The two junior authors rated each article independently. Each was randomly assigned an approximately equal number of articles from all three journals. To test for interrater reliability, twenty-three issues were randomly selected from all three journals: five from *AJCP*, ten from *CMHJ*, and eight from *JCP*. There was a 96 percent agreement between the two raters: they agreed with each other's ratings for 222 articles, while they differed on 10 articles. Reliability was also determined for "ethnic" versus "nonethnic," "empirical" versus "nonempirical," and "ethnic-white comparison" versus "ethnic" on an article-by-article basis. For the 222 articles that the raters agreed on, agreement on the "ethnic" versus "nonethnic" distinction was 93 percent, agreement on the "empirical" versus "nonempirical" distinction was 86 percent, and agreement on the "ethnic-white comparison" versus "ethnic" distinction was 98 percent. To correct for chance agreement, we performed the kappa statistic for "ethnic" versus "nonethnic" (.78), "empirical" versus "nonempirical" (.65), and "ethnic-white comparison" versus "ethnic" (.77).[15]

Table 1

Number and Proportion of Published Articles by Cultural Content

	AJCP		*CMHJ*		*JCP*		Total	
Single Ethnic	37	(6.8%)	24	(3.0%)	42	(7.6%)	103	(5.5%)
Inter/Multi-ethnic	3	(0.6%)	4	(0.5%)	2	(0.4%)	9	(0.5%)
Ethnic-White Comparison	45	(8.3%)	30	(3.8%)	21	(3.8%)	96	(5.1%)
International	8	(1.5%)	14	(1.8%)	23	(4.2%)	45	(2.4%)
White	440	(80.7%)	702	(89.2%)	453	(82.2%)	1595	(84.7%)
Token	12	(2.2%)	13	(1.7%)	10	(1.8%)	35	(1.9%)
Total Articles	545	(28.9%)	787	(41.8%)	551	(29.3%)	1883	

Results

All Journals Combined

Of the articles published in the three community psychology journals, 13 percent (n = 253) furthered the goals of cultural diversity and relativity and 86 percent (n = 1,630) did not. As shown in Table 1, of those articles that did so, 5.5 percent (n = 103) were studies of "single ethnic" minority populations, 5.1 percent (n = 96) compared ethnic minorities with whites, 2.4 percent (n = 45) were studies of "international" populations, and 0.5 percent (n = 9) were studies that compared two or more ethnic minority groups ("interethnic").

Among the articles that promoted cultural diversity, greater coverage was given to U.S. ethnic minority groups than to non-U.S. cultural populations (11 percent compared to 2 percent). In addition, cultural diversity was primarily furthered by articles on a single ethnic minority group or by studies that compared ethnic minorities with whites; "single ethnic" and "ethnic-white comparison" articles were published in roughly similar proportions (about 5 percent each). Very few "interethnic" articles were published.

Journal Comparisons

Of the three journals, *AJCP* and *JCP* published a larger proportion of articles devoted to cultural diversity than did *CMHJ*: 17 and 16 percent (n = 93 and 88), respectively, compared to only 9 percent (n = 72) in *CMHJ*. Moreover, the proportion of articles on single ethnic minority populations published in *AJCP* and *JCP* was at least twice as large as that in *CMHJ*. The largest proportion of articles comparing an ethnic minority sample with a white sample appeared in *AJCP* (8 percent); this was twice as large as that found in either of the other two journals (4 percent each). The largest proportion of articles on international cultural groups was published in *JCP*: 4 percent compared to only 2 percent in the other two journals. There were no differences among the three journals with regard to the proportion of articles on two or more ethnic minority groups; such studies were few in number in all three journals (under 1 percent each).

Table 2

Articles that Fostered Cultural Diversity by Specific Ethnicity

	Blacks	Hispanics	Asian Amer.	Native Amer.	Total
AJCP					
Single Ethnic	24 (4.4%)	9 (1.7%)	2 (0.4%)	2 (0.4%)	37
White/Single Ethnic	9.5	5	0	0	14.5
White/Multiethnic	5.2	5.2	0.58	0.33	11.31
Inter/Multiethnic	1.5	1.5	0	0	3
Total	40.2 (7.4%)	20.4 (3.8%)	2.58 (0.5%)	2.33 (0.4%)	65.81
CMHJ					
Single Ethnic	13 (1.7%)	7 (0.9%)	2 (0.3%)	2 (0.3%)	24
White/Single Ethnic	7.5	1.5	0	0	9
White/Multiethnic	2.84	3.17	0.2	0.53	6.74
Inter/Multiethnic	1.58	1.58	0.58	0.25	3.99
Total	24.92 (3.2%)	13.25 (1.7%)	2.78 (0.4%)	2.78 (0.4%)	43.73
JCP					
Single Ethnic	19 (3.4%)	15 (2.7%)	8 (1.5%)	0 (0%)	42
White/Single Ethnic	4.5	1.5	0	0	0
White/Multiethnic	2.81	2.81	0.5	0	6.12
Inter/Multiethnic	0.75	0.75	0.25	0.25	2
Total					
TOTAL					
Single Ethnic	56	31	12	4	
Single Ethnic w/ fractional breakdown	92.18	53.35	14.11	5.36	

Breakdown by Ethnicity

As seen in Table 2, analysis of the "single ethnic" articles reveals that there were substantially more articles published on blacks than on other U.S. ethnic minority groups: for the three journals combined, 56 articles (54 percent of all "single ethnic" articles) were studies of blacks. Hispanics and Puerto Ricans came next with a total of 31 articles (30 percent of all "single ethnic" articles in the three journals). Compared to blacks and Hispanics/Puerto Ricans, far less attention has been paid to Asian Americans: only twelve articles (12 percent of all "single ethnic" articles published in the three journals) dealt with them. Minimal attention was devoted to Native Americans: they were the subject of only four articles (4 percent of all "single ethnic" articles).

The difference in the amount of attention paid to the various ethnic minority populations increases when fractional breakdowns are calculated for articles that studied more than one ethnic minority group or compared ethnic minorities to whites (i.e., "ethnic-white comparisons," "interethnic/multiethnic" studies). In articles that compared whites to blacks, for example, credit would be divided so that blacks would be assigned a value of 0.5, while an article comparing Asian Americans, Native Americans, and Hispanics would be divided so that each group would be assigned a value of 0.33.

When "single ethnic" and fractional breakdowns were combined, there were 92.18 articles on blacks, 53.35 articles on Hispanics/Puerto Ricans, 14.11 on Asian Americans, and 5.36 on

Native Americans. Among all articles dealing with U.S. ethnic minorities, the attention given to specific ethnic minorities (when combining "single ethnic" and fractional breakdown for "ethnic-white" and "interethnic/multiethnic" articles) amounted to 56 percent for blacks, 32 percent for Hispanics/Puerto Ricans, 9 percent for Asian Americans, and 3 percent for Native Americans.

The order of attention given to each major U.S. ethnic group did not differ among the three journals: all gave the most attention to blacks, followed by Hispanics, then Asian Americans, and lastly Native Americans. *AJCP* has given slightly more attention than the other journals to the study of blacks, as they published more studies comparing blacks to whites.

For "single ethnic" articles published in *AJCP* from 1973 to 1985, 4 percent were on blacks, 2 percent on Hispanics, and less than 1 percent each on Asian Americans and Native Americans. When combining "single ethnic" with fractional breakdowns for "ethnic-white comparisons" and "interethnic," *AJCP* devoted 7 percent of its articles to blacks, 4 percent to Hispanics, and less than 1 percent each to Asian Americans and Native Americans.

For "single ethnic" articles published in *CMHJ* from 1965-1985, 2 percent were on blacks, 1 percent on Hispanics/Puerto Ricans, and less than 1 percent each on Asian Americans and Native Americans. When combining "single ethnic" with the fractional breakdowns for "ethnic-white comparisons" and "interethnic," *CMHJ* devoted 3 percent of its articles to blacks, 2 percent to Hispanics/Puerto Ricans, and less than 1 percent each to Asian

Americans and Native Americans.

For "single ethnic" articles published in *JCP* from 1973-1985, 3 percent were on blacks, 3 percent on Hispanics/Puerto Ricans, 2 percent on Asian Americans, and zero percent on Native Americans. When "single ethnic" are combined with the fractional breakdowns for "ethnic-white comparisons" and "interethnic," *JCP* devoted 5 percent of its articles to blacks, 4 percent to Hispanics/Puerto Ricans, 2 percent to Asian Americans, and none to Native Americans.

Trends Over Time

Year by year. We first examined the proportion of articles devoted to cultural diversity on a yearly basis for the three journals combined and for each journal separately (see Table 3). Cultural diversity was defined as the total of "single ethnic," "interethnic/multi-ethnic," "ethnic-white comparison," and "international." For all journals combined, the year and journal having the smallest proportion of articles on cultural diversity was the 1966 volume of *CMHJ*, with only 3 percent of its articles covering minority groups. The year and journal with the largest proportion of articles on cultural diversity was the 1985 volume of *JCP*, with 38 percent of its articles focussing on nonwhites. Thus, on a yearly basis, the proportion of articles on minorities in the three journals of community psychology ranged from 3 to 38 percent. Looking at each journal separately, the percent of articles devoted to cultural diversity by year ranged from 3 (1966) to 21 percent (1981) for *CMHJ*, from 10 (1978 and 1985) to 29 percent (1980) for *AJCP*, and from 5 (1975) to 38 percent (1985) for

Table 3. Published Articles that Fostered the Goal of Cultural Diversity by Year of Publication for the *Journal of Community Psychology (JCP)*, *American Journal of Community Psychology (AJCP)*, and the *Community Mental Health Journal (CMHJ)* 1965-1985.

		Year of publication													Year of publication							
		'65	'66	'67	'68	'69	'70	'71	'72	'73	'74	'75	'76	'77	'78	'79	'80	'81	'82	'83	'84	'85
AJCP	# articles "ethnic"									3	5	7	5	6	5	9	14	6	12	9	6	4
	% articles "ethnic"									10%	14%	21%	15%	16%	10%	19%	30%	17%	21%	20%	13%	10%
	# articles "other"									0	0	0	2	1	3	0	4	1	0	1	0	0
	% articles "other"									0%	0%	0%	6%	3%	6%	0%	8%	2%	0%	2%	0%	0%
	Total # articles									31	36	33	33	38	52	48	48	48	56	44	47	41
CMHJ	# articles "ethnic"	5	1	3	3	4	7	3	1	4	7	3	5	2	2	2	2	6	3	1	4	4
	% articles "ethnic"	11%	3%	6%	6%	8%	14%	9%	3%	11%	14%	6%	10%	5%	6%	8%	8%	21%	13%	4%	17%	15%
	# articles "other"	0	0	0	0	2	0	1	0	0	0	0	3	3	0	0	3	0	1	0	0	0
	% articles "other"	0%	0%	0%	0%	4%	0%	3%	0%	0%	0%	0%	6%	8%	0%	0%	11%	0%	4%	0%	0%	0%
	Total # articles	46	40	48	54	52	49	32	30	38	49	52	49	38	33	25	26	29	24	23	24	26
JCP	# articles "ethnic"									6	6	2	1	4	9	6	11	7	7	10	6	13
	% articles "ethnic"									12%	11%	5%	3%	9%	21%	14%	24%	17%	17%	30%	16%	38%
	# articles "other"									0	1	0	1	2	2	0	0	0	0	3	1	0
	% articles "other"									0%	2%	0%	3%	4%	5%	0%	0%	0%	0%	9%	3%	0%
	Total # articles									51	56	41	39	45	43	44	46	40	41	34	37	34
TOTAL	# articles "ethnic"	5	1	3	3	4	7	3	1	13	18	12	11	12	16	15	27	21	22	20	16	21
	% articles "ethnic"	11%	3%	6%	6%	8%	14%	6%	3%	11%	13%	10%	9%	10%	13%	13%	23%	18%	18%	20%	15%	21%
	Total # articles	46	40	48	54	52	49	32	30	120	141	126	121	121	128	117	120	117	121	101	108	101

[1]Ethnic = Total of single ethnic, interethnic, White/ethnic comparison, and international articles published.

JCP.

Since ethnic minorities are estimated to be 20 percent of the U.S. population, we calculated the number of years that the proportion of articles published in each of these journals reached 20 percent or more to see how close to the benchmark each journal came. (Note that 20 percent is a very conservative benchmark because "international" is included in the "cultural diversity" category, though such groups are not ethnic minorities in the U.S.). In only one out of twenty-one years (1981) did *CMHJ* devote more than 20 percent of its articles to cultural diversity. In *AJCP*, the proportion of articles on cultural diversity reached over 20 percent in three out of thirteen years (1980, 1982, 1983). In *JCP*, four out of thirteen years (1978, 1980, 1983, 1985) had more than 20 percent of its articles fostering cultural diversity.

Table 4
Percent of Ethnic/Cultural Diversity Articles for All Journals by Three-Year Periods

	All Journals	*AJCP*	*CMHJ*	*JCP*
1965-67	7%	–	7%	–
1968-70	9%	–	9%	–
1971-73	10%	10%	8%	12%
1974-76	15%	17%	10%	1%
1977-79	12%	14%	6%	14%
1980-82	20%	22%	14%	20%
1983-85	18%	14%	12%	28%
Means	x=13%	x=17%	x=9%	x=16%

Three-year intervals. Since it was difficult to decipher trends over time on a year-to-year basis, we divided the entire 1965-1985 period into seven intervals of three years each and calculated the frequencies and percentages of articles that fostered cultural diversity for each period. Overall, there has been a general increase in the percentage of articles focusing on ethnicity over time when the data from all three journals are combined (see Table 4). It should be noted that two of the three journals (*JCP* and *AJCP*) did not commence publication until 1973.

For the three-year intervals, the proportions ranged from 7 percent (1965-1967) to 20 percent (1980-1982). *CMHJ* showed little variation between 1965 and 1979, with the proportion hovering in the 6-10 percent range. Between 1980 and 1985, attention to ethnicity and cultural diversity increased slightly, with the proportion rising to the 12-14 percent range. For *AJCP*, attention to ethnicity and cultural diversity has been relatively steady over the three-year periods. The proportion for the 1971-1973 period was only 10 percent but the journal only began in 1973. The percentage rose to 22 percent in the 1980-1982 period. Overall, during 1974-1985, attention to culture and ethnicity was in the 14-22 percent range. Between 1974 and 1985, *JCP* has shown a more dramatic increase than the other two journals, leaping from 1 percent in the 1974-1976 period to 14 percent in the 1977-1979 period and 20 percent in the 1980-1982 period. The rising percentages in the last two periods were due to two special issues--one in 1981 on the "Training of Asian American Clinical-Community Psychologists" and one in 1985 on "Community Psychology in Cuba."

(We found, with the exception of articles on blacks, that articles on minorities were most often published in special issues.) Overall, *JCP* had the smallest (1 percent) as well as the largest (18 percent) proportion of articles devoted to ethnicity and cultural diversity for the three-year periods.

Table 5

Proportion of U.S. Ethnic Articles that Were "White-Ethnic Comparisons" and Those that Were Ethnic Minority Only For All Community Psychology Journals

	Single Ethnic	Interethnic	White-Ethnic Comparison	Total U.S. Ethnic
1965-67	2 (33%)	2 (33%)	2 (33%)	6
1968-70	3 (30%)	0 (0%)	7 (70%)	10
1971-73	7 (44%)	2 (13%)	7 (44%)	16
1974-76	19 (53%)	3 (8%)	14 (39%)	36
1977-79	22 (59%)	1 (3%)	14 (38%)	37
1980-82	32 (52%)	6 (10%)	24 (39%)	62
1983-85	20 (50%)	3 (7%)	17 (43%)	40

There was no consistent trend of increase in the proportion of ethnic minority articles ("single ethnic" plus "interethnic/ multiethnic") compared to "ethnic-white comparison" articles over time (see Table 5). For all journals taken together, the proportion of "U.S. ethnic" articles that compared whites to ethnic minorities was

33, 64, 44, 39, 38, 39, and 43 percent for the seven successive three-year intervals, respectively, while the proportion of articles on ethnic minorities alone was 66, 27, 57, 61, 62, 62, and 57 percent, respectively.

Table 6

Empirical and Nonempirical Articles for Total and "Ethnic" among All Community Psychology Journals

	AJCP	*CMHJ*	*JCP*	Total
Total Empirical "Ethnic Articles"	89 (96%)	49 (68%)	64 (73%)	202
Total Nonempirical "Ethnic" Articles	4 (4%)	23 (32%)	24 (27%)	51
Total "Ethnic" Articles	93	72	88	253
Total Empirical Articles	436 (80%)	443 (56%)	409 (74%)	1,288 (69%)
Total Nonempirical Articles	108 (20%)	343 (44%)	142 (26%)	593 (31%)
Total Articles	544	786	551	1,881

Empirical and Nonempirical

As shown in Table 6, of all the articles published in the three community psychology journals, 69 percent (n = 1,288) were empirical and 31 percent (n = 593) nonempirical.[16] Of the three journals, *AJCP* had the largest proportion of empirical articles (80 percent) compared to nonempirical articles (20 percent). *JCP* followed with 74 percent of its articles being empirical and 26 percent nonempirical. Compared to the other journals, *CMHJ* had the smallest proportion of empirical articles (56 percent) and the largest proportion of nonempirical articles (44 percent).

For all journals combined, of those articles that promoted cultural diversity, 80 percent were empirical and 20 percent non-empirical; on a journal-by-journal basis, the proportions were 96 percent empirical and 4 percent nonempirical for *AJCP*; 72 percent empirical and 27 percent nonempirical for *JCP*, and 69 percent empirical and 32 percent nonempirical for *CMHJ*.

Discussion

The intent of our study was to evaluate how well the field of community psychology has accomplished one of its original goals: furthering cultural diversity by publishing more research on, and offering more service to, ethnic minority populations. Using the proportion of articles published in three professional journals as a rough measure of the extent to which the field has met this goal over the last twenty years, our findings are both discouraging and encouraging. On the discouraging side, only 6 percent of all articles published in the three journals focused exclusively on U.S. ethnic minorities, with another 5 percent comparing ethnic minorities to whites. Combining these two categories, 11 percent of all articles related to ethnic minorities in the United States. In our judgment, 11 percent is low, considering the fact that this includes a period when ethnic activism was at its peak (the late 1960s and 1970s), and when ethnic minorities constituted 20 percent of the U.S. population (1980). We had hoped that the amount of research on such populations would approximate their proportion in the population at large, that is, be at least 20 percent. Some might argue the proportion of articles on ethnicity and culture should be even higher than the representation of ethnic minorities in the U.S. population, since the field of community psychology should give greater-than-parity attention to the underserved, among whom ethnic minorities are overrepresented.

On the encouraging side, three-year period trends reveal that, for all journals combined, there has been a general increase in the proportion of published articles devoted to ethnicity and cultural diversity. The proportion of articles on ethnicity and culture rose noticeably in the 1971-1973 period (when *AJCP* and *JCP* began their publications), then increased again in the 1980-1985 period (when each journal showed a jump of 6-8 percent in the proportion of ethnic and culture-oriented articles). Since 1980, for these three journals combined, the average proportion of articles on ethnicity or cultural diversity for the three-year periods was in the 18-20 percent range.

We encourage the field of community psychology to continue to increase its attention to U.S. ethnic minority research. Given the almost-nil existence of interethnic comparative research, we also recommend increased attention to this topic. Finally, noting that only 2 percent of the articles published concerned non-U.S. cultures, we encourage a greater global scope to include the study of cultures outside of our own.

In more general terms, we urge community psychology to move beyond the mainstream perspective. Quite possibly, there are scholars who are unable to cast off the dominant paradigm applicable to white, middle-class America. Clearly, it is easier to study a culturally-familiar population that is easily accessible to academic researchers. Yet, as Watts points out, unless community psychologists are trained to understand and respect cultural differences, the "reach" of community psychology is likely to be very narrow.[17] Unless community psychologists actively seek to serve and study ethnic minorities and culturally diverse communities, their fear and "vulnerability" will constrain them to studying only familiar, accessible, and "safe" subjects.[18]

Rappaport and Ramirez and Castenada contend that psychologists may recognize cultural differences in the abstract but not respect them in reality.[19] In our judgment, the mission of studying and serving ethnic minorities requires more than respect; it requires a concerted, active intent to make this commitment a reality. Such endeavors can only enlarge and invigorate the field, for psychologists have much to learn from Native Americans, Chinese Americans, Korean Americans, Vietnamese Americans, Hispanics, and blacks, many of whom have ethnically-distinct communities. Indeed, in several areas of this nation, ethnic "minorities" may soon constitute the majority.

Future research is needed in a variety of other areas as well. First, it would be valuable to investigate whether the acceptance and rejection rates of articles submitted on (or by) ethnic minorities differ from those on (or by) whites. Secondly, much can be learned from a study that compares various disciplines (e.g., history, ethnic studies, sociology, anthropology, and psychiatry) in terms of their attention to ethnicity, race, and culture, in order to see the pattern of coverage on ethnic minorities in journals in those disciplines. Is there greater receptivity to these issues on the part of ethnic studies, history, sociology, anthropology, and psychiatry? If so, does the "reputation" of specific disciplines and/or journals affect the submission and acceptance rates of articles dealing with ethnicity and/or culture? Third, there are many contemporary conditions in need of study, such as the effects of residential displacement on ethnic minorities in inner cities, successful and unsuccessful struggles to preserve ethnic enclaves from the "destructive" forces of urban renewal and gentrification, the race relations issues that emerge as new nonwhite immigrants move into previously all-white neighborhoods,[20] the increasing political power and participation of ethnic minorities in this country, and the conditions faced by recent refugees.

Finally, community psychology as a field has been concerned with a broad array of topics, from mental health, to prevention, to consultation, to drug and substance abuse, and to program evaluation. If researchers in these areas would *apply* their insights to how service is delivered to ethnic minorities or culturally diverse populations, the "timetable" by which community psychology can achieve its mandate to promote cultural diversity and serve this nation's ethnic minority populations will be substantially shortened.

We need to answer several questions. What are the barriers to publication of studies on ethnicity and culture? Do they lie in the review process, in submission, or in lack of research due to its "costs"?[21] Why is it that a larger proportion of "ethnic" articles published in *AJCP* were empirical (96 percent) compared to all articles published in that journal, and why has this not been the case for *JCP* and *CMHJ*? What accounts for differences in attention to ethnicity and culture among these three journals?

In our opinion, the commitment to ethnic minority populations and cultural diversity remains community psychology's toughest challenge. Community psychology needs to expand beyond mainstream concerns if these goals are to be achieved. Otherwise, the underserved remain underserved and the underrepresented continue to be underrepresented. Progress has been made toward the goals set twenty years ago, but more needs to be done.

Notes

This research was supported in part by an Institute for American Cultures grant from the University of California at Los Angeles and Asian American Studies.

We thank Sonia Alvarez-Hernandez, Irma Serrano-Garcia, and John Moritsugu for their suggestions and Judy Chan, Tina Yee, and UCLA's Word Processing for Social Sciences unit for their assistance in manuscript preparation.

1. John W. Lounsbury, Michael P. Cook, Dianne S. Leader, and Elizabeth Meares, "A Content Analysis of Community Psychology Research," in *Community Research: Methods, Paradigms and Applications,* ed. Donald Klein and Edwin Susskind (New York: Praeger, 1985), 39-105; Ray W. Novaco and John Monahan, "Research in Community Psychology: An Analysis of Work Published in the First Six Years of the *American Journal of Community Psychology,*" *American Journal of Community Psychology* 8 (1980): 131-145.

2. Everett Moitoza and Charles Hersch, "Community Psychology: Past, Present, and Future: 1965 Boston Conference Revisited," *American Journal of Community Psychology* 9 (1981): 225-232.

3. Novaco and Monahan, "Research in Community Psychology," 142-143.

4. Nicholas Hobbs, "Mental Health's Third Revolution," *American Journal of Orthopsychiatry* 34 (1964): 1-20; Ira Iscoe, Bernard L. Bloom, and Charles D. Speilberger, eds., *Community Psychology in Transition: Proceedings of the National Conference in Training in Community Psychology* (Washington, D.C.: Hemisphere Press, 1977); Bernard Lubin, "Issues Briefly Considered at the Conference," in *Community Psychology in Transition: Proceedings*

of the National Conference in Training in Community Psychology, ed., Ira Iscoe, Bernard L. Bloom, and Charles D. Speilberger (Washington, D.C.: Hemisphere Press, 1977), 247-250; Ernest R. Myers and Henry Pitts, "Community, Psychology and Racism," in *Community Psychology in Transition: Proceedings of the National Conference in Training in Community Psychology*, ed., Ira Iscoe, Bernard L. Bloom, and Charles D. Speilberger (Washington, D.C.: Hemisphere Press, 1977): 267-270; President's Commission on Mental Health, *Report to the President* (Washington, D.C.: U.S. Government Printing Office, 1978).

5. Seymour B. Sarason, *The Psychological Sense of Community: Prospects for a Community Psychology* (San Francisco: Jossey Bass, 1974), 202.

6. Julian Rappaport, "Cultural Relativity and Diversity in the Pursuit of Science," *American Psychological Association: The Community Psychologist* 19 (1977): 13-14.

7. Thomas Moore, "Editorial Opinion: Will Community Psychology be Committed to Minority People?" *Journal of Community Psychology* 5 (1977): 388-391.

8. Loni R. Snowden, "The Peculiar Success of Community Psychology," *Division of Community Psychology Newsletter* 18 (1985): 9-10.

9. Annette U. Rickel, "Community Psychology's Emerging Identity," *Division of Community Psychology Newsletter* 18 (1985): 1-2.

10. Lounsbury et al., "A Content Analysis"; Novaco and Monahan, "Research in Community Psychology."

11. John W. Lounsbury, Karol Rosium, Lois Pokorny, Abigail Sills, and Gregory Meissen, "An Analysis of Topic Areas and Topic Trends in the *Community Mental Health Journal* from 1966-1977," *Community Mental Health Journal* 15 (1979): 267-276.

12. Julian Rappaport, *Community Psychology: Values, Action, and Research* (New York: Holt Rinehart, 1977), 22.

13. Novaco and Manahan, "Research in Community Psychology"; Lounsbury et al., "A Content Analysis."

14. Lounsbury et al., "An Analysis of Topic Areas."

15. Jacob Cohen, "A Coefficient of Agreement for Nominal Scales," *Educational and Psychological Measurement* 20 (1960): 37-46.

16. Two articles were not coded due to an error of omission. This accounts for the discrepancy between the total of 1,881 articles (empirical and nonempirical combined) and the total of 1,883 articles for all journals (as indicated in Table 1).

17. Roderick Watts, "Cultural Diversity Perspectives in Training," *American Psychological Association: The Community Psychologist* 19 (1986): 12.

18. Richard Katz and Mario Nunez-Malina, "Researching Realities? A Method for Understanding Cultural Diversity," *American Psychological Association: The Community Psychologist* 19 (1986): 7-8.

19. Rappaport, "Community Psychology"; Manuel Ramirez and Antonio Castaneda, *Cultural Democracy, Bicognitive Development and Education* (New York: Academic Press, 1974).

20. *Los Angeles Times* (6 April 1987).

21. Stanley Lehmann, "Community and Psychology and Community Psychology," *American Psychologist* 26 (1971): 554-565; James Kelly, "Qualities for the Community Psychologist," *American Psychologist* 26 (1971): 897-903; Kenneth Heller, Richard Price, Shulamit Reinharz, Stephanie Riger, Abraham Wandersman,

Psychology and Community Change (Homewood, Ill.: Dorsey Press, 1984); Chalsa Loo and Don Mar, "Asian American Communities: Social Change or Empty Prize?" *Amerasia Journal* 12 (1985): 85-93.

Notes on Contributors

Adalberto Aguirre, Jr. is Associate Professor of Sociology at the University of California, Riverside. He received his Ph.D. in 1977 from Stanford University. He has published *An Experimental Sociolinguistic Investigation of Chicano Bilingualism* (San Francisco: R&E Research Associates, 1978); *Intelligence Testing, Education and Chicanos* (Princeton: Educational Testing Service, 1980); *Language in the Chicano Speech Community* (The Hague: Mouton, 1985); and "An Interpretative Analysis of Chicano Faculty in Academe," *The Social Science Journal* 24 (1987).

Edwin B. Almirol is Assistant Professor of Asian American Studies at the University of California, Davis. He received his Ph.D. in 1977 from the University of Illinois. He has published "Chasing the Elusive Butterfly: Gossip and the Pursuit of Reputation," *Ethnicity* 8 (1981): 293-304; "Rights and Obligations in Filipino American Families," *Journal of Comparative Family Studies* 12 (1982): 291-306; "Exclusion and Acceptance of Filipinos in America," *Asian Profile* 13 (1985): 395-408; *Ethnic Identity and Social Negotiation: A Study of A Filipino Community in California* (N.Y.: AMS Press, 1985); and "Filipino Adaptation and Voluntary Associations," *Philippine Studies* 34 (1986): 41-60.

Lisa M. Bohon-Hock is a graduate student in Psychology at the University of California, Riverside. She is doing research on intergroup relations and will receive her Ph.D. in 1990.

Amado Cabezas is Assistant Professor of Asian American Studies at the University of California, Berkeley. He received his Ph.D. (in physics) in 1961 from the University of California, Berkeley. He has published (with H. T. Yee), *Discriminatory Employment of Asian Americans: Private Industry in the San Francisco-Oakland SMSA* (San Francisco: ASIAN, Inc., 1977); (with Pauline Fong), "Economic and Employment Status of Asian Pacific Women," *Proceedings of the Conference on the Educational and Occupational Needs of Asian Pacific Women* (Washington D.C.: National Institute of Education,

1980); *Social Support: A Cross-Cultural Investigation* (San Francisco: California Department of Mental Health, 1982); "Employment Issues," in *Civil Rights Issues of Asian and Pacific Americans: Myths and Realities* (Washington, D.C.: U.S. Government Printing Office, 1980); *Social Support and Mental Health Promotion in Americans of Chinese, Filipino, and Japanese Descent* (San Francisco: ASIAN, Inc., 1986); (with Larry Shinagawa and Gary Kawaguchi), "New Inquiries into the Socioeconomic Status of Pilipino Americans in California," *Amerasia Journal* 13 (1986): 1-22.

Sucheng Chan is Professor of History and Asian American Studies at the University of California, Santa Barbara. She received her Ph.D. from the Univerisity of California, Berkeley in 1973. She is the author of *This Bittersweet Soil: The Chinese in California Agriculture, 1860-1910* (Berkeley and Los Angeles: University of California Press, 1986); "Chinese Livelihood in Rural California: The Impact of Economic Change, 1860-1880," *Pacific Historical Review* 53 (1984): 273-307; "European and Asian Immigration into the United States in Comparative Perspective, 1820s to 1920s," in *Immigration: History, Sociology, Politics,* ed. Virginia Yans-McLaughlin (New York: Oxford University Press, 1990); and the editor of *Ethnic and Gender Boundaries in the United States: Studies of Asian, Black, Mexican and Native Americans* (Lewiston, N.Y.: The Edwin Mellen Press, 1989); and *Quiet Odyssey: A Pioneer Korean Woman in America* (Seattle: University of Washington Press, 1990).

Jenni Currie is a lecturer in English at San Francisco State University. She received her M. A. from San Francisco State University in 1988. She served as the assistant editor of *Ethnic and Gender Boundaries in the United States: Studies of Asian, Black, Mexican and Native Americans* (Lewiston, N.Y.: The Edwin Mellen Press, 1988); and *Quiet Odyssey: A Pioneer Korean Woman in America* (Seattle: University of Washington Press, 1990); and as an editor of *Ink* 2 (1987) and *Ink* 3 (1988).

Adela de la Torre is Assistant Professor of Health Care Administration at California State University, Long Beach. She received her Ph.D. in 1982 from the University of California,

Berkeley. She has published (with Lynda Rush) "The Economic Determinants of Breastfeeding for Mexican Migrant Women," *International Migration Review* 21 (1987) :728-742; (with Lynda Rush) "The Effect of Health Care Access on Maternal and Infant Health of California Seasonal Farm Worker Women," *Border Health* 1 (1987) :18-25; "Maternal and Infant Health Care of Seasonal Farmworkers in California" in *Agriculture and Economic Instability,* ed. M. Bellamy (Aldershot, Hants, England: Gower Publishing, 1987), 183-186; and (with Refugio Rochin) "The Current Status and Future of Chicano Studies Programs: Are They Academically Sound?" *La Red--The Net* 1 (1987) :11-30.

Kenneth T. Fong is a research assistant in Psychiatry and Behavioral Sciences at Stanford University. He received his B. A. from the University of California, Santa Cruz in 1985.

Raymond T. Garza is Professor of Psychology at the University of California, Riverside. He received his Ph.D. from Purdue University in 1975. He has published (with F. W. Widlak), "The Validity of Locus of Control Dimensions for Chicano Populations," *Journal of Personality Assessment* 41 (1977): 635-643; (with J. P. Lipton) "Culture, Personality and Reactions to Praise and Criticism," *Journal of Personality* 46 (1978): 743-761; (with J. P. Lipton), "Foundations for a Chicano Social Psychology," in *Chicano Psychology*, ed. J. L. Martinez, Jr. and R. H. Mendoza, 2nd ed. (New York: Academic Press, 1984); (with J.A. Espinoza), "Social Group Salience and Interethnic Cooperation," *Journal of Experimental Social Psychology* 21 (1985): 380-392; (with P. I. Gallegos), "Environmental Influences and Personal Choice: A Humanistic Perspective on Acculturation," *Hispanic Journal of Behavioral Sciences* 4 (1985): 365-379; and (with S. A. Isonio and P. I. Gallegos), "Community Development in Rural Mexico: The Social Psychological Effects of Adult Education," *Journal of Applied Social Psychology,* forthcoming.

Gayle Y. Iwamasa is a graduate student in Clinical Psychology at Purdue University, where she will receive her Ph.D. in 1990.

Gary Kawaguchi is a graduate student in Ethnic Studies at the University of California, Berkeley, where he will receive his Ph.D. in 1989. He has published "Face and Moon," *Fusion-San: A Japanese American Anthology* (San Francisco: Asian American Studies Dept., San Francisco State University, 1986) and (with Amado Cabezas and Larry Hajime Shinagawa), "New Inquiries into the Socio-Economic Status of Pilipino Americans in California," *Amerasia Journal* 13 (1986): 1-22.

Chalsa Loo is Adjunct Associate Professor of Ethnic Studies at Santa Clara University. She received her Ph.D. from Ohio State University in 1971. She has published "Measures for Predicting Therapeutic Skill and the Effects of Training," *Psychotherapy: Theory, Research, and Practice* 16 (1979): 460-466; (with Paul Ong), "Slaying Demons with a Sewing Needle: Feminist Issues for Chinatown's Women," *Berkeley Journal of Sociology* 27 (1982): 77-88; (with Paul Ong), "Crowding Perceptions, Attitudes, and Consequences Among the Chinese," *Environment and Behavior* 16 (1985): 55-87; (with G. Rolison), "Alienation of Ethnic Minority Students at a Predominantly-white University," *Journal of Higher Education* 57 (1985): 58-77; "The 'Biliterate' Ballot Controversy: Language Acquisition and Cultural Shift Among Immigrants," *International Migration Review* 19 (1985): 493-515; and "Neighborhood Satisfaction and Safety in a Low Income, Ethnic Area," *Environment and Behavior* 18 (1986): 109-131.

Paul Ong is Assistant Professor of Urban Planning at the University of California, Los Angeles. He received his Ph.D. from the University of California, Berkeley in 1983. He has published "An Ethnic Trade: The Chinese Laundries in Early California," *Journal of Ethnic Studies* 8 (1981): 95-112; "Chinatown Labor in Early San Francisco: Racial Segmentation and Industrial Expansion," *Amerasia* 8 (1981): 69-92; "Chinatown Unemployment and the Ethnic Labor Market," *Amerasia* 11 (1984): 35-54; "The Central Pacific Railroad and Exploitation of Chinese Labor," *Journal of Ethnic Studies* 13 (1985): 119-124; (with Chalsa Loo) "Slaying Demons with a Sewing Needle: Feminist Issues for Chinatown's Women," *Berkeley Journal of Sociology* 27 (1982): 77-87; and "Labor Force Participation of Chinese Immigrant Wives," *Industrial Relations,* forthcoming.

Gin Yong Pang is a graduate student in Ethnic Studies at the University of California, Berkeley, where she will receive her Ph.D. in 1991. She is writing her dissertation on "Marriage Patterns Among Asian Americans in California."

Refugio Rochin is Associate Professor of Agricultural Economics at the University of California, Davis. He received his Ph.D. from Michigan State University in 1971. He has published "Farmworker Service and Employment Programs," in *Seasonal Agricultural Labor Markets in Markets in the United States,* ed. R. D. Emerson (Ames: Iowa State University Press, 1984); "Mexico's Agriculture in Crisis: A Study of Its Northern States," *Mexican Studies/Estudios Mexicanos* 1 (1985): 255-275; "The Conversion of Chicano Farmworkers Into Owner-Operators of Cooperative Farms, 1970-85," *Rural Sociology* 51 (1986): 97-115; (with Ricardo Amon), "Agribusiness and Migrant Labor in Mexico: Networks of Dependency," in *Contemporary Business and Economic Issues in Latin America, 1988: Proceedings of the Business Association of Latin American Studies,* ed. H. Kuklan, J. Anderson and D. Dimon (North Carolina: North Carolina Central University School of Business, 1988); (with Adela de la Torre), "Strengthening Chicano Studies Programs: A Study of Correlates for Success," *La Red: The Hispanic Journal of Education* 1 (1988); (with Heliodoro Diza Cisneros), "Peasant Cooperatives and Rural Development: An Indigenous Model from Mexico," *The Rural Sociologist* 8 (1988):218-225; and "The Changing Workforce: A Challenge for Hispanics of the 21st Century," *Hispanic Books Bulletin* 2 (1988):12-15.

Silvia Santos is a graduate student in Psychology at the University of California, Riverside. She is writing her dissertation on "The Impact of Perceived Illegitimacy of Status Relations on Social Identity" and will receive her Ph.D. in 1990. She has written (with R. Garza), "Social Group Salience and Interethnic Competition and Cooperation," submitted to *Journal of Experimental Psychology.*

Larry Hajime Shinagawa is a graduate student in Sociology at the University of California, Berkeley, where he will receive his Ph.D. in 1989. He has published (with Amado Cabezas and Gary Kawaguchi)

"New Inquiries into the Socioeconomic Status of Pilipino Americans in California," *Amerasia Journal* 13 (1986): 1-22. He has also written "The 'Family' and the Issue of Ethnic Success: The Case of Asian Americans," in *Frontiers in Asian American Studies*, ed. Gail Nomura, Shirley Hune, and Gary Okihiro (Pullman, WA: Washington State University Press, forthcoming); "Asian American Intermarriage: The Current State of Research," *Asian American Intermarriage and Multicultural Identity*, ed. Russell Endo (Boulder, CO: University of Colorado Press, forthcoming); and "Racial Identification of Households and Members of the Household: The Impact of Census Procedures," in *Demography and Public Policy*, ed. Larry D. Branett (Wilmington: University of Delaware Press, forthcoming).

Federico A. Subervi-Velez is Assistant Professor of Communication Studies at the University of California, Santa Barbara. He received his Ph.D. from the University of Wisconsin, Madison in 1984. He has published "La violencia y los medios de comunicacion," *Etiologia de la violencia en Puerto Rico* (San Juan, Puerto Rico: Technical Services of Puerto Rico, Inc., 1976); (with Yayoi Anzai and Juliet Dee), "Mutual Images: Americans and Japanese in T.V. Commercials," *Human Communication Studies* 13 (Spring1986): 1-33; "The Mass Media and Ethnic Assimilation and Pluralism: A Review and Research Proposals with Special Focus on Hispanics," *Communication Research* 13 (1986): 71-96; (with Richard Herrera and Michael Begay), "Toward an Understanding of the Role of the Mass Media in Latino Political Life," *Social Science Quarterly* 68 (1987): 185-196; and "Spanish Language Daily Newspapers and the 1984 Elections," *Journalism Quarterly* 65, forthcoming.

MELLEN STUDIES IN SOCIOLOGY

1. Sucheng Chan (ed.), **Social Gender and Boundaries in the United States**

2. Mathew J. Kanjirathinkal, **A Sociological Critique of Theories of Cognitive Development: The Limitations of Piaget and Kohlberg**

3. Sucheng Chan (ed.), **Income and Status Differences Between White and Minority Americans: A Persistent Inequality**

4. Eugene G. d'Aquili and Hans Mol, **The Regulation of Physical and Mental Systems: Systems Theory of the Philosophy of Science**

5. Frances Woods, **Value Retention Among Young Creoles: Attitudes and Commitment of Contemporary Youth**

6. Michael Stein, **The Ethnography of an Adult Bookstore: Private Scenes, Public Place**